The
YANKEES
READER

The
YANKEES
READER

Edited by
Miro Weinberger
and
Dan Riley

HOUGHTON MIFFLIN COMPANY

Boston • 1991

For information about permission to reproduce selections from
this book, write to Permissions, Houghton Mifflin Company,
2 Park Street, Boston, Massachusetts 02108.

Library of Congress Cataloging-in-Publication Data
The Yankees reader / edited by Miro Weinberger and Dan Riley.
    p.   cm.
ISBN 0-395-58777-8
1. New York Yankees (Baseball team) — History. I. Weinberger,
Miro. II. Riley, Dan.
GV875.N4Y26   1991   90-28467
796.357'64'097471 — dc20 CIP

Printed in the United States of America

Book design by Robert Overholtzer

BTA 10 9 8 7 6 5 4 3 2 1

Grateful acknowledgment is made to the following for permission to
reprint previously published material:

Lesley Hazleton for "Hers" column by Lesley Hazleton, *The New
York Times Magazine,* May 22, 1986. Copyright © 1986 by Lesley
Hazleton.

"The New York Yankees" by Grantland Rice, *Sport* magazine,
September 1951.

"74,200 Fans See Yankees' Opening" by Frederick G. Lieb, *New
York Evening Telegram,* April 18, 1923.

Excerpt from *The Greatest of All* by John Mosedale. Copyright ©
1974 by John Mosedale. Used by permission of Doubleday, a division of
Bantam, Doubleday, Dell Publishing Group, Inc.

Excerpt from *The Old Man and the Sea* by Ernest Hemingway,
reprinted by permission of Charles Scribner's Sons, an imprint of
Macmillan Publishing Company. Copyright © 1952 by Ernest Hemingway; renewal copyright © 1980 by Mary Hemingway.

"1956: New York Yankees 2, Brooklyn Dodgers 0" by Shirley Povich.
Copyright © 1956 by the *Washington Post.*

Excerpt from *Sixty-One* by Tony Kubek and Terry Pluto, reprinted

This book is dedicated
to the memory of my grandfather,
Theodore Jacoff
who, despite caring little
for the Yankees or baseball,
would have been proud to
read this book.

— M. W.

Acknowledgments

Highest thanks go to my parents, Bruce Wood, and especially Ted Levin.

The advice and resources provided by Erik Enquist and Brooks Thompson — Yankee fans from the penultimate tier — and by Alexander Theroux were invaluable. Research assistance was also graciously provided by the Hall of Fame Library and the New York Public Library.

For a vast range of reasons, the book would not be what it is without Paul LaFarge, Richard Freeman, Tom Larkin, Larry Niles, Mary-Rose Papandrea, Sam Power, John Schumann, Kristin Seitz, Kevin Watts, Peter Welch, Elizabeth White, and Jeff Zacks.

— M.W.

Contents

THE ATMOSPHERE WAS GRIM

Introduction

On January 5, 1920, the Supreme Court ruled that the Volstead Act was constitutional. What followed was a decade full of some of the most colorful, jazzy images of twentieth-century America: Scott and Zelda, Gatsby, Hemingway, Capone, bootlegging, "Joe sent me," the Charleston, St. Valentine's Day celebrated with bonbons and machine guns.

In New York, on the same January 5, it was announced that the Boston Red Sox had sold Babe Ruth to the Yankees for cash. And thus the dominant cultural icon of the age took center stage, and the long and glorious reign of the New York Yankees began.

There is no room for the "chicken-or-egg" argument here. In their seventeen pre-Ruth seasons, not a single Yankee squad finished first — few were even close — while in the six decades that followed the arrival of the Bambino, the Pinstripes won half of all American League pennants (32) and a full third of the World Championships (22). When he arrived the Yankees were a debtor, tenant team, while the franchise he left was the wealthiest in all of sport and possessor of the most lordly ballpark the country had ever seen.

Not that he did it alone. Ruth may have been the first Yankee Hall of Famer, but thirty-two more have been inducted since him. With Gehrig, DiMaggio, Berra, Mantle, and Jackson there was seemingly a new Yankee hero for every decade. Countless legends were spawned: from the simple eloquence of the condemned Gehrig to the convoluted Stengelese of the Ol' Perfesser (and ten pennants in twelve years), from DiMaggio's grueling 56-game hitting streak to Larsen's singular perfect day in the sun — each act but a thin page in the bulging volume entitled "Yankee Tradition." Even larger, perhaps, was the scene that surrounded the Yanks: Ernest Hemingway was part of it, and then Marilyn and Paul Simon, Mr. Coffee and Reggie Bars. The tradition grew, the scene expanded, and the Yankees came to represent the hegemony — cultural, military, and otherwise — that was America.

But then the 1980s arrived, and suddenly it wasn't such a good time to be a Yankee fan. Sure the club beat their division twice, and they made it to the Series once — but they didn't win it. You have to go back a very long way, back to the nearly mythical years when the Red Sox were actually World Series victors, to find the last decade in which the Yankees didn't win at least one World Championship. Managers were shuffled in and out, and faceless players were paraded through the New York roster.

Now we are in the '90s. Bad management did the impossible by making it an embarrassment to be a Yankee fan. In 1990, for only the second time in seventy-eight years, the Yankees finished last, with the worst record in the league, the second-worst in all of baseball.

For Yankee rooters the good old days are not figments of selective memory. The years past truly were better, simpler, more predictable times. Much of this book is about returning to those finer periods in Yankee history. The victories, the heroes, the grand personalities that colored the New York game — all of this was captured in print, and in this book we have tried to recapture it. The writing is richly diverse. The entries come from different Yankee eras and a variety of Yankee observers, from both in and out of the game. You will find that a range of intellects — great novelists, sportswriters, and the players themselves — have lent their voices to these pages. Some entries were included because they are funny in a very baseball kind of way; others could not be ignored because they so brilliantly evoke the sheer drama of the game.

But for all the variety, there is a basic thread that binds the bulk of these pieces together. It is never stated; it is too obvious for that in a way. Rather it is a given, like the laws of gravity or the fundamental economic principles of supply and demand. It is the underlying belief based on the premise that the Yankees are, have been, and always will be superior.

It is hard to admire what is taken for granted, and for all the worship and respect that the Yankees received during their greatness, perhaps it is possible to truly marvel at the team's string of remarkable accomplishments only now that it is over, not just for the Yankees but for teams in all our major sports. Maybe with the realization that these pieces are rooted in a logic that currently seems distant and utterly defunct, the writing becomes nostalgic and even more appealing.

In any case, there has never been a better time for Yankee fans to reminisce than the present. Enjoy the pages ahead.

M.W.
October 1990

A MYTHICAL PLACE CALLED AMERICA

In the first essay in our collection, Lesley Hazleton, newly arrived in the United States, recalls finding a mythical place called America during her first visit to Yankee Stadium. Where else? The house that Ruth built . . . lordly, majestic Yankee Stadium balanced like the earth itself on the back of a poor, uneducated Atlas from Baltimore with spindly legs and a ferocious appetite for hot dogs and drama. The Yankees, of course, have been a central part of the American myth throughout much of the twentieth century, an efficient, indomitable colossus, bestriding a world it overwhelms with a richness of talent and good fortune.

The three pieces that follow Hazleton's are almost shameless in their praise of the Yankees but instructive in showing us how storytellers have always played a pivotal role in the making of myths. Grantland Rice was a legendary sportswriter in his day; today his history of the Yankees through the DiMaggio era fairly reads like a creation of the Yankee PR department, but then what did Homer do for the myth of the early Greeks if not provide some very effective PR? On the other hand, John Mosedale's 1974 appraisal of the 1927 Yanks was written during the debunking age of American sportswriting; but even that perspective doesn't dissuade him from proclaiming that legendary team as the greatest of all. And in his eyewitness account of the day Yankee Stadium opened, Fred Lieb innocently observes, "The kids are all for the Babe, and he is for the kids." Cynicism about modern-day ballplayers is rampant, of course, but it may actually be easier to find one or two about whom such a line could be written than it would be to find a writer who'd dare to write it.

No writer in this century had more to do with the creation of the mythic American hero — defined as grace under pressure — than Ernest Hemingway. The perfect embodiment of Hemingway's ideal was the great DiMaggio, whose deeds provided solace and inspiration for Hemingway's fictional fisherman in our excerpt from *The Old Man and the Sea*. Oh, for the days when real heroes inspired fictional ones, but today's heroes all seem to be wearing two-hundred-dollar sneakers on their feet of clay, and the fictional ones are all cartoon characters. DiMaggio was no cartoon.

Some of Hemingway's famous bullfighting scenes, with their exquisite descriptions of a solitary man at the center of the ring drawing on all his natural reserves to confront a fierce and mighty foe, practically provide a paradigm for the events reported in the next three pieces — Shirley Povich on Don Larsen's perfect afternoon in the October sun, Tony Kubek on Roger Maris's grueling confrontation with the ghost of the Babe in 1961, and Roger Angell on Reggie Jackson transcending his prodigious self-promotion with four swings of the bat in October 1977.

In another region of the country, Thomas Boswell's masterpiece on the Greatest Game Ever Played, which concludes this section, echoes the myth of the Trojans, history's tragic losers, done in at the last by the ultimate hidden ball trick. Play it where Yankee fans gather, however, and it reaffirms, again, the still enduring American/Yankee myth of inevitable victory.

Lesley Hazleton

"Hers" Column

The New York Times Magazine, May 22, 1986

It was a sunny, dry September Sunday — the kind of day that can convince an unsuspecting stranger that New York is a wonderful place to spend the summer. I was fresh off the plane from Israel. It was only my second day in the United States, but my friends here had made the shocked discovery that I had never even seen a baseball diamond. So they took me out to the ball game. Thurman Munson had been killed in a plane crash a few weeks before, and the Yankees weren't going to be in any World Series that year. But this particular Sunday had been declared Catfish Hunter day. Ole Catfish was retiring, and New York had turned out for him.

Maybe it was in comparison with the parched browns of Israel at summer's end. Maybe it was the combined smell of hot dogs and marijuana drifting over the stands. Maybe it was the light. All I know for sure is that when I emerged from the tunnel and stood there in the first tier, looking out over home base, I gasped at the perfect greenness of it. So this was a diamond.

What happened then was everything I expected from America. A brass band, heavy on the epaulets and the drums. High-stepping marching girls in white rubber bootees and pompons, throwing silver plywood rifles twisting into the air. A whole ceremony right on the field, including Catfish's mother, wife and two young boys, and of course Catfish

himself — the archetype of the huntin'-shootin'-fishin' man.
Speeches were made and messages read out from presidents
of various organizations, including one President called Jimmy
Carter. Gifts were hauled, driven and led out onto the field
(television sets, Toyota cars and a live elephant, respectively). And then came a hush as Catfish approached the
microphone.

"There's three men shoulda been here today," he said.
"One's my pa" — riotous applause — "one's the scout that
signed me" — more riotous applause — "and the third one"
— pause — "is Thurman Munson." Riot. Fifty thousand people up on their feet and roaring, including my friends. The
fifty thousand and first — myself — looked on in bewilder-
ment. I missed Catfish's next sentence, but I'll never forget
the last one of that brief speech. "Thank you, God," he said,
"for giving me strength, and making me a ballplayer."

And suddenly I too was up on my feet and cheering. It was
the perfect American day, the perfect American place, the
perfect American sentence. That combination of faith and
morality, sincerity and naiveté, was everything my Old-World
preconceptions had led me to expect, and as I watched Catfish
walk off the field into the sunset of the Baseball Hall of Fame,
leading his little boy with one hand and the elephant with the
other, I felt that I had had my first glimpse of a mythical place
called America.

Three hot dogs, two bags of peanuts, three glasses of beer
and nine innings later, I was amazed to find out how much I
already knew about baseball. In fact I'd played a simpler form
of it as a schoolgirl in England, where it was called rounders
and was played exclusively by rather upperclass young ladies
in the best public schools, which in England of course means
the best private schools. Yet though we played on asphalt and
used hard cricket balls, and played with all the savagery that
enforced good breeding can create, we never dreamed of
such refinements as I saw that afternoon. The exhilaration of
sliding into base! That giant paw of the glove! The whole
principle of hustle! A world awaits the well-bred young

Englishwoman in the ballpark. But for me the most splendid of these splendors was to watch the American language being acted out.

Though I knew no Americans when I lived in England — those were the years when America was still considered a brash black sheep of the family, so to speak, and was not mentioned in polite society — I came to know many in the years I lived in Israel. And since they were the only people with whom I spoke English, I picked up their language. I could touch base, give a ballpark figure, strike out and reach first base long before I ever realized that these were baseball terms. I could be out of the ball game, let alone out of the ballpark. I could play ball — even hardball when I had to. There were times when I climbed the walls, and accused others of being off the wall. And it seemed I had a talent for throwing the occasional curve ball in an argument. . . .

That September Sunday in Yankee Stadium, the American language loaded the bases and gave me a grand slam home run. It came alive for me, and with it, American culture. Baseball was suddenly my code to understanding this culture, the key to the continent. And I knew that I'd really arrived in America one rainy afternoon a couple of years later, the kind of afternoon that lends itself to sitting at your desk, staring out the window and daydreaming. Slowly, I realized that I had just emerged smiling from the classic 10-year-old-boy's all-American fantasy: seventh game of the World Series, three runs down, bases loaded, two out, and I'm up at bat. I take a strike on the first pitch. The crowd is roaring. Another strike on the second pitch. The crowd roars even louder. And then comes the third pitch, right where I want it. . . .

Grantland Rice

The New York Yankees

Sport Magazine, September 1951

It was in the spring of 1904 that I first saw the New York Yankees, or Highlanders as they were known then. A fairly nondescript outfit, or so they appeared at the time, they were in Atlanta, Georgia, during their spring training period. I remember particularly Clark Griffith, their manager and a veteran pitcher at the time; the little sharpshooter, Wee Willie Keeler; and Jack Chesbro, the smiling, right-handed pitcher who went on to win 41 games that year. As I watched them work out under the warm Georgia sun, I of course never realized I was watching the formation of the greatest baseball dynasty of them all, one that would reign as world champion 13 times and American League leader 17 times in the next 46 years.

Call the roll of Yankee greats, past and present, and you name so many of baseball's all-time heroes — Babe Ruth and Lou Gehrig and Joe DiMaggio and Herb Pennock and Bill Dickey and Tony Lazzeri and others. Even now, you get a special tingle of excitement when you read over their names and picture them as they were in their many hours of triumph at Yankee Stadium — and in all the other parks around the league.

It is easy to say that they alone made the Yankees, but it is not that simple. The great Yankee record and the pride and tradition that go with it is the product of many years of effort, mixed with anguish and success. No one man is responsible for the achievement; many great ballplayers, managers and front-office executives have contributed their share to baseball's proudest success story.

The American League first started boasting about the Yankees 48 years ago. They weren't the Yankees then, of course. In that first year of their history, 1903, the newspapers referred to them as the Greater New York Club of the American League. But Ban Johnson, the enterprising ex-sportswriter who founded the new group of baseball teams to compete with the well-established National League, was understandably proud and happy with the New York franchise. The success or failure of his project depended a great deal on getting a club in the nation's biggest city. It had been no easy job.

The New York Giants had a firm stranglehold on the town's baseball patronage and owner John T. Brush wasn't anxious to share it with anyone. Brush and the former millionaire owner of the Giants, Andrew Freedman, an influential man in town, continually threw up road blocks in Johnson's way. For two years, his attempts to move the Baltimore team into New York and lease property for a ball park were thwarted.

But in January, 1903, representatives of the two leagues got together and came to an agreement of sorts over the admission of a New York American League club into the majors. Brush continued his private fight against the plan, but Johnson found two men with the necessary money and influence to push the deal through. One, Frank Farrell, was a big-shot gambler and racing-stable owner and the other, William S. Devery, was an ex–chief of police and a successful realtor. In those days, there was no Judge Landis to fuss about a magnate's private business associations. Farrell and Devery were just what Johnson had been looking for. They paid $18,000 for the Baltimore franchise, selected coal dealer Joseph Gordon to act as their president, and named Clark Griffith manager.

The greatest of all major-league baseball teams certainly

had a humble beginning. On a bright May Day afternoon, 16,243 fans crowded into the wooden grandstands and lined up around the outfield to watch the new American League team in action. The right-field area was still somewhat rough and rock-strewn, but special ground rules were made. Before the game, Bayne's 69th Regiment band played "Yankee Doodle" and other lively airs while the crowd waved tiny American flags that had been distributed at the gate. Most eyes were on the Highlanders, as the New Yorkers were called, in their shiny new white uniforms and white flannel caps with black lacing. They watched Willie Keeler, the team's one big-name star, as he warmed up. Willie was on the downgrade then, but he still could punch out hits. The visiting Washington club boasted big Ed Delahanty, who had led the league in batting the previous year and had hit four home runs in one game in 1896. Big Ed looked under-trained and over-fed that afternoon. He was to meet an untimely death two months later.

Griffith brought the Highlanders in a respectable fourth that first season. And before the spring of 1904, Ban Johnson was sure he had supplied the New Yorkers with enough ammunition to battle the Giants on even terms for the city's patronage. Jack Chesbro had been persuaded away from Pittsburgh the year before. Johnson rigged a trade that brought the classy shortstop Norman (The Tabasco Kid) Elberfeld to the Highlanders from Detroit. Pat Dougherty and Dave Fultz were other standout players who joined the team.

Griff's hand-picked crew, often referred to as the "All-Stars," chased the Red Sox right down to the wire in the 1904 season. In fact, the race closed with nearly the same dramatic twist as at the end of the 1949 season. On the final day, the Highlanders were one and a half games behind the Red Sox and a doubleheader between the two clubs was scheduled for Hilltop Park. A sweep would mean the flag for New York.

The records say 28,540 people pushed their way into a park built for half that number. They packed the stands and crowded around the outfield, standing on benches and boxes. They saw one of the most famous games in American League history.

Happy Jack Chesbro, who won a total of 41 games that year (still a modern major-league record), was locked in a 2–2 pitching duel with Bill Dinneen going into the ninth inning of the first contest. In the ninth, with a Red Sox runner on third, Chesbro wild-pitched to shortstop Fred Parent. The run beat the Highlanders and won the pennant for Boston. New York took the anti-climactic second game, 1–0, in ten innings.

That was as close as the New Yorkers were to come for 17 years, although they finished second in 1906 and again in 1910. In fact, if it hadn't been for the presence of some exciting personalities in the lineup, particularly Hal Chase, the great defensive first-baseman, the club might have dropped right out of the public's sight during the next few seasons. There was little reason why the fans should go to Hilltop Park instead of the Polo Grounds, home of the highly successful and popular Giants.

Chase was one of the few bona fide stars to play for the Yankees in the early years. (I'll refer to them as the Yankees from now on, because that nickname became popular around 1908, especially with the newspapermen who had a hard time fitting "Highlanders" into one-column heads.)

Whatever small progress the Yankees had made in their box-office battle with the Giants disintegrated in 1908. Farrell and Devery took more active interest in the club and it wasn't long before they were feuding with manager Clark Griffith. The team started to slump in mid-season after a fair start and Griff, loudly resenting front-office interference, quit. The owners promoted shortstop Elberfeld to the pilot's job but their troubles only increased. The Kid was a belligerent, hard-talking player whose normal actions would be enough to get him bounced out of any game today. He had a playful habit of stomping on an umpire's feet when he was disputing a call.

There was considerable bitterness between Elberfeld and Hal Chase. The feeling increased as soon as the appointment was announced. It wasn't exactly a secret that Hal had wanted Griff's job, too.

On September 4, Chase packed up and left for San Jose, California, his hometown. Before leaving New York, Chase told newspapermen that the club management circulated stories "detrimental to his character and honesty." Besides losing a crack first-baseman, the team lost its highest-paid employee, which was no great blow to the anemic Yankee treasury. Two years before, Chase had balked at signing for $4,100 and got a pay boost to nearly $6,000 — the best wage any ballplayer, other than a pitcher, was receiving in the game at the time.

If you could get a look at the league standings in September of 1908, you'd never believe your eyes. On Labor Day, shortly before Orville Wright astounded military observers at Fort Meyer, Virginia, by staying aloft in an "aeroplane" four minutes and 15 seconds, the Yankees were in the cellar, 16 games behind the seventh-place Washington Senators! In a four-game series with the Nats, the lowly New Yorkers were shut out three times by Walter Johnson. At the same time, the Giants were leading the National League and drawing crowds up to 30,000 at the nearby Polo Grounds. Yankee fortunes were at their lowest ebb.

Farrell and Devery had to do something to pump a little blood into their impotent team. They weren't making enough to pay laundry bills, and neither of the magnates was in a position to throw any more money into the operation. Chase was persuaded to rejoin the team and George Stallings, who made baseball history with the 1914 Boston Braves five seasons later, was named manager. The Yankees pulled up to fifth in 1909 and finished second the following year. But before the close of the season in 1910, Stallings, like Griffith before him, had run out of patience with his second-guessing bosses, Farrell and Devery. He resigned.

Like most unstable, tottering baseball organizations, the Yankees went through managers as quickly as they did uniforms in the next four years. Because of his tremendous fan appeal, Chase was picked to lead the club after Stallings. But as talented and shrewd as Hal was, he couldn't handle a big-league team. A minor-league manager with big-league color and theatrics, Harry Wolverton, was tried out. But after a last-place finish, Farrell and Devery decided on another switch. In 1913, they called on Frank Chance, the great Chicago Cubs hero, to lead them out of the woods. As capable as Chance was, he never should have managed the Yankees, or any other big-league team, in 1913. Frank had been hit by so many baseballs in his career that his hearing and eyesight were failing.

New York advanced one notch to seventh under Chance. But an undercurrent of trouble and resentment that ran through the club gained momentum the next season. Chance argued long and heatedly with Farrell and Devery over the need for new players and they complained of his field tactics. Chase revolted against his manager by refusing to carry out orders and playing comedian at Chance's expense in the clubhouse and dugout. The situation became intolerable for manager, owner and team. Chase was traded to the White Sox and Chance, after nearly tangling with Devery, departed for California without finishing the season. A young shortstop named Roger Peckinpaugh filled in as manager of the disorganized band.

The future of the Yankees was obviously limited under the Farrell-Devery banner, and no one knew it better than Ban Johnson. Farrell was in the habit of betting heavily at the race tracks and neither he nor Devery was a good financial risk. Club debts increased and there was no prospect of more revenue at the gate.

Johnson became more and more anxious to have a solvent, successful American League entry in New York. He talked to Colonel Jacob Ruppert, who had inherited a profitable brewery from his immigrant father and was one of the city's most prominent — and best-heeled — sportsmen, about the Yankee franchise. While serving in Congress in 1900, Ruppert had made a $150,000 offer for the Giants, but had shown little other interest in baseball. The Colonel spent more time with his other hobbies such as a racing stable, his yacht, a private zoo, and his rare collections. After that first offer for the Giants, he apparently lost interest in baseball. He went to the Polo Grounds occasionally but never saw the Yankees play at the old American League hilltop park and watched them but twice after they became co-tenants with the Giants in 1913.

"When I bought the Yankees, I went into it in a sporting spirit, like buying a lake or a shooting preserve," Ruppert later admitted.

Johnson got Ruppert together with Captain Tillinghast L'Hommedieu Huston, a self-made millionaire and a close pal of John McGraw. The two quickly became interested in purchasing the club. They were as different as two million-aires could possibly be. Ruppert was an impeccable example of the rich, society-minded sportsman, a man of aesthetic taste. Huston was a rough-hewn old Army man who had made his fortune as an engineer in Cuba after the Spanish-American war. He liked a good drink and enjoyed the rough, coarse-talking sports crowd that hung around the ball parks.

Their first look into the status of the American League club was discouraging. The property was overburdened with notes and obligations that had accumulated during the losing box-office battle with the Giants. But both were excited by the possibilities of running a major-league franchise in the biggest city in the country. On January 11, 1915, the deal was completed and Ruppert and Huston paid $400,000 for the New York ball club. They went in 50–50, an arrangement that Ruppert was soon unhappy about.

The new owners found that, among other things, they needed a new manager. They picked Bill Donovan, once a star pitcher with the Tigers and then a successful minor-league manager, to replace Roger Peckinpaugh, who had filled in for Frank Chance during the last season. They made their first important player acquisition when they influenced Frank (Home Run) Baker, property of the Philadelphia A's, to come out of his self-imposed retirement.

But Baker wasn't enough to lift the team into the class of a pennant contender. After a fifth-place finish in 1915, the Yankees pushed into the first division the following year, only to drop to sixth in 1917. Cap Huston had taken a far more active interest in the club's fortunes than his partner, Ruppert. He loved to pal around with the players and the newspapermen who followed the team. The threat of war was growing darker in those days and, as a result of Cap's military mind, the Yankee players were the first to hold squad drills with bats substituted for rifles at spring training. He even had some of the newspaper crowd marching around with Louisville Sluggers over their shoulders — an experience that Bill McGeehan, Damon Runyon and myself, among others, never forgot. Huston went off to France with the Army Engineers in 1917 and Ruppert was left to worry about the team and its rapidly decreasing patronage.

Jake liked Bill Donovan personally but had little faith in him as a team builder, so his first post-season move was to look for a new manager. He went to his friend and adviser, Ban Johnson, and asked for suggestions. Johnson didn't hesitate to name Miller Huggins, the dwarfish fellow who was then leading the St. Louis Cardinals in the National League. In France, Huston had his own ideas about a manager. He was determined to get Wilbert Robinson, a good friend of his and the manager of the Brooklyn Dodgers. Ruppert agreed to talk to Robinson, but neither he nor Robby was impressed by the interview.

Jake went ahead with Johnson's choice, even though he was skeptical about Huggins. He had met him once and was a bit startled at his appearance and manner. They were introduced in a hotel lobby and Huggins, a little man wearing an over-sized cap on his head and a worried expression on his small face, merely said "Hi" and walked away. The Colonel wasn't used to a quick brush-off.

But a formal meeting with Huggins changed Ruppert's first impression. The Colonel liked the little man's straightforward speech and was impressed with his thorough knowledge of the game. He signed Huggins to a two-year contract, the first and only formal agreement the two had in Miller's 12 years as manager of the Yankees.

Ruppert was satisfied that he had made a wise choice, but when word got to Huston overseas, there was an explosion that broke their partnership wide open. Angered because Ruppert had by-passed Robinson, Cap Huston (soon to become a Colonel) carried on a long-distance campaign against the managerial choice. He wrote letters and spoke bitterly about it to Army friends. Huggins, all five feet, three inches of him, found himself in the middle between two feuding employers. Hug, who was to survive some turbulent years with the Yankees, later asserted he never had to go through anything like that early period — 1919 to 1923.

He was such a little man that it was a constant shock to see him with Ruth, Gehrig and the other big ballplayers. His uniform never fit and the letters that spelled out "New York" across his chest always drooped as they did when the shirt was hung over a peg in the locker room. He was a champion worrier and fretter and, Lord knows, he had enough to worry about. His constant struggle to take and keep charge of the greatest collection of high-priced prima-donnas the game has ever seen wore him down and, eventually, killed him.

Huggins' first Yankee team struggled through the abbreviated 1918 season with a patch-work lineup that was constantly being changed by the demands of the armed forces. The club finished a creditable fourth.

If you must pick a single turning point in Yankee history, the moment when the team shed the cloak of mediocrity and started its triumphant climb to its place of domination in baseball, it would be January 5, 1920. That was the day the New York Yankees purchased Babe Ruth.

I'm sure no ballplayer had so much to do with the swift, sure success of a team as did Ruth with the Yankees. And yet, at the same time, I feel the Babe was indebted to New York for providing him with an appropriate stage for his tremendous heroics. The greatest figure the game has known needed baseball's greatest team, and vice versa. The Yankees probably would have become the fabulous success they are now without the Babe, but, I'm certain, the road to the top would have been much longer and much less exciting.

When the Yankees purchased Ruth that winter, he was 25 years old, a well-constructed, six-foot, two-inch left-handed pitcher-outfielder who had a fine reputation as a hurler and had just astonished the baseball public by hitting 29 homers in 1919.

Ruth's sale to New York was headline news. As announced by Harry Frazee, the Red Sox owner, the Yankees paid $100,000 for Babe — the biggest deal the game had seen. The sale of Ruth caused a near mutiny among Boston fans. Newspapers ran cartoons showing "For Sale" signs on the Boston Common and some people threatened to boycott the Red Sox. Frazee quickly countered with the statement: "It would be an injustice to keep him with the Red Sox, who were fast becoming a one-man team." Later, he said, "Ruth had simply become impossible and the Boston club could no longer put up with his eccentricities." But the truth was that Frazee, hounded by baseball and theatrical debts, desperately needed money. The transaction for Ruth also included a $350,000 loan from Ruppert, who took over the mortgage on Fenway Park.

So the Yankees acquired baseball's greatest drawing card for a sum less than what they have paid Joe DiMaggio in annual salary. During the next ten years, Ruth received $579,397 in pay checks and World Series earnings. The club took out a $300,000 life insurance policy on him. He was the most profitable investment a team ever made. Ruppert and Huston were nearly $1,000,000 in the red with the Yankees of 1919. Within a decade, the club was the richest in baseball, one of the soundest enterprises the sports world has ever known.

The Babe made a smashing success out of his first season in Yankee uniform. He hit .376 and a total of 54 home runs for the third-place club.

Less than a year after the coming of Ruth, the Yankees

made another important acquisition that had a great influence on their future success. Some critics feel that the Yankee story was written by Ed Barrow, who became business manager on October 28, 1920, more than anyone else. Until he retired as president in 1945, Barrow saw the Yankees win 14 of their pennants and ten World Series. Under his direction, the club went from tenants at the Polo Grounds to owners of the greatest baseball plant in the world: from a struggling organization surviving on the accumulated wealth of two sport-loving millionaires to the most successful franchise in the majors; from just one of eight American League clubs to the epitome of everything that is class and "big league" in baseball.

The Yankees' first pennant in 1921 came a lot harder than most of those that followed. The Cleveland Indians, defending champs in the AL, battled the New Yorkers right down to the wire. The clincher came on October 1 at the Polo Grounds when the Yanks whipped the A's in a doubleheader. The Yankee lineup in those days was not filled with many of the names that were to become famous a half-dozen years later on. The batting order usually ran something like this: Elmer Miller, cf; Roger Peckinpaugh, ss; Babe Ruth, lf; Bob Meusel, rf; Wally Pipp, 1b; Aaron Ward, 2b; Frank Baker, 3b; Wally Schang, c. The front line of pitchers included Waite Hoyt, Carl Mays, Bob Shawkey, and Jack Quinn. But it was a well-rounded combination of youth and experience and it had the mightiest hitter in the game batting third.

On the final day of the season against the Red Sox, Ruth belted his 59th home run into the upper right-field deck at the Polo Grounds — the climax of a terrific year for the Yankee outfielder.

Because of Ruth's prodigious home-run feats, the Yankees were slightly favored over the Giants in the World Series. It was baseball's first five-cent — or Subway — Series and New York was steamed up over the prospects of a showdown battle between the landlords and the tenants of the Polo

Grounds. Needless to say, much of the excitement was generated by one man — the Babe.

The newspapers played up the clash between the city rivals to such a degree that fans stayed away from the park, fearing they couldn't even buy standing room. All-night lines formed for the rush seats, but at game time the first afternoon, there were nearly 8,000 empty seats in the upper stands and only 30,203 people attended. They saw Carl Mays pitch airtight ball and beat the Giants, 3–0. After Hoyt shut them out by the same score the next day, there was talk of a sweep for the Yanks. Ruth, who had walked three times and stolen second and third in the second game, led the cheers in the Yankee locker-room. Decked out in that familiar yellow cap and big polo coat of the same color, the boisterous Babe was more confident than anyone that the Yanks were in.

But in the third game, the silent Giant bats suddenly exploded, sending in eight runs in the seventh inning, enough to win a 13–5 decision. The next day, Mays weakened in the eighth after allowing but two hits and the Giants beat him, 4–2. Ruth thrilled the fans with a tremendous homer that struck the upper right-field tier and bounded into the bleachers. The fifth game went to the Yankees when Waite Hoyt, not far removed from the classroom at Erasmus Hall, Brooklyn, beat the Giants, 3–1.

The Yankees suffered a bad blow when the Babe was forced to the bench with a badly swollen elbow. He didn't appear in the lineup again until the eighth game when he was used as a pinch-hitter. The Giants took the seventh, 2–1, and clinched the five-out-of-nine Series by taking the final, 1–0. An error by Peckinpaugh leaked in the run, but the Yankees put on a dramatic ninth-inning rally that failed to score.

Something of a shock to their prestige, the Series nevertheless gave the Yankees a big financial boost. Each player took home $3,510; the Giants realized $5,265 apiece.

Following their first pennant success in 1921, the Yankees comported themselves like a bunch of champion prima donnas the next spring. Ruth and Bob Meusel had started out by defying Judge Landis and engaging in a long barnstorming tour in the fall soon after the Series. The law-breaking venture cost them their World Series money, a month's pay, and 38 days' suspension at the start of the '22 season. Ruth spent his term playing golf while teammates growled about his attitude and the front office fretted over the loss of his batting.

Huggins' task of running the club on the field was nearly over-shadowed by the problems he encountered riding herd on his roisterous, cocky crew after business hours. The management even hired a detective to report on the late-hour shenanigans of the players.

In St. Louis one afternoon, Huggins had to pry Ruth and first-baseman Wally Pipp apart in a short but spirited fight that climaxed a name-calling feud between them. Ruth's belated start and all that golf didn't help his home-run swing, and he finished up with a fairly modest output of 35 homers. But the Yankees won again, outlasting the Browns by a slim margin at the finish. And once more, the Giants and Yankees met at the Polo Grounds.

For the first and only time in their history, the Yankees were shut out without a single victory in the World Series. They played a ten-inning, 3–3 tie in the second game, called because of darkness, but that's as close as they came to Mc-Graw's outfit. Ruth got only two hits in the set and batted a disheartening .118. Performances of other club members were nearly as dispirited as Ruth's.

Fred Lieb tells about riding downtown to the old Commodore Hotel after the final game. Colonel Huston shared the cab with him and was speechless the whole journey. But once in the hotel, Huston suddenly gave vent to the rage that had been burning within him all afternoon. He slapped the top of the bar, rattling glasses and spilling some on the floor, and shouted: "Miller Huggins has managed his last Yankee team!"

It was an old cry for Huston, of course, one that he had made to friends before. Cap never got over his anger at

Ruppert for ignoring Wilbert Robinson. In three years' time, he had failed to warm up to Huggins.

But instead of Huggins managing his last Yankee team, Huston was spending his last year as part-owner of the New Yorkers. On May 21 the following spring, Ruppert bought out Huston's interest in the organization for $1,500,000. Despite his enthusiasm for the Yankees and many deep friendships among the baseball writers, Huston started to lose interest when it became apparent the team would have to invest in its own ball park. He was not eager to put up the kind of money it would take to construct an adequate stadium in New York and he advised Ruppert to sell out with him.

The Yankee Stadium was finished for opening day of the 1923 season. An estimated $2,500,000 was poured into the structure. It was, beyond challenge, the most magnificent baseball plant in the world at the time. A lot of people referred to it as "The House that Ruth Built" and that was a very accurate description of the Stadium.

Some of Ruppert's friends advised him that New Yorkers wouldn't patronize a club housed in the Bronx section, across the river from Manhattan. But on opening day, April 18, 1923, an announced crowd of 74,217 filled the new stadium, even though it was as cold and windy as it gets in New York in April. A few days later, the Yankees published a revised estimate on the crowd and the second figure was closer to 60,000. But it was still a major-league record throng and it saw Babe Ruth hit a home run — an appropriate start to a new era in Yankee history.

Although no one was remotely aware of the significance at the time, it's interesting to note that on the afternoon the Stadium opened, a Columbia University pitcher named Lou Gehrig struck out 17 Williams College batters in a game played at nearby South Field. The young hurler for the Lions was so wild he lost the game, 5–1, but he got a pair of hits to lead his team at bat.

Two months later, Gehrig was in Yankee uniform and caused a lot of raised eyebrows among the champions by hitting the ball hard and safely in 11 of 26 pinch-hitting and substitute appearances before he was sent to Hartford. The Yankees of '23 were fast company, too, the best in baseball. Bob Meusel, Ruth and Whitey Witt played the outfield. Wally Pipp was at first, Aaron Ward at second, Everett Scott, the iron man of baseball at the time, was the shortstop, and the talented Joe Dugan played third. Wally Schang did most of the catching for a crack hurling staff that included Herb Pennock, Sam Jones, Bob Shawkey, Joe Bush and Waite Hoyt. Pennock, incidentally, had been purchased from the Red Sox, another handsome addition to the Yankee fold, from Harry Frazee in Boston. No one could stop the Yanks from racing to their third straight flag, which they took by a margin of 16 games.

The 1923 Series provided the same old Giant–Yankees match, but the locale changed and so did the outcome. The games didn't get under way until October 10. The Giants won the opener, 5–4, before 55,307 at the Polo Grounds when outfielder Casey Stengel cracked a ninth-inning homer. But the next day, Ruth hit two and the Yanks and Pennock took a 4–2 decision. The Series shifted to Yankee Stadium, site of so many future October classics, and the Giants (with Stengel) spoiled the occasion for the hosts. The ubiquitous Stengel slapped one of Sam Jones' screwballs over Ruth's head for a home run and a 1–0 victory. A record 62,430 saw the game.

On Saturday, the Yankees evened the Series with an 8–4 win, but I missed it, one of the few times I've failed to see the Yankees in post-season play. I was assigned to cover the Army–Notre Dame battle, held before a mob of 35,000 at Ebbets Field the same afternoon. It was a good game, too, the Irish with a backfield of Crowley, Layden, Miller and Stuhldreher winning, 13–0. In the Series finale at the Polo Grounds, the Yankees worked out from under a Giant lead in the eighth and won, 6–4. Ruth hit his third homer in that one.

New York fans charged the Yankees' second-place finish in 1924 to overconfidence, complacency and the inevitable letdown after a run of triumphs. If nothing else, it was a glorious year for Ruth, who hit .378 and led the league in batting for the first and last time in his career. Maybe it was too much of a year for the Babe. Because the next season all he hit was trouble.

It started April 7 in Asheville, North Carolina, where the club was making an exhibition appearance on its way north from St. Petersburg. The Babe suddenly collapsed in the railroad station, falling against a radiator. He was quickly taken to the hospital. The first bulletins announced he was suffering from a severe attack of grippe and indigestion. The whole country was alarmed by the news.

Babe recovered from the illness but his trouble had only started. His batting dipped far below his 1924 pace — and stayed there. In late August, he was batting .260 and his relations with Huggins were at a new low. So were the Yankees, who floundered around the second division. Ruth was in the habit of popping off to Huggins and disregarding his orders. He carried his rugged individualism too far in St. Louis one day.

The Babe came into the Hotel Buckingham hours after Miller's one A.M. curfew and reported late to Sportsmans Park for the game that afternoon. Huggins was waiting for him. The actual exchange of words between the two has become distorted in retelling, but there were plenty of fireworks. The fact remains that Huggins, who had swallowed his pride so many times in "showdowns" with Ruth, called the big fellow's bluff, slapped a $5,000 fine on him and suspended him indefinitely.

The next day, no one could find Ruth but the story was on page one in every New York newspaper and most others around the country. On August 29, Ruth showed up in Chicago and promised to carry out a threat to quit the Yankees as soon as he had talked to Judge Landis. Interviewed by Chicago sportswriters, the Babe spouted: "Why, I know of guys killing people . . . and even bootleggers, who don't get that tough a fine. It ain't right! I'll never play for that —— Huggins again."

Landis was unavailable to Ruth so he packed up and headed for New York and a conference with Jake Ruppert.

Ruth roared into his employer's office like a lion. He came

out like a lamb a half hour later. Newspapermen packed into the hall, waiting for Ruth, were unbelieving. The Babe admitted he had gotten "a bit hot-headed." He was ready to apologize to Huggins. Yes, he wanted to play again right away. Ruppert announced the fine of $5,000 — baseball's all-time high — would stick. It did until after Huggins died, when Ruppert returned the sum to Ruth.

There is one other event in 1925 that needs recording. Unlike the other highlights of the season, this is remembered as a bright spot in Yankee history. On June 1, Lou Gehrig, back from training at Hartford, was used as a pinch-hitter for shortstop Pee Wee Wanninger. The next day, he replaced the ailing Wally Pipp at first base and started his remarkable streak of consecutive games that spanned 15 seasons. He was a big, awkward youngster in 1925, but from the day he took over at first, he began to improve himself.

From the dismal end of the 1925 season, the Yankees quickly took the shape of contenders early in 1926 and showed unmistakable signs of coming greatness. The outfield of Meusel, Combs and Ruth was unmatched in the game. The infield was short on experience but bursting with talent and enthusiasm. Mark Koenig, the shortstop, and Gehrig, at first base, didn't have a complete major-league season between them. Joe Dugan was a veteran third-baseman. At second was a rookie from San Francisco by the name of Tony Lazzeri.

The 1926 Yankees did not breeze to a pennant as their immediate successors did. They won only after a last-ditch battle with Cleveland. The World Series that year is still remembered as a personal triumph for the aged St. Louis Cardinal pitcher, Grover Cleveland Alexander. Old Pete's storied feat of striking out young Lazzeri with the bases loaded in the seventh inning of the seventh game is, of course, one of baseball's most famous episodes.

If the Yankees were shaken by that close defeat in the World Series, they showed no signs of it when 1927 rolled around. When you mention 1927 in baseball chronology, you have to say the Yankees, too. Was there ever a more awesome combination of naked batting power, pitching talent, and plain and simple class in the game? This was a matchless collection of baseball players, led by the most lethal one-two punch baseball has known — Ruth and Gehrig. The Babe set the home-run figure they are still shooting at by knocking 60 out of American League parks, and Gehrig, who followed him in the batting order, hit 47. Ruth hit .356; Gehrig .373. But that wasn't all by any means. There was the cold, emotionless Bob Meusel who batted a stout .337 and could fire bullet-like throws from his post in left field. There was tall, gray Earle Combs who led off and had 231 hits during the season. His average was .356. There was Koenig and the dangerous Lazzeri, who hit .309 and had 102 RBI's. The catchers — John Grabowski, Pat Collins and Benny Bengough — knew how to use a bat. So, of course, did third-baseman Joe Dugan. Key men on the best pitching staff in the league were Herb Pennock, Waite Hoyt, George Pipgras, ace reliever Wilcy Moore and Urban Shocker.

The conservative Miller Huggins once said this was the only team that didn't need luck to win. I think he was right.

The '27 Series was the one in which the Yankees, who had taken the AL pennant with a record total of 110 victories, swept right through the apparently awe-struck Pittsburgh Pirates in four games. Although the Yanks did not exactly crush the Pirates with their bats, they did whip Donie Bush's men at every turn, with sharp pitching, timely hitting and the old Yankee ability to cash in on opportunities, which the National Leaguers supplied in abundance. Pittsburgh errors and a single gave the Yankees three runs and a 5–4 triumph in the first game, much to the disappointment of 41,567 fans at Forbes Field. Pipgras and Pennock took the next two in impressive fashion, and when Miljus wild-pitched with the bases loaded in the ninth inning of the fourth game, the Yankees had a 4–3 victory and their first World Series sweep.

A proper conclusion to the great Yankee success of 1927 came when 24-year-old Lou Gehrig was named the league's most valuable player.

Those were great days for all the Yankees, but especially for Babe Ruth. How the fans of the country loved him and how he loved the adulation and hero-worship! I doubt if any American hero ever succeeded in developing such a degree of smiling tolerance among his followers as did Ruth. There were times when the press got fed up with his antics and raked him severely. But the public was inclined to shrug and smile. "That's the Babe," was the normal reaction when Ruth popped off or got into a wrangle with the club.

Everyone expected the Yankees to come down to earth in 1928. They did, but they didn't reach the level of the other clubs in the league right away. Off to a whopping lead by the middle of the race, the club first started to show signs of strain in August. Yankee pitching was off form and the team lost ground in big chunks. In early September, the Athletics caught up with them. On the ninth of the month, the two clubs met at Yankee Stadium in a battle for first place. The crowd was announced as 85,265 — a few thousand more than could actually be squeezed into the place. Anyway, the huge mob saw a performance that has become characteristic of Yankee teams whenever they are faced with a crucial battle. The Yankees whipped the A's in both ends of a doubleheader and fought on to their third straight flag.

If the '28 team was less invincible than its famous predecessors, it was nevertheless a superb club. Ruth produced 54 homers and the great man in his shadow, Lou Gehrig, batted .374. Their spectacular hitting performances in the Series shattered the St. Louis Cardinals and gained a revengeful four-straight triumph over the National League champs. Ruth knocked Cardinal pitching for a record .625 average and Gehrig smacked four homers, a double and a single in compiling a .545 mark. Waite Hoyt three-hitted the Redbirds in the opener at the Stadium and the Yankees turned on 41-year-old Grover Cleveland Alexander, hero of the 1926 set, to pile up a 9–3 margin in the second game. At St. Louis, the Yankees took the last two by identical 7–3 scores. The Babe, who had thrilled a Sportsmans Park crowd in the 1926 Series by hitting three home runs in a single game, duplicated his stupendous feat in the fourth game — another great Ruthian record.

The first period of Yankee domination came to an end in 1929. The heroes of 1926-'27-'28, or most of them, at least, simply ran out of gas. There were obvious weaknesses at third and short, Bob Meusel was much slower, and the pitching of Pennock, Pipgras and Hoyt failed to measure up to previous years. If time was beginning to tell on some of the Yankee players, it was taking a serious toll from their little manager, Miller Huggins. He worried and fretted and sweated his way through the summer months of 1929, realizing that his club would not make it again. By the middle of September, he was at the breaking point. After a losing game on September 20, Huggins went to the hospital with what was diagnosed as a carbuncle on his face. Five days later, he died.

The passing of Huggins put a period to a Yankee era.

There was a brief interlude in the Yankee success story between the passing of Huggins and the coming of Joe McCarthy. The hopeful start and failure of Bob Shawkey as pilot came in 1930 after Ed Barrow and Jake Ruppert had offered the job to three other men. Donie Bush was a first choice but the former Pittsburgh manager signed a contract with the White Sox hours before Barrow contacted him. Eddie Collins and Art Fletcher both refused the offer.

Shawkey, a likable veteran on the Yankees who had turned to the coaching lines after he retired as a pitcher, took the job knowing that Babe Ruth was sharply disappointed because he had not been picked. At 36, Ruth knew his playing days were nearly over and he wanted nothing more than to become manager of the Yankees. Ed Barrow has said that Ruth never was considered for the job. "After all, Ruth couldn't manage himself," Barrow said.

The Yankees finished a respectable third under Shawkey. That wasn't good enough for a team accustomed to league championships. Bob, who lasted only a couple of months longer than one season, found his long association with many of the players a tough handicap. He didn't have the temperament to crack the whip over the heads of old friends and teammates.

That the Yankees, in search of a new manager, and Joe McCarthy, looking for another job in the majors, should get together was inevitable. Joe had built a strong reputation as an efficient, sound pilot with the Chicago Cubs, whom he had led to a pennant in 1929. Ed Barrow, who had kept a close eye on McCarthy's progress, was sure he was the right man for the Yankees.

McCarthy's appointment was announced during the World Series between the Cardinals and Athletics. Thus began one of the most successful partnerships in baseball. During the next 16 years, Joe managed eight pennant winners and seven world champions. McCarthy's success was achieved in such a cool, businesslike way that many fans minimized his talents and gave all the credit to the players. If Joe's material was the finest in the game, he did the very most with the best.

The Yankees' new manager was not long in coming up with a winner. With the considerable help of two recent additions to the pitching staff, Red Ruffing, a big right-hander obtained from the Red Sox in May, 1930, and an angular young lefty named Vernon Gomez, the Yankees won another flag in 1932. McCarthy's satisfaction in his early success in the American League was redoubled in the Series when the Yanks knocked over the Chicago Cubs, his old employers, in four straight.

The Series would be recorded as just another rout of a National League foe by the Yankees except for a famous Ruthian episode in the third game at Chicago. With the score tied at 4–4 in the fifth inning, a Wrigley Field crowd of 49,986 was whooping it up as Babe Ruth, who had homered in the first, came to bat. What happened next belongs to baseball legend.

I was there and I saw the Babe point toward center field. Only he knew what, if anything, the gesture meant. But the crowd interpreted it as meaning one thing — he was going to knock the next one out of the lot. He did, too. As Ruth trotted across the plate with that hippopotomic grace of his, Gabby Hartnett, the Chicago catcher, said to him: "You incredible ——!"

That night, I saw Ruth in his hotel room. He was beaming from ear to ear. "Got the ball, too," he said. "The damned thing's lop-sided."

The Series ended in anti-climax the next afternoon as the Yankees trounced the Cubs, 13–6.

After the 1932 success over the Chicago Cubs and their fifth world championship, the Yankees slipped into one of those short-lived interludes during which they regrouped their forces before swaggering to the front again. Some of the club's key players were at the end of their careers and it was necessary to plug some big gaps. When Herb Pennock, a veteran of 39, was unconditionally released in 1934, the Yankees said goodbye to one of their all-time pitching stars. "He's the only pitcher I never gave a signal to," Bill Dickey said later.

But even more important than Pennock's departure was the close of Babe Ruth's career in Yankee uniform. The Big Fellow had tailed off rapidly after 1932, slipping down to a .301 batting average and a homer output of 34 the following season. In 1934, he dropped below .300 for the first time since the disastrous year of 1925. It was clear to everyone that the Babe, at 39, was through as a player.

The manner of disposing of Ruth was, of course, a delicate problem. The tremendous public sentiment for Ruth had deepened during his declining years and nearly everyone seemed to think he deserved a prominent job in the Yankee organization. It was no secret that Ruth coveted the post as manager of the Yankees and was unhappy with McCarthy's apparently well-entrenched position. Ruth decided to settle the issue in a talk with Jake Ruppert.

The Babe asked Ruppert point-blank if McCarthy was to

be retained after the 1935 season (the Yankees had finished second). Jake replied, evasively, "He has another year on his contract."

"And what happens after that?" asked the Babe in so many words.

"We'll see," said Ruppert.

A happy solution, from a Yankee standpoint anyway, came in the mid-winter of 1935 when Judge Emil Fuchs of the Boston Braves made a bid to obtain Ruth in an effort to put a little gate sock into his rather drab team. He offered Ruth a job as player and vice-president. The Yankees immediately gave Babe his unconditional release, receiving no money for a ballplayer who had been a priceless commodity for years.

Ruth left the Yankees on February 25, 1935. Despite his bitter disappointment at his failure to replace McCarthy as manager, he parted from Jake Ruppert with a smile and a handshake. In fact, the Babe went up to Ruppert's brewery and had a farewell bottle of beer, the first time he had ever had one in that building.

The loss of Ruth came as the Yankees were set to launch a drive that would sweep them into power for another lengthy period. The 1935 team lacked the solid hitting and pitching strength of a championship club, yet it had enough to chase Detroit through the summer and finish second.

With Ruth gone, the famous Ruth-Meusel-Combs picket line passed into memory. Combs was still on the roster but he played only part of the time with the other outfielders — Ben Chapman, George Selkirk, Jesse Hill and Myril Hoag. Gehrig led the team in batting in 1935 with .329, something of a mediocre year for the Iron Horse.

While the Yankees were experiencing what could be termed an off season, a young outfielder, who was to play an historic role in future years at the Stadium, was burning up the Pacific Coast League. He was Joe DiMaggio, a 21-year-old Italian ballplayer, hitting at a .398 clip in 1935 and making some of baseball's top scouts bitterly unhappy.

*   *   *

Joe was a product of the San Francisco sand lots, the son of a Sicilian fisherman. His interest in baseball had been kindled by an older brother, Vince, who was playing for San Francisco at the time. A trial with the Seals in 1932 resulted in a three-game turn at shortstop at the end of the season. The next year, he was a regular outfielder, having edged his brother out of a job, and he hit safely in 61 straight games. Scouts from most major-league teams were hot on Joe's trail until a freak, off-the-field accident to his knee cooled them off. Yankee scouts Bill Essick and Joe Devine took time to check into the rumors that young DiMaggio suffered from "chronic knee trouble." They found nothing to scare them off, and the Yanks got DiMag for $25,000 and five players, instead of the $75,000 or more that the Seals had originally anticipated.

DiMag fitted brilliantly into the Stadium scene in 1936. The Yankees grabbed the lead on May 10 and pumped up such an advantage that they clinched the pennant on September 9, the earliest date it had ever been won. Joe justified the faith Essick and Devine had shown in him by batting .323 in his freshman year. Major-league fans and players were surprised at the power the young Coast star generated from a wide-open, flat-footed stance and the accomplished ease with which he handled balls in the outfield.

DiMaggio was the junior member of a cast of standout players in 1936. The apparently indestructible Lou Gehrig was at first, maintaining his streak of playing in every game and swinging the most feared bat in the majors. The tried and true second-base combination of Tony Lazzeri and Frank Crosetti gave the Yankees real class in that vital area. Red Rolfe was developing into the league's best third-baseman. The outfield started with Selkirk, DiMaggio and Ben Chapman, but early in the campaign, McCarthy traded the temperamental Chapman for Jake Powell of the Washington Senators. The deal brought a chorus of criticism from the press and public but it stood up well during the year.

Not since the Yankees of 1927 had baseball seen such brute batting power as was displayed by the 1936 Bronx Bombers.

Five members of McCarthy's wrecking crew batted in 100 or more runs: Gehrig (152), DiMaggio (125), Lazzeri (109), Dickey (107) and Selkirk (107). The team total of 2,703 total bases is still a record and their mark of 182 home runs has not been touched by an American League team.

For the first time since 1923, baseball had a "Subway Series." The Giants had taken the National League flag after a grueling, season-long battle. They had made it chiefly on the pitching mastery of Carl Hubbell, who won a grand total of 26 games and lost but six.

What little solace the Giants got out of their fourth world championship match with their rivals from across the Harlem River came from Hubbell's trusty left arm. In a steady drizzle at the Polo Grounds on September 30, he opened the Series with a well-fashioned 6–1 triumph over the Bombers. The second game was postponed a day because of wet weather, delaying the record carnage perpetrated by the Yankees against five Giant hurlers. The score of that one was 18–4. Tony Lazzeri hit a grand slam in a seven-run third inning. President Roosevelt was one of the 43,543 who watched the unprecedented scoring spree. The next day, the Yankees were held to four hits by Fred Fitzsimmons but won, 2–1. It was all over for the Giants, although they did win the fifth game. The Giants came to the same conclusion that the seven other American League clubs had during the season — there was no successful way of checking the Yankee power for any length of time. This was to prove true for a four-year period.

In 1937, for instance, the Yankees came through with a season almost identical with the preceding one. They won 102 games again, taking the flag in early September. Everywhere they went, they were expected to win — and they usually did. Gomez and Ruffing were 20-game winners, Gehrig and DiMaggio batted .351 and .346, respectively, and the veterans and newcomers came through in Yankee style. Personnel changes were few, although the club did come up with a promising young free agent in Tommy Henrich, who was used as a replacement for Selkirk and hit .320 in 67 games.

Unanimous choice to win the Series, they did just that with ease. The Giants again supplied the opposition and the Yankees slugged through them in five games, losing only a fourth-game, 7–3 decision to Carl Hubbell. Lefty Gomez won two of the Yankee victories and veteran Tony Lazzeri, playing his last year with the team, batted .400.

Ed Barrow and manager Joe McCarthy were in the habit of standing pat with a championship club, unless there were some obvious repairs to be made. After the '37 Series, the Yankees released Tony Lazzeri so he could accept an attractive offer from the Chicago Cubs. His departure left only one member of the famous 1927 team on the active roster — Lou Gehrig.

The replacement for Lazzeri, Joe Gordon, was no ordinary ballplayer. A dangerous long-ball hitter, Gordon was spectacular in his fielding. With Frank Crosetti, he promised to give the Yankees the best double-play combination in the game. Other changes in 1938 saw Henrich move to a regular outfield post and team with DiMaggio and Selkirk. The pitching strength came from reliable Red Ruffing (21–7), Lefty Gomez (18–12), Monte Pearson (16–7) and Spud Chandler (14–5). Johnny Murphy, a right-hander, was a good relief man. On August 27 at the Stadium, Pearson shut out Cleveland without a hit or run, facing only 27 batters. He walked two and fanned seven.

Oddly enough, the Yankees got off to an unpromising start in the spring that year. Joe DiMaggio was a stubborn holdout during the training season. He sat out the entire exhibition schedule in San Francisco, refusing to weaken in his demand for a contract of about $40,000. The holdout by DiMag lasted so long that there was talk that it had been "staged" to advertise owner Ruppert's beer! Joe finally came to terms when the Yanks returned to New York for the start of the AL season. For a while, he was booed in every park the Yankees visited. His delayed start obviously hurt the team's performance for a few weeks.

By mid-July, however, the Yankees were out in front. The

pennant — the club's tenth in the last 18 years — was celebrated on the night of September 18.

The Yankees polished off the National League champs, the Cubs, with familiar ease, winning in the shortest time possible. The only exciting moment in the four games occurred in the second contest at Chicago when a sore-armed Dizzy Dean stopped the Yankee bats for seven innings before weakening. Dean and the Cubs lost, 6–3. Huge crowds turned out at Wrigley Field for the first two games, but the below-capacity gatherings at Yankee Stadium indicated that the New York baseball public was only mildly interested in seeing the Yanks outclass another Series foe.

The Yankees' line of success remained unbroken in 1939, yet two widely separated happenings cast a pall of tragedy over the Stadium.

First, on January 13, Colonel Jacob Ruppert died at his home at 1120 Fifth Avenue, New York. Recurrent attacks of phlebitis had kept him home during most of the 1938 season. His condition worsened early in the winter and he passed away before his 72nd birthday. Few members of the team had ever had close relations with the Yankee owner. But there was a general realization that he was a central figure behind the club's success. When he died, there was concern about the future of the Yankees. It was soon alleviated by the appointment of Ed Barrow as president and the announcement that Ruppert's stock had been divided among his nieces and a friend.

Another blow fell on May 2 when the Yankees were in Detroit for a series with the Tigers. Lou Gehrig dropped out of the lineup for the first time since June 1, 1929, his amazing streak of consecutive games ended at 2,130.

All of us who watched the Yankees during spring training at St. Petersburg that year were puzzled and concerned about Lou. It was obvious that he was fading rapidly and we knew that, sooner or later, he would have to take a rest. But none of us was prepared for the news that came from the Mayo

Clinic in Rochester, Minnesota, where Lou went for an examination in June. It was announced that he was suffering from amyotrophic lateral sclerosis — a form of chronic poliomyelitis — and that it was necessary for him to give up his baseball career.

A few weeks later, Yankee fans and many of us who were friends and admirers of Gehrig gathered at Yankee Stadium to pay tribute to him who had served his club — and baseball — so well. Many of us knew we were saying goodbye to Lou for the last time.

I like to think of Gehrig in the Twenties and Thirties when he was compiling his untouchable record of 2,130 games without a miss and blasting American League pitchers at a tempo that earned him a .340 lifetime batting average. Lou, a man of great physical power who had to mould himself into an exceptional player, clung to the background, unsure of himself at first and unsure that the crowds would accept him. As long as Ruth was in the lineup, he never did take the center of the stage, but when the Babe left, he carried the leading role well.

One evening in 1938, when many of us were wondering what had happened to the old Gehrig power, Bill Dickey and I dropped in to see him at his Larchmont home. We were able to kid about his "slump" then because none of us knew that he was suffering from a fatal disease. Bill and I said to him, "What you need is a good stiff drink, Lou."

Gehrig didn't drink, except for an occasional beer, during the season, but he kept a supply on hand for the friends, newspapermen, etc., who frequently swarmed around his place. But he went along with the suggestion. When it came time to pour the drinks, he couldn't handle the cocktail shaker and had to let Bill take over. I guess we were all upset for a moment. There was no room for a joke then.

The Yankees, without Gehrig, raced to another pennant in relentless, monotonous fashion that summer of 1939, finishing 17 games ahead of the Boston Red Sox. They were in first place 156 days of the season and ended up with a staggering total of 106 victories against 45 defeats. Lou was gone but Joe DiMaggio, who batted .381, newcomer Charley Keller with a first-year mark of .334, and veterans Selkirk and Dickey supplied more than enough offensive punch. Reliable Red Ruffing won 21 games and Atley Donald, Marius Russo and Steve Sundra contributed a big share.

It mattered little to the Yankees that Cincinnati had won its first pennant in 20 years in the National League and that the city on the banks of the Ohio was in a state of frenzy over its championship team. The Series opened under the shadow of a European war and the newspapers were full of the ominous details of Hitler's triumphant march into Warsaw as the two clubs squared away at Yankee Stadium.

The Yankees revealed all aspects of their greatness in this short Series. They captured the tight ones with the help of superb pitching, blasted the opposition with a typical Yankee home-run barrage, displayed an impregnable defense anchored by Gordon and Crosetti, and exploited Cincinnati weaknesses whenever possible. Cincinnati didn't win a game.

After taking their fourth straight world championship, the Yankees heard an old cry echoing around baseball: "Break up the Yankees!" The complaint that they were ruining the game had been made ten years before, only this time it was a bit louder — there seemed to be more reason for it.

It was just as well for baseball that the Yankees slipped down to third place in 1940. The club was the same, except for a few new faces on the bench and some signs of old age in such stalwarts as Ruffing, Selkirk, Dickey and Gomez. Joe McCarthy had first-base trouble. He said he was no longer satisfied with Babe Dahlgren. "His arms are too short," was Joe's curious reply to inquiring newspapermen. In '41, he experimented with Joe Gordon at first and Jerry Priddy at second. It didn't last long. Johnny Sturm was given the job, and although none of the pitchers won over 15 games, the Yankees took another pennant — their 12th — by 17 games.

High note of the season was the record-smashing streak of

Joe DiMaggio, who hit in 56 successive games from May 15 through July 16. Joe's string, which bettered Willie Keeler's old mark of 44, was finally broken on the night of July 17 before 67,468 at Cleveland. Al Smith and Jim Bagby were the Indians' pitchers. As DiMag's bat grew hotter in early July, so did the Yanks. They reeled off 14 wins in a row at one point to build up a big advantage in the league standings.

The year was not without its sorrow for Yankee fans. On June 2, Lou Gehrig died at his home in New York. Lou had been sinking rapidly since 1940, yet his death was a blow to the Yankees, past and present, and sent the entire baseball world into mourning.

The result of the 1941 World Series was just what it had been on eight of the 11 previous times the Yankees had played in the October classic. The Yanks beat their NL rivals in five games. But this was no ordinary Series. The event was super-charged with color and excitement simply because the Brooklyn Dodgers were representing the National League for the first time in 21 years. The whole nation was intensely worked up over the Dodgers' success. In fact, the public, including most New Yorkers, forgot all about the Yankees during the last weeks of September. All that mattered was that Brooklyn had edged St. Louis in a ding-dong race and was champ at last.

The Yankees and Dodgers split the first two games at Yankee Stadium, Ruffing winning his sixth Series game in the first and Whit Wyatt taking the second for the Dodgers. The third went to New York when the venerable Fred Fitzsimmons was literally knocked out of the box by a Marius Russo line drive that bounced off his leg. Hugh Casey lost the game in relief of Fitz.

The ninth inning of the fourth game had to be seen to be believed. Remember? Two Yankees were out in the top of that inning and the Dodgers were leading, 4–3. When Tommy Henrich cut at a Casey pitch and missed it for a third strike, the Dodger fans were up whooping and yelling. Police dashed out on the field to protect the diamond from the happy mob. The Brooks had tied the Series! But had they? The third strike had bounced off catcher Mickey Owen's mitt and was rolling toward the stands. Henrich streaked for first. There was no chance to get him. The Yankees were still alive.

The rest was a nightmare for Brooklyn — and a superb example of the Yanks' traditional talent for making the most of enemy mistakes. DiMaggio, the next up, lined out a single. Charley Keller had two strikes on him when he smashed a double off the right-field screen. Henrich scored the tying run and the swift DiMaggio slid across the plate with the fifth. Two more Yanks scored before the hapless Casey could retire the side. It killed the Brooks. The next afternoon, Tiny Bonham restricted them to four hits and the Yanks won, 3–1.

The world was in chaos in 1942 but things were normal in the American League. The Yankees won again. It was not a great Yankee team, but even with obvious imperfections it was stronger than the rest of the field. The Yankees met a brash, free-wheeling team in the St. Louis Cardinals, and for the first time since 1926, were whipped by a National League entry. The Cards did it with amazing ease in five games. After taking the opener, the Yankees lost to Card rookie Johnny Beazley, 4–3, in the second game; were shut out by Ernie White, 2–0, in the third; and lost the fourth, 9–6, before 69,902 at the Stadium. Apparently upset by the Cardinals' reckless speed and cocky attitude, the Yanks dropped the fifth game — and the Series — as Beazley cooled them again, 4–2.

The nation's baseball critics found themselves in the uncommon position of being able to second-guess Joe McCarthy. "Do you have to win all the time?" was Joe's indignant reply.

Like most major-league clubs, the Yanks were nearly unrecognizable in 1943. Spring training was held in Asbury Park, instead of St. Petersburg, and McCarthy spent a lot of time with unfamiliar players like Nick Etten at first base, rookie Billy Johnson at third, Bud Metheny and Tuck Stainback, outfielders, and infielder George Stirnweiss.

The team that successfully defended the Yankees' 1942 flag was a hodgepodge of old Yankee pros, farmhands and replacements from other clubs. No one pretended it was a very good Yankee team. The only regular to hit over .300 was Bill Dickey, who appeared in 85 games. But veteran Spud Chandler, who had an earned-run average of 1.64, and Tiny Bonham gave McCarthy strong pitching.

In the Series, the Yankees got back at the slightly deflated Cardinals, beating them decisively in five games.

The Yankees' string of pennant victories came to a temporary end in 1944. Service calls had left but a skeleton of the once invincible Bombers. Chandler, Gordon, Johnson, Keller and Murphy all went into the armed forces and the usually dependable pipelines from Newark and Kansas City were unable to furnish adequate replacements.

Although the club stopped making big news on the field, it was involved in a headline story in late January, 1945. That was the announcement that the heirs of the late Jake Ruppert — Mrs. Joseph Holleran, Mrs. J. Basil Maguire and Miss Helen Weyant — had sold their interests in the Yankees for the sum of $2,800,000. In a separate negotiation, president Ed Barrow, who had been with the club for 25 years and had seen it win 15 pennants and ten world championships, disposed of his ten percent share for an estimated $300,000. The new owners were Larry MacPhail, recently retired from the Army as a Lt. Colonel and a man who had made quite a mark running teams at Cincinnati and Brooklyn in the National League; Dan Topping, an Army captain and owner of the Brooklyn pro football franchise; and Del Webb, a prosperous contractor from Phoenix, Arizona.

Under the new directorship, Joe McCarthy brought the Yanks home fourth in 1945, the lowest finish for the team in his 15 years as manager.

Meanwhile, MacPhail was busy streamlining the Yankee

organization and modernizing Yankee Stadium in a manner
that brought a few growls of disapproval from old New York
fans and writers. Light towers went up and the Yanks played
their first after-dark game at home on May 28, 1946. Capital-
izing on the easy flow of money at the time, MacPhail built a
plush "Stadium Club" behind the grandstand for subscribers
to the new season box-seat plan ($600 for four). But the new
appeal wasn't aimed exclusively at the carriage trade. For the
plain fan, there were fashion shows, foot races, clown acts
and other sideline attractions. Old-timers expressed their
dismay with MacPhail's operations but crowds poured into
the park in such numbers that new attendance records were
made.

Yankee turnstiles played a merry tune but there were
occasional bursts of disharmony within the organization. One
of the dissatisfied employees was manager McCarthy. The ill
feeling between him and MacPhail was an open secret. No
one was particularly surprised when, on May 24, 1946, Joe
announced his resignation. The most successful manager in
baseball history, winner of eight pennants in 15 years, left
with his team five games behind the Boston Red Sox.

Bill Dickey was moved up from his catching job to replace
McCarthy. But Dickey resigned as manager on September
12, when MacPhail refused to assure him that he would be
retained in 1947. Coach Johnny Neun finished the season as
field boss. Three managers in one season set a Yankee
record. The three previous pilots — Huggins, Shawkey and
McCarthy — covered a 29-year period.

Bucky Harris was MacPhail's choice to lead the Yankees in
1947. And after three years without a championship, the club
drove to its first flag under the new regime. A streak of 19
consecutive wins in July gave the Bombers the momentum
they needed to finish 12 games in front of Detroit.

The '47 Series with the Dodgers went seven games, was
the richest ever, and was one of the most exciting of all
October classics. It was highlighted by the never-to-be-

forgotten fourth game at Ebbets Field when, with right-hander Bill Bevens pitching no-hit ball with two out in the ninth, Cookie Lavagetto lined a double off the right-field wall, scoring the two runs which gave the Brooks a 3–2 triumph. Then, too, there was Al Gionfriddo's amazing catch in front of the 415-foot sign in left-center at Yankee Stadium that robbed DiMag of a homer and shut off a Yankee rally. The big seventh game went to the Yankees when Joe Page, making his fourth relief appearance in the Series, stopped the Dodgers for five innings.

It seemed as if there had never been a victory celebration like the one that followed the Yankees' 1947 success. In the midst of all the yelling and whooping in the jam-packed Yankee clubhouse, a teary-eyed Larry MacPhail announced that he was quitting. The news took the edge off the happy celebration, of course, and a lot of people blamed MacPhail for muscling his way into the headlines that deservedly belonged to the team. Asked why he was pulling out at the time, MacPhail blurted, "Because I want to . . . "

That night, while champagne corks popped in the festivities at the Hotel Biltmore, MacPhail took a wild punch at John MacDonald, former Dodger road secretary. Before the evening was over, he had nearly tangled with the new Yankee president, Dan Topping. In all the furor and excitement, it was somehow determined that George Weiss, the director of the farm system, would be the new general manager.

MacPhail had ended his 33 months as president of the Yankees with some typical MacPhailian fireworks. Whether or not they were glad to see him go, Yankee fans had to admit he had brought a period of prosperity never before realized by the richest of all baseball teams. During the 1946 season, for example, the Yanks became the first major-league team to attract more than two million customers when 2,265,512 fans paid their way into the Stadium.

1948 was not a particularly happy year for the Yankees. They finished behind Cleveland and Boston in the pennant race and in midsummer they lost the greatest ballplayer they ever had when Babe Ruth died. From the wet June afternoon when New York paid its respects to the Babe with a "day" at the Stadium until August 16, the day he died, we were all grimly aware that Ruth was fighting a losing battle with the sickness that had plagued him for some time. Like Gehrig, it was a shock to see him in those last days of his life, and when he passed on, it was a shock to realize he had gone. Even now, when I go to the Stadium, I find it hard to believe that Babe and Lou, who meant so much to the Yankees, are no longer around.

The Yankees have won so many championships by sheer weight of power, talent and class that the pennant victory in 1949 rates as a special achievement in the club's bright history. It, more than anything else, proves that the Yankees boast an indomitable spirit, too.

You will remember that the '49 team was not ranked very high. It didn't figure to stand much of a chance when the great DiMaggio missed the first 65 games of the season with an ailing heel. A new manager, Casey Stengel, was directing play from the bench, Bucky Harris having been fired at the end of 1948. Casey, of course, had a reputation for being a droll wit and for his comical stunts as the skipper of second-division teams. A lot of people said he just wasn't the Yankee type. Tommy Henrich was also on the injured list that grew to an enormous length during the season.

Apparently, enough of the great Yankee character had rubbed off on guys like Yogi Berra, the fast-improving catcher; Jerry Coleman, a rookie second-baseman; and Hank Bauer and Gene Woodling. For the Yanks stuck right up there despite their troubles in fielding a healthy nine. As the season came to a close, the Yankees were a game out of first place and had two to play with the leading Red Sox at the Stadium. They took both of them, tying the race with a 5–4 comeback triumph on Saturday and clinching the pennant the last day with a 5–3 decision. No Yankee team ever came through so heroically in the last ditch as did this one. It was one of the most popular of all Yankee triumphs and it was appropriately crowned with a world championship when Stengel's spirited gang flattened the Dodgers again in a five-game Series.

It was another Yankee year in 1950 — the 17th American League flag and 13th World Series triumph, this time over the Philadelphia Phillies in four straight games.

No baseball team can match that Yankee record. At this time, it seems doubtful that any ever will. For the Yankees are still the Yankees and who is there in the baseball world to stop them from going on to more victories, more pennants, and more world championships?

Frederick G. Lieb

74,200 Fans See Yankees' Opening

Biggest Crowd in History of Baseball at Dedication of New Stadium

New York Evening Telegram, April 18, 1923

Yankee Stadium, Wednesday — It takes more than a cold blast or two to keep the average New Yorker from his baseball game, as was evidenced by the long lines of struggling men and women pouring toward the gates from the elevated and subway stations. Thousands of others came by trolley and auto. A majority were attired in heavy overcoats and wore long mufflers.

74,200 were in the huge stands when the first ball was thrown in the opening contest between the Yankees and the Boston Red Sox. There was little confusion about the Stadium. One hundred and fifty policemen in charge of Inspector Thomas Ryan and Deputy Inspector James H. Post were on duty and kept the crowds moving toward the gates. Twenty-five traffic men and five mounted policemen prevented any traffic snarls.

A man — a rotund, red faced man — puttered around home plate just before the New York squad took batting practice. He received scant attention, and did not want any. He was busy with his rake and apparently unconscious to his surroundings, yet who can imagine the emotions that beat under that breast?

Even the Yankee Colonels, Ruppert and Huston, owners of the Yanks, bag, baggage, franchise, players and stadium, felt no greater pride on this day of days than this stubby, deep-chested man in the overalls. To the wealthy Colonels the dream of a championship Yankee club in a Yankee stadium has come true. To our friend with the rake a twentieth century fairy tale has reached its climax.

It was Phil Schenck, whose occupation long was a jest, who pounded the earth around the home plate. For many years Phil was a groundkeeper without grounds. He was landscape gardener for Frank Farrell on the hilltop terrace on Broadway, and when the Yankees moved to the Polo Grounds ten years ago Phil was left without a ball field. But he managed to stick on the payroll, assisting with the trunks and baggage, helping out the trainer and dreaming of the days when he again would have a ball field to give his tender care.

His Dream Comes True

But year after year the dreams appeared further away. The Yanks apparently had imbedded themselves at the Polo Grounds. But Phil clung on to the club. Evidently only he and Roger Peckinpaugh were hold-overs from the Farrell regime and when Peck was traded a year ago Schenck was the lone survivor. And then the fairy tale came true. Over a year ago the Yanks purchased their present plot in the Bronx and last fall Phil Schenck carefully sodded the ball field with a carpet of green and put in the turtle back infield. And today, as the Yankees open their twenty-first American League opening, with the Boston Red Sox, the former groundkeeper, without grounds, looks over his finished work in the greatest shrine erected to old king baseball.

The fans were on hand early for this historic American League opening. A goodly crowd was assembled around the massive structure of concrete when Cousin Egbert Barrow, Yankee business manager, ordered the locks taken off the stadium at twelve o'clock. Thereafter each subway train reaching 161st street and each "L" arriving at Jerome avenue brought a steady stream of new customers. By half-past one practically all the unreserved section of the lower stand was occupied. At that time there were 10,000 in the stands. From the top of the stand they looked like ants as they wended their way to seats in the large lower stand. The mezzanine floor and upper stands began to fill up around two o'clock. These seats probably will be entirely "decorated" when the real rush comes between two and three o'clock.

Everything Is New

Everything smelled of a newness of fresh paint, fresh plaster and fresh grass. Perhaps a few minor details are still to be completed, but the contractors practically are through with their toil. A few painters still were busy outside, but inside all was spick and span. The stands have been painted a pleasing green, and, with a lavish display of the national colors, made a beautiful background for a ball game.

Not only is the stadium the most commodious in baseball, but it is a beautiful piece of baseball architecture, with graceful, pleasing lines, and should take its place among the show places of America. Unlike the Polo Grounds, which is built in a hollow, the stadium can be seen for miles, and its triple-deck grandstand majestically rises from the banks of the Harlem. Approaching it from the 150th street viaduct one is impressed with its bigness. It looks only a short walk ahead, but as one approaches from Edgecombe avenue he soon discovers it to be quite a hike.

Once inside the fans' eyes become dizzy as they rove over the rows and rows of seats. The ball field is deceptive. The stands are so big and high that the field looks smaller than it is.

Yet, we can't overlook the fact that this is an American

League opening and that the Yanks, two time champions, are rather intent on turning the trick a third time. It is their purpose, with the aid of Bob Shawkey's good right arm, to make a good start in that direction today. Only the Red Sox, recruited almost wholly from Yank discards, are in the way.

The Yanks appeared in neat, new uniforms at 1:00 o'clock. The club house is under the grand stand, and the players scrambled out of their dugout. Sam Jones, Charley O'Leary, the coach, and Freddy Hofmann, the catcher, were the first to appear. Most of the athletes were well bundled up in their gray sweaters.

Ruth Given Big Hand

Ruth appeared several minutes after the rest of the team and the crowd gave the Big Boy a great hand. Jones was the practice pitcher and Ruth slammed the first pitch into the right field bleachers near the exit which reads "This way out." Pipp, Meusel, Ward, Scott and other favorites were loudly cheered as they went to the plate for a crack at Jones' offerings. Scott took a good swing at the ball and apparently shows no bad effects of his injury in Springfield, Mo., last week.

The weather man was fairly decent, though he might have provided a little more warmth without hurting anybody. But the sky was blue and the sun was out: The players wore their sweaters except when batting. The Red Sox appeared on the field shortly before two o'clock. They wore a new uniform of light gray and crimson. The Boston sweaters are a brighter red than anything ever seen on a baseball uniform. Chance was in the lead of his team.

Fate has played a strange game with the one-time peerless leader of the Cubs. Ten years ago, when the Yanks moved to the Polo Grounds, Chance was in charge of the then New York tail-enders. Ten years later he comes to assist in the opening of the great Yankee Stadium, the manager of the Red Sox tail-enders, the team which was the world's championship club ten years ago.

Great as is the grand stand capacity of the new Yankee

Stadium, it was evident that the club had overtaxed it in its first contest.

Hylan Unable to Attend

Colonel Ruppert, president of the Yanks, announced that Mayor Hylan would be unable to be present because of illness.

The Seventh Regiment Band and the antics of the photographers helped to amuse the crowd. The stadium is so large that the band sounds far away. Babe Ruth, as usual, was taken in every possible pose. He was snapped with several urchins, one about five years old, in a baseball uniform. The kids are all for the Babe, and he is for the kids.

Late comers say that there are thousands of persons outside unable to get in. Subway expresses rumbling by on River avenue are jammed with human freight. All the grand stand seats have been sold and lines of three hundred are standing in front of the bleacher entrances. There is no doubt that the park will be filled to capacity, and it may be necessary to turn back some of the crowd.

The corner of the right field grand stand looks like an easy home run zone. During batting practice both Yanks and Red Sox repeatedly drove the ball into this "pocket" and the right field bleachers.

Landis Photographed

The crowd gave the white-haired Commissioner, Kenesaw Landis, quite an ovation as he came walking through the stands. Colonels Ruppert and Huston escorted the Commissioner, and he promptly had his picture taken with the Yankee Colonels in front of the New York dugout. Shortly after Landis the two Colonels, Charley Stoneham and Jim Tierney, of the Giants, and Eddie Bennett, the Yankee mascot, posed for another picture. Only patches of the bleachers remained vacant when the Yanks went for fielding practice at three o'clock. The fans were mostly interested in Everett Scott, the man who has played 986 successive games. Scotty flitted around the infield without showing any bad effects of his injury.

At fifteen minutes past three o'clock the guests of honor appeared in the offing, while the Seventh Regiment Band, in full regalia, formed at the plate to head the parade of tossers to the outfield. John Philip Sousa, the famous band leader, was escorted on the field by Lieutenant Sutherland, the Seventh Regiment leader, and Sousa took command of the expedition. The Yanks in their blue caps and gray sweaters made a pretty color scene with the gaudy red sweaters of the Red Sox.

Pennant Is Raised

The guests, Governor Smith, Judge Landis, Generals Bullard and Walgland and other high military men, met the parade at the center field flagpole. To the inspiring strains of "The Star Spangled Banner," Managers Huggins and Chance first raised the American flag and then the American League pennant for 1922.

With Sousa leading the "Stars and Stripes Forever" the entire assembly marched back to the plate, greeted by the cheers of the entire stands. Judge Landis, Mrs. Landis, Governor Smith and Colonel Ruppert were in the first line of march.

Bob Shawkey, veteran right hander and a gob during the war, began warming up at quarter-past three for the Yankees, and Howard Ehmke, the long, angular heaver, for the Red Sox. He beat the Yanks five times in 1920, but since then has not been so effective.

Just before game time there were around 68,000 in the stands. While there still were a few unoccupied spots in the bleachers, the fans stood three deep behind the lower stand and mezzanine floors. There were at least 5,000 standees.

Before the game the Yankees were presented with a large horseshoe made of red carnations, while Babe Ruth was called to the plate and presented with a large box containing a gilded bat and other knickknacks.

John Mosedale

From *The Greatest of All*

On Thursday, September 22, 1927 — the afternoon of the night Gene Tunney defeated Jack Dempsey in the Battle of the Long Count in Chicago — Babe Ruth hit a home run in the bottom of the ninth inning at Yankee Stadium.

It was his fifty-sixth home run of the year, more than any man except he himself had hit in a single season, and it was Ruthian, to use a popular adjective of the day, meaning timely, surrounded by emotion, and simply stupendous.

Timely because it also scored Mark Koenig from second base, thus defeating the Detroit Tigers, 8–7, after the Tigers had struggled from behind to take a lead. Ruth liked to uppercut the ball, lofting it so that it soared dramatically, like an artillery shell, or a rocket, and this one, according to a careful report in *The New York Times,* chipped a piece out of a seat six rows from the top of the bleachers.

One of the witnesses to the event was the doorman of the Yankee private offices in the Stadium. All season long he waited in darkness, the crowd noise his only reporter, locked away from adventure. Now he had been given a message to take to the dugout, and he stuck his head into Stadium sunlight during game action for the first time that season, just in time to see Ruth deliver his blow.

And then an affecting thing happened, symbolic of the love Ruth engendered and of the gulf which separates our times from 1927, which is more than just a matter of half a century. All afternoon long, a boy in knickerbockers sat in the grandstand, imploring Ruth to hit a home run.

When the Babe delivered, the boy did not wait to see the ball land in the bleachers, but leaped from his seat and, as Ruth rounded first, onto the field. He dashed across the diamond and intercepted Ruth at third base.

Ruth was still carrying his bat, and the idolatrous lad grabbed the handle with one hand, patting Ruth on the back with the other, and together the two trotted home. Together they touched home plate and swept together into the dugout, the boy hanging on like the tail of a comet, before they could be engulfed by the fans who streamed from the stands.

Altogether, not a tableau likely to be repeated these days. For one thing the fan in the newer stadium sits so far from the field of action that even a twelve-year-old's vital signs would flag before he reached the diamond, and he would collapse somewhere around Row BB. For another, a police officer would likely collar anyone headed for the field, fearing an assassination attempt on any popular figure. For another there would be an entirely proper concern that the lad was armed with pickax or Molotov cocktail. For yet another the player's lawyer or business affairs consultant surely would inform him that the incident — contact by a third person — constituted an interview, for which the player's fee was five hundred dollars, and would push on to the question of ancillary rights.

But this was 1927, when the gods seemed kinder to the United States of America, and so the incident passed with no more than the commotion customary when Ruth touched off an explosion. Rather typically, Lou Gehrig earlier in the day drove in two runs, bringing his season's total to 172, breaking Ruth's 1921 record of 170. Gehrig got the subheadlines, under the big news about Ruth, but then, Gehrig would always be remembered, in Franklin P. Adams' rueful observation, as "the guy who hit all those homers the year Ruth set the record."

Not that many people at the beginning of the season expected either Ruth or the Yankees, who led the league by some sixteen games, to be in such exalted states that autumn afternoon. It was figured that Ruth would hit home runs, but when he shocked baseball by hitting fifty-nine in 1921, it was believed that the mark would last, in baseball time, forever.

The phrase is that he revolutionized the game. It has been said so many times that it slides easily on the tongue, and its truth is forgotten. Until Ruth came along, the home run was eschewed as almost vulgar. Although he worked as a pitcher, he first tied for the home run lead with 11 in 1918. The previous year, Wally Pipp, then Yankee first baseman, led the league with 9; Gavvy Cravath of the Phils led all hitters with 12, and there were just 339 major league home runs. By 1921, in only his third year as a full-time outfielder, Ruth set the record for home runs, lifetime, with 132, breaking a mark set in the nineteenth century by a man named Roger Connor, variously of New York, Philadelphia, and St. Louis. One hundred and thirty-seven home runs, lifetime, will not get you batting practice today.

Before the Babe the man perhaps most closely associated with the home run was J. Franklin Baker of the Philadelphia Athletics, who led the league from 1911–13, never collecting more than twelve in a single season. His nickname of "Home Run" came from the fact that he once hit two of them in a World Series — not World Series game, *World Series* — in successive games against the Giants in 1911.

By 1927 a lot of major leaguers were grabbing the bat at the bottom of the handle and swinging hard, conscious of the fact that the Babe's salary had jumped from ten thousand his first year in the outfield to seventy thousand. The club owners publicly, and perhaps in the heart of their hearts (for who knows what is in a club owner's heart?), deplored the financial element of Ruth's climb to fame — he and Charlie Chaplin were called the two best-known men in America, not excepting President Coolidge — but every ball park in the major leagues had been enlarged since Ruth's debut. And by the simple, flawless stroke of his bat he changed the pay scale for athletes for all time.

As to the club itself, it was figured to be a good team, one of the favorites for the pennant, but only one of them. Its 16½-game lead by September 22 did not seem likely back in the spring of the year. There were questions about its pitching, catching, and infield and about the ages of Ruth and pitchers Herb Pennock and Urban Shocker.

The myth of the Yankee pinstripe, which insisted that merely putting on the Yankee uniform made you part of a remorseless, invincible team, did not yet exist. The 1927 club carved out its beginnings.

True, the team had won the pennant in 1926. But it lost an historic World Series to the St. Louis Cardinals, and its league championship was regarded more as a collapse of the opposition than as any demonstration of lasting superiority. The 1925 club had finished seventh, and by winning the '26 pennant, the Yankees made the biggest jump to a flag in American League history up to that time, and there was a feeling that the pendulum might swing back.

So the Yankees that gathered in St. Petersburg, Florida, in March were respected but regarded as wearing no cloak of immortality. To begin with, there was Ruth. You always begin with Ruth. He was regarded as the game's Titan or, more aptly, its Gargantua, heroic from the cradle, but it was wondered how much longer he had to go; he was thirty-three, and there was some talk that his bat might be running out of home runs. He had hit forty-seven in 1926, but he had a way of following good years with bad.

In recent years there have been various attempts to strip away something called the legend of Babe Ruth, but there is no way to do this, for even after you strip away, you are left with the legend. Almost all the responsible things said about the man were true, the good and the bad, so the legend strippers usually settle by pointing out that the Babe liked women and drinking, which separates him from most healthy young men, and sometimes behaved badly, which sets him apart from humanity. And what is left is the swashbuckler who shaped the course of baseball and much else in modern sports, who set records that lasted for decades. In other words, a legend intact.

As early as 1921 there were attempts made to show just how singular and homeric a figure he was. Unlike the case with most giants, the stature was not stretched on the rack of nostalgia, retrospectively. With Ruth people immediately knew what they had, something outsize and unique. *Baseball* magazine in 1921 argued that he could be compared to no other player, that Christy Mathewson in his prime had rivals, that Tris Speaker, then generally acknowledged as the greatest of center fielders, had competitors, that Ty Cobb even then was challenged by other base-stealers, but that Ruth stood alone, unchallenged.

Besides Ruth, the Yankees of 1927 had Lou Gehrig, in his third season as a regular, a .313 hitter the previous year, with 16 home runs and 107 runs batted in. Already his name was bracketed with Ruth's, although not in the way it would be after 1927, but he was not yet "the Iron Horse" who played in a record 2,130 consecutive games or Gary Cooper–Gehrig, whose farewell speech at Yankee Stadium is now part of a rite of passage for American youth, fixed in celluloid in one of Hollywood's few honorable approaches to the national game. He was called "Columbia Lou," because he had attended Columbia University, or "Biscuit Pants," for his running back's center of gravity, six inches off the ground, or, more often, "Buster," a name favored by Ruth, who never remembered anyone's name.

Tony Lazzeri was the second baseman, coming off a rookie year in which he played every game, batting .275, which would be well below his lifetime average. He was "Poosh 'Em Up," a name dating back to his first year in organized baseball, with Salt Lake City, when he was struggling, and a restaurant owner named Tony Roffetti took pity on him, feeding him spaghetti dinners three nights running, and urging him to "poosh 'em up," meaning hit. In 1925, when he was twenty-one, Tony Lazzeri set a couple of Pacific Coast League records with 60 homers and 222 runs batted in.

Mark Koenig was the shortstop, in his second full year, like Lazzeri and, like Lazzeri, a San Francisco native and a product of its sandlots. He was regarded, preseason, as a potential flaw in the formidable front the Yankees presented the world. He hit .271 the previous year, but he committed fifty-two errors, more than any other shortstop in the American League. It was asked if he ever would make a major league infielder. He had been the World Series goat, striking out seven times, sometimes at critical points, hitting into three double plays, and committing three errors, one of them crucial, in the seventh and deciding game.

Joe Dugan, who hit .288 in 1926, was called "Jumping Joe," and, in previous years, "the best third baseman in baseball." He could hit, field, run, and throw. He handled the bunt famously, dashing in to barehand it and whip it across the diamond in one of baseball's patterned graces, and the old Yankees and some newspaper accounts credit his nickname to this rare talent, but the name was first attached to him by a sportswriter named Tiny Maxwell with the Philadelphia *Ledger,* after one of Joe's frequent disappearances from the Athletics, his first major league club, which did not pay him enough, he thought, and which he did not believe was going any place. "Jumping Joe," according to one teammate, jumped the A's thirty-six times, a modern record, going home to New Haven, or to Boston, or simply to check the ocean at Atlantic City a couple of days. In the spring of 1927 he was suspect because of an old knee injury.

With Ruth in the outfield there was Earle Combs, the best lead-off man in the major leagues, who hit .299 in 1926, more than 25 points below his lifetime average, but there was no doubt about him, a line-drive hitter who specialized in triples. Pitchers cried the couplet, "Hark! to the tombs / Here comes Earle Combs." He was a ghost on the bases, who, with Louisville in the minor leagues, was timed in ten flat for the hundred-yard dash in uniform and spikes by a clocker with

Churchill Downs. Combs was a greatly respected southern gentleman, and, oddly, a cheerleader. He had only an average throwing arm, but no one was faster getting rid of the ball, and he covered a tremendous amount of outfield, having been advised to take all the space he wanted with no fear of running into Ruth or Bob Meusel.

Perhaps one of the reasons that Combs's throwing arm was so questioned was that he played next to Ruth, who had been a great pitcher, capable of making the Hall of Fame through that arduous calling alone, having once, as every schoolboy learns along with the pledge of allegiance, pitched $29\frac{2}{3}$ scoreless World Series innings, a record that stood for forty-three years. He had become an outfielder only because his bat was too explosive to leave out of the daily lineup, but he retained his marvelous arm, so that base runners seldom challenged him, and it was said that he never made a mechanical error, never threw to the wrong base.

On the other side of Combs was Meusel, who had the best arm, by common consent, in baseball, a rifle, and who also hit for the average — .315 in 1926 — and with power. The only year during the 1920s that Ruth did not lead the league in home runs — 1925 — Meusel was the leader, with thirty-three, and the runs-batted-in leader, too. He stood six feet, three inches, and was called "Long Bob," also "Languid Bob," because he was uncommunicative and because he tended to play the way he felt that day.

Fans remembered his performance in the 1921 World Series, when he lazed to first base and cost the Yankees a run that would have saved the game and, with Koenig, he was a 1926 Series goat, muffing a fly in the deciding game, but his manager once said, "I don't want to brag, but it looks to me as though Meusel is going to be the greatest batter-in of runs that baseball has seen in recent years." He traditionally led the league in assists for an outfielder.

There were three catchers with the 1927 Yankees. The nominal first-stringer was Benny Bengough, twenty-nine years old and in his fifth season with the club, a Merry

Andrew who, at five feet seven and 145 pounds, looked more like the batboy than the catcher. He hit .381 in 1926 but played in only thirty-six games, having been hit on the right arm by George "The Bull" Uhle, a great Cleveland pitcher on his way to twenty-seven wins. Having unsuccessfully consulted medical specialists, X-ray artists, osteopaths, Bengough was visited by eccentrics and quacks claiming restorative powers for the damaged arm. One, a St. Louis dealer in hope, put Bengough in something like an electric chair, and the catcher leaped out at the current's first jolt and turned his ankle, thus becoming simultaneously sore of nonmatching limbs.

Tharon Patrick "Pat" Collins was a bigger man, solider, in the traditional catcher's mold, and he caught in 102 games in 1926, hitting .286 and, in the Series, .600, but he, too, had an injured throwing arm and doubted his own capacity to make the throw to second. He claimed, but gingerly, that he regained its strength through bowling — he was owner of a bowling alley in Kansas City — and he advised bowling in moderate amounts as the cure for ailing arms.

To back up this shaky duet, the Yankees dealt during the off-season for John Grabowski, inelegantly called "Nig," who hit .262 in forty-eight games with the Chicago White Sox in 1926, his third year in the major leagues. Grabowski handled pitchers well, it was felt, but there was concern about his dexterity, particularly in going after foul balls.

Baseball magazine observed unconvincingly, "The Yankee catchers are methodical, mere plodders, but, brother, these type are the salt of the earth, the backbone of the game."

The biggest question of all about the 1927 Yankees involved the pitching.

The ace was Herbert-Jeffries Pennock, the Squire of Kennett Square, Pennsylvania, where he bred silver foxes. He won twenty-three games in 1926, losing only eleven, but this would be his fourteenth year in the big leagues. He had come up with the Athletics in 1912 and pitched for the Boston Red Sox before joining the Yankees in 1923 to win nineteen games en route to a World Series, and there was speculation as to how much longer he could be useful, particularly since he was a serious holdout at thirty-three.

But a Yankee coach said, "If you were to cut that bird's head open, the weakness of every batter in the league would fall out." One tremendous Detroit hitter, Bob "Fatty" Fothergill (lifetime batting average .326) said to an even more tremendous Detroit hitter named Harry Heilmann (lifetime batting average .342 and four times American League batting champion), that no left-hander could get him, Fothergill, out, and then went zero for four against Pennock. "What the hell happened?" said Fothergill. Heilmann explained, "You didn't face a left-hander, you faced Herb Pennock," a line that would be repeated, under other circumstances, before 1927 was over.

Right up with Pennock on the Yankee pitching staff was Waite Charles Hoyt, twenty-seven and in his tenth major-league season, but still called "Schoolboy," a name attached to him when he signed a baseball contract at sixteen out of Brooklyn's Erasmus High School. He won sixteen and lost twelve in 1926 and had not yet won twenty games in a season, but in 1921 he emerged from three complete World Series games with an earned run average of 0.000, a record he was to share with the legendary Christy Mathewson and one of those rare marks that will never be lowered.

Urban Shocker was back with the Yankees for his third year in 1927. He first joined the team in 1916, when he was twenty-six, but two years later he was traded to the St. Louis Browns, a move regretted later, for he became a Yankee nemesis, credited with knowing more about pitching to Ruth, in particular, than any other man in the game except for the great, tarnished Eddie Cicotte of the Black Sox. Shocker won 127 games and lost 79 for the Browns, a club even then studying for its role as the essence of big-league ineptness, before the Yankees finally got him back in 1925. The spitball was outlawed in 1920, but pitchers already using it were allowed to continue. Shocker was one of only seven legal practitioners in 1927, but he had such an assortment of curves and other dirty tricks that he said he sometimes got through a game without resorting to the spitter. He was thirty-seven now, clearly nearing the end of the baseball road, but with a reputation as "the greatest in the game at pitching to a batter's weakness or pitching to a dangerous batter," and only Shocker that spring had any intimation, which he kept to himself, that the drum banged slowly for him.

When Walter "Dutch" Ruether, a left-hander with ten major league years behind him after stops in Chicago, Cincinnati, and Brooklyn of the National League, and Washington of the American, came to the Yankees in 1926 for "cash well exceeding the waiver price," the deal elicited comment, since he was still regarded as one of the league's better pitchers, the Senators' staff was short of left-handers, and six clubs still in contention had to pass on him before he got to the Yankees. "One possible explanation is that Dutch's salary may have scared them away," wrote Rud Rennie in the New York *Herald Tribune*. "Another is that he may have been unruly. Dutch has been unruly."

This meant, in the code of a boozy era, that Ruether drank. He was accused of getting drunk before the first game of the 1919 World Series, when he beat Cicotte and the heavily favored White Sox, 9–1, in a game later accepted as being fixed.

"I beat them easily," Ruether later recalled. "What hurt me was the disclosure that they were merely fooling around. It's hard to believe. I thought I had worked a tight game."

He was nineteen and six with the Reds that season, and he may have pitched a winning game, at that. It was something a man could think about, over a drink.

Another veteran, Bob Shawkey, the oldest Yankee in terms of years with the team, was not counted on for much. After two and a half seasons with the Athletics, starting in 1913, he came to the Yankees, winning twenty-four games for them in 1916, thirteen the following season, before entering the Navy in World War I, picking up the lasting nickname of "Sailor Bob," resuming with six big seasons, twice winning twenty games but clearly wearing out and winning only eight in 1926.

Since the staff was in need of more dependable arms, it was time the cup not pass from the lips of George Pipgras, called "the Danish Viking," a Minnesota farm boy tagged by that fatal baseball cliché, "world of stuff, no control," coming out of the dugout only often enough to win one game, lose four over two seasons, before being farmed out to pitch 102 minor league games in two years, and this spring he was back for what could be a final look. All the pressure was on him to prove he could be a major league pitcher.

"One of the most amazing characters ever to wear a Yankee uniform" and attracting instant notice was William Wilcy Moore, a big, yellow-haired Oklahoma dirt farmer who turned thirty that spring but was a rookie after a six-year career in the obscurity of places like Paris, Texas, and Ardmore and Okmulgee, Oklahoma. Two seasons earlier, his wrist was fractured by a batted ball, and, after he came back, he began throwing sidearm to relieve the strain and so developed a sinker, a low fast ball that breaks sharply as it reaches the plate. In 1926 he was thirty and four with Greenville, South Carolina, in the Sally League, walking only seventy men all season. A pitcher with a thirty and four record is worth looking at, it was said, even if he is pitching in the Scandinavian League, and so Wilcy Moore, who had thought the previous year of packing it in, going home, and settling down to the farm life, would be looked at closely that spring.

There were, of course, others in camp, rookies of great promise, utility men, veterans, a gaggle of substitutes like pitchers Myles Thomas, a Penn State man with a six–six record the previous year, and Joe Giard, thirteen–fifteen after two seasons; and backup outfielders like Ben Paschal, in his third season with the Yankees, who could field and who hit .360 in eighty-nine games in 1925 (but how do you, realistically, *how do you* break into an outfield of Ruth, Combs, and Meusel, unless you pray for a selective outbreak of the plague?); and infielders like Roy Morehart, out of Stephen Austin College in Texas, who hit .315 in seventy-three games with the 1926 White Sox, Julian Wera, and Mike Gazella, a weak hitter in his third year, who proved that a spear-carrier can mean more than his average the previous season, when the Yankees, having all but dissipated a huge July lead, lost a double-header to Cleveland, the second-place club, for their fourth defeat in a row. At dinner that night Gazella, a former baseball and football hero at Lafayette College, said approximately, "All right, you birds have been kidding me all season about the old college spirit. If you gutless bums had a little of that spirit, you would not have quit the way you did today." That little speech was credited with helping the team turn around and beat the Indians the next day and go on to the pennant.

Such were the men who gathered in St. Petersburg for training camp in the spring of 1927.

Ernest Hemingway

From *The Old Man and the Sea*

"If you're not tired, fish," he said aloud, "you must be very strange."

He felt very tired now and he knew the night would come soon and he tried to think of other things. He thought of the Big Leagues, to him they were the *Gran Ligas,* and he knew that the Yankees of New York were playing the *Tigres* of Detroit.

This is the second day now that I do not know the result of the *juegos,* he thought. But I must have confidence and I must be worthy of the great DiMaggio who does all things perfectly even with the pain of the bone spur in his heel. What is a bone spur? he asked himself. *Un espuela de hueso.* We do not have them. Can it be as painful as the spur of a fighting cock in one's heel? I do not think I could endure that or the loss of the eye and of both eyes and continue to fight as the fighting cocks do. Man is not much beside the great birds and beasts. Still I would rather be that beast down there in the darkness of the sea.

"Unless sharks come," he said aloud. "If sharks come, God pity him and me."

Do you believe the great DiMaggio would stay with a fish as long as I will stay with this one? he thought. I am sure he would and more since he is young and strong. Also his father was a fisherman. But would the bone spur hurt him too much?

"I do not know," he said aloud. "I never had a bone spur."

Shirley Povich

1956: New York Yankees 2, Brooklyn Dodgers 0

Washington Post, October 9, 1956

The million-to-one shot came in. Hell froze over. A month of Sundays hit the calendar. Don Larsen today pitched a no-hit, no-run, no-man-reach-first game in a World Series.

On the mound at Yankee Stadium, the same guy who was knocked out in two innings by the Dodgers on Friday came up today with one for the record books, posting it there in solo grandeur as the only Perfect Game in World Series history.

With it, the Yankee right-hander shattered the Dodgers, 2–0, and beat Sal Maglie, while taking 64,519 suspense-limp fans into his act.

First there was mild speculation, then there was hope, then breaths were held in slackened jaws in the late innings as the big mob wondered if the big Yankee right-hander could bring off for them the most fabulous of all World Series games.

He did it, and the Yanks took the Series lead three games to two, to leave the Dodgers as thunderstruck as Larsen himself appeared to be at the finish of his feat.

Larsen whizzed a third strike past pinch hitter Dale Mitchell in the ninth. That was all. It was over. Automatically, the massive 226-pounder from San Diego started walking from the mound toward the dugout, as pitchers are supposed to do at the finish.

But this time there was a woodenness in his steps and his stride was that of a man in a daze. The spell was broken for Larsen when Yogi Berra ran onto the infield to embrace him.

It was not Larsen jumping for joy. It was the more demonstrative Berra. His battery mate leaped full tilt at the big guy. In self-defense, Larsen caught Berra in mid-air as one would catch a frolicking child, and that's how they made their way toward the Yankee bench, Larsen carrying Berra.

There wasn't a Brooklyn partisan left among the 64,519, it seemed, at the finish. Loyalties to the Dodgers evaporated in sheer enthrallment at the show big Larsen was giving them, for this was a day when the fans could boast that they were there.

So at the finish, Larsen had brought it off, and erected for himself a special throne in baseball's Hall of Fame, with the first Perfect Game pitched in major-league baseball since Charlie Robertson of the White Sox against Detroit 34 years ago.

But this was one more special. This one was in a World Series. Three times, pitchers had almost come through with no-hitters, and there were three one-hitters in the World Series books, but never a no-man-reach-base classic.

The tragic victim of it all, sitting on the Dodger bench, was sad Sal Maglie, himself a five-hit pitcher today in his bid for a second Series victory over the Yankees. He was out of the game, technically, but he was staying to see it out and it must have been in disbelief that he saw himself beaten by another guy's World Series no-hitter.

Mickey Mantle hit a home run today in the fourth inning and that was all the impetus the Yankees needed, but no game-winning home run ever wound up with such emphatic second billing as Mantle's this afternoon.

It was an exciting wallop but in the fourth inning only, because after that Larsen was the story today, and the dumbfounded Dodgers could wonder how this same guy who couldn't last out two innings in the second game could master them so thoroughly today.

He did it with a tremendous assortment of pitches that seemed to have five forward speeds, including a slow one that ought to have been equipped with back-up lights.

Larsen had them in hand all day. He used only 97 pitches, not an abnormally low number because 11 pitches an inning is about normal for a good day's work. But he was the boss from the outset. Only against Pee Wee Reese in the first inning did he lapse to a three-ball count, and then he struck Reese out. No other Dodger was ever favored with more than two called balls by Umpire Babe Pinelli.

Behind him, his Yankee teammates made three spectacular fielding plays to put Larsen in the Hall of Fame. There was one in the second inning that calls for special description. In the fifth, Mickey Mantle ranged far back into left center to haul in Gil Hodges' long drive with a backhand shoetop grab that was a beaut. In the eighth, the same Hodges made another bid to break it up, but Third Baseman Andy Carey speared his line drive.

Little did Larsen, the Yankees, the Dodgers or anybody among the 64,519 in the stands suspect that when Jackie Robinson was robbed of a line-drive hit in the second inning, the stage was being set for a Perfect Game.

Robinson murdered the ball so hard that Third Baseman Andy Carey barely had time to fling his glove upward in a desperate attempt to get the ball. He could only deflect it. But, luckily, Shortstop Gil McDougald was backing up, and able to grab the ball on one bounce. By a half-step, Mc-Dougald got Robinson at first base, and Larsen tonight can be grateful that it was not the younger, fleeter Robinson of a few years back but a heavy-legged, 40-year-old Jackie.

As the game wore on, Larsen lost the edge that gave him five strikeouts in the first four innings, and added only two in the last five. He had opened up by slipping called third strikes past both Gilliam and Reese in the first inning.

Came the sixth, and he got Furillo and Campanella on pops,

fanned Maglie. Gilliam, Reese and Snider were easy in the seventh. Robinson tapped out, Hodges lined out and Amoros flied out in the eighth. And now it was the ninth, and the big Scandinavian-American was going for the works with a calm that was exclusive with him.

Furillo gave him a bit of a battle, fouled off four pitches, then flied mildly to Bauer. He got two quick strikes on Campanella, got him on a slow roller to Martin.

Now it was the left-handed Dale Mitchell, pinch hitting for Maglie.

Ball one came in high. Larsen got a called strike.

On the next pitch, Mitchell swung for strike two.

Then the last pitch of the game. Mitchell started to swing, but didn't go through with it.

But it made no difference because Umpire Pinelli was calling it Strike Number Three, and baseball history was being made.

Maglie himself was a magnificent figure out there all day, pitching hitless ball and leaving the Yankees a perplexed gang, until suddenly with two out in the fourth, Mickey Mantle, with two called strikes against him, lashed the next pitch on a line into the right-field seats to give the Yanks a 1–0 lead.

There was doubt about that Mantle homer because the ball was curving and would it stay fair? It did. In their own half of the inning, the Dodgers had no such luck. Duke Snider's drive into the same seats had curved foul by a few feet. The disgusted Snider eventually took a third strike.

The Dodgers were a luckless gang and Larsen a fortunate fellow in the fifth. Like Mantle, Sandy Amoros lined one into the seats in right, and that one was a near thing for the Yankees. By what seemed only inches, it curved foul, the umpires ruled.

Going into the sixth, Maglie was pitching a one-hitter — Mantle's homer — and being outpitched. The old guy lost some of his stuff in the sixth, though, and the Yankees came up with their other run.

Carey led off with a single to center, and Larsen sacrificed him to second on a daring third-strike bunt. Hank Bauer got the run in with a single to left. There might have been a close play at the plate had Amoros come up with the ball cleanly, but he didn't and Carey scored unmolested.

Now there were Yanks still on first and third with only one out, but they could get no more. Hodges made a scintillating pickup of Mantle's smash, stepped on first and threw to home for a double play on Bauer, who was trying to score. Bauer was trapped in a rundown and caught despite a low throw by Campanella that caused Robinson to fall into the dirt.

But the Yankees weren't needing any more runs for Larsen today. They didn't even need their second one, because they were getting a pitching job for the books this memorable day in baseball.

Tony Kubek and Terry Pluto

From *Sixty-One*

The last time I talked to Roger Maris was about two months before he died. It was one of his good days when the pain wasn't so bad, and he was able to talk with an old friend for about ninety minutes.

For a while, we asked about each other's families and some friends we had in common, but it wasn't long before our conversation turned back to the 1961 Yankees. That's how it usually went with us.

That year, Bobby Richardson led off, I batted second, Roger hit third, and Mickey Mantle was fourth. Roger liked to talk about the lineup, how I used to dig a hole with my back foot in the batter's box. We kept our back feet in the same spot, and Roger's swing was in such a groove that season he could tell if the hole was just a little off. He'd come back to the dugout and ask me why I was standing in the wrong place.

It's kind of crazy the things you end up remembering and talking about after twenty-five years. It's also strange that Roger's one home run I remember the most was not his sixty-first, but his fifty-eighth. We were playing in Detroit, and I was on second base. Roger was at the plate and stepped out of the batter's box. He seemed to be staring at the upper deck in right field. I looked out there, but I didn't see anything. Suddenly, a flock of about 250 Canadian geese appeared on the horizon, flying right over the right-field roof in Tiger Stadium. Roger took off his cap, wiped his brow, and just watched the geese. I know it couldn't have been more than a minute, but it seemed like about ten before he put his cap back on and got into the batter's box. Nester Chylak was the umpire, and I could see he was getting a little nervous because Roger was holding up the game, but Chylak let Roger stand there looking at the geese. Terry Fox was the Detroit pitcher, and he wasn't thrilled with the delay. He stood on the mound, rubbing up the ball and wondering what Roger was doing. But like Chylak, Terry never said a word. The game just stopped because Roger Maris wanted to watch some geese.

Finally, Roger was ready to hit. Fox threw him a pitch that was about a foot outside and six inches off the ground. I could see it perfectly from second base. Roger went out and got it, pulling a four-hundred-foot homer into the upper deck in right, just under where the geese had flown.

I mentioned this to Roger, and he said, "Tony, I can still see those geese. Watching them was so peaceful."

In 1961, I think the only place Roger felt any peace was at home plate. In the outfield, he was in danger of having some jerk rip out a chair and throw it at him, as happened in Detroit. In the clubhouse, there were countless reporters with endless questions. In the hotels, there were fans wanting time and autographs. But at home plate in 1961, Roger Maris could do anything he wanted.

"I always loved to hit," Roger would say. "I loved everything about playing baseball. As for the other stuff, well, you can have it."

"Roger was in such a groove in sixty-one," said Ralph Terry. "He really had that three-and-one shot down pat. Roger would be at the plate, and some poor guy on the mound would be pitching him carefully. Then the count would run to three-and-one, and the pitcher would look at the on-deck circle and see Mickey Mantle. So what is he supposed to do, walk Roger and get to Mickey? He had no choice but to come in there, and Roger was ready. Roger hit 61 homers and didn't draw one intentional walk. That shows you how strong our lineup was and how much the pitchers feared Mickey."

During the last few months of the 1961 season, Roger was getting about three thousand letters a week. I received about one hundred, a lot of them admonishing me not to make the last out of a game, depriving Roger Maris and Mickey Mantle of a last at bat and another shot at a record.

I was twenty-five, the starting shortstop for the New York Yankees. I used to walk out of the park three hours after a day game and see over one hundred kids wanting to know if Roger and Mickey had left the dressing room. I used to go to a place called The Dutchman's, which was really Daube's Steak House, with Roger and Mickey. It was just off 161st Street, over a hill from Yankee Stadium. Babe Ruth and Lou Gehrig used to eat there, and so had a lot of old National League players since the Polo Grounds wasn't far away. Supposedly, the Gas House Gang would come into the place, literally tear it up, and then leave a pile of cash on the table to pay for the damages. The place raised rustic to an art form with sawdust floors and a couple of Dobermans guarding the door. One of the waiters told us that Babe Ruth would have a few beers and start sliding headfirst into the tables. You ordered your steak by the ounce and felt as though you had stepped back in time.

Ruth seemed to be everywhere in 1961. For most of the season, he haunted Roger and Mickey as they chased his home run record. After Mickey was hurt, it was Roger versus the Babe, a duel neither man would have ever imagined. And in many ways, it was just one of many ironies. For example, not only did Ruth lose his home run record to Roger, his record for consecutive scoreless innings in World Series competition was topped by Whitey Ford.

Our team won 109 games. We hit a record 240 homers without the benefit of a designated hitter and playing in a much bigger Yankee Stadium than exists today. Also, there weren't the homer havens that have opened since, such as the Kingdome, the Metrodome, and Exhibition Stadium. It was the first time Whitey won twenty games and the last time a hardheaded pitcher named Jim Coates ever insulted Ellie Howard. It was the end of Casey Stengel and the beginning of Ralph Houk. For Luis Arroyo and Rollie Sheldon, it was the beginning and end of their careers, all in one year. It also was the last time a shortstop named Tony Kubek would play a big-league season without suffering from back problems.

"All I can tell you about the 1961 Yankees," said former Detroit manager Bob Scheffing, "is that they had the best infield in the league, and they had so much power that a guy like Moose Skowron hit seventh, and that seemed to be the right spot for him."

Bud Daley came to the Yankees on June 14, 1961, one day before the trading deadline. He had been with Kansas City and in last place. "What struck me about the Yankees was the confidence. The hitters would tell us to keep the score within a run in the last three innings and the other team would crack. The other team usually did because one of our guys was cracking a home run."

"The 1961 Yankees may have been the best team of all time," said Johnny Sain. "We had defense no one knew about. We had pitching no one knew about. We had a manager in Ralph Houk no one knew would become a great one. And we had Roger hitting 61 homers. You know that no one ever expected that to happen."

"The year belonged to Roger and Mickey," said Clete Boyer. "Those guys were just such great players. I remember a doubleheader in Chicago where I hit two home runs. That was pretty good, considering the White Sox' pitching. What the hell, you hit a couple of homers, and you expect to see your name in the paper. But Roger hit four that day. His name was in the headlines and mine was only in the box score. But no one was jealous of Roger and Mickey getting all the publicity because they deserved it."

It was also the story of three men — Roger, Mickey, and Babe Ruth. And in the end, it came down to two men — a very human Roger Maris versus Babe Ruth, who had become so great that even his very human failings became legendary.

Sixty-one.

That's the number of home runs Roger hit, and it was a year when we all wore crew cuts. Roger always preferred to have his hair cut near his home in Kansas City, because "New York barbers give you that glamour-boy look I can't stand."

Sixty-one was when I lived at a place called The Stadium Motor Lodge, a two-story motel about eight blocks from Yankee Stadium. It was a place fans would spend a night or two when they came to town to catch a game. I shared a room there with an infielder named Joe DeMaestri and, early in the year, pitcher Johnny James. Bill Stafford, Clete Boyer, and Moose Skowron also spent some time there. For us, it was a place to hang our clothes and watch television. It was close enough to the park so we could walk. When we went on the road, we'd check out of all the rooms but one, throwing all of our stuff in there. Hey, it saved a few bucks. As for Roger, he lived with Mickey and Bob Cerv in an unpretentious apartment in Queens. That's where Roger cooked breakfast for the three of them. They would spend hours in their living room, playing for pennies by putting a golf ball into a little tin hole that sat on top of the carpet. They rode to the Stadium in Roger's convertible, the top down and the wind in their faces serving as the air conditioner.

At the park, Roger kept to himself. Between innings early in the game, Roger sometimes went into the clubhouse, smoking one of his Camels or sipping coffee. The Yankees also had a television in the clubhouse, and Roger used it to get a better look at what the pitcher was throwing. You could hear the scraping of his spikes against the concrete as he came down the runway just before it was his turn to bat or to go out and play right field. He prized the quiet you find in an empty clubhouse during a game.

Before the game, Roger often sat at the huge oak table that was in the middle of the clubhouse. That table went back to the days of Ruth and Gehrig, and clubhouse man Big Pete

Sheehy would never let the front office replace it. As usual, his coffee and Camels were near. He had this game, it was a box about a foot wide and three inches deep. Inside, there were two small wooden platforms with forty holes. The idea was to maneuver a little steel ball from one hole, through a maze, and one level to another. Roger was fascinated by it and would play the game for hours. He had a routine in which he could smoke his Camels, drink coffee, and play the game all at the same time.

The first things I thought about when Roger died were him staring at those Canadian geese and him playing that labyrinth game. Then I started to think about the team, and I remembered a picture we had taken by *Look* magazine. They dressed us in suits and handed us briefcases. The theme of the photo was that the Yankees were like U.S. Steel — cold, corporate, businesslike. That wasn't the Yankees I knew, and it was Roger's death that convinced me to contact the guys who were a part of sixty-one. Most of us are in our fifties, and some are over sixty. In our last conversation, Roger said, "You know, Tony, we're all getting kind of old. There were some pretty good guys on that club. Not too many people know that."

And Roger was one of them. It was easy to get the wrong impression of Roger. He was suspicious of strangers and could care less about his public image. He didn't crack many jokes, and when he did, they often came out wrong when he was in the company of strangers. The first time people met Roger, it wasn't surprising if they came away with the misconception that Roger was one morose guy.

But Roger had his moments. In Baltimore, he loved to order hardshelled crabs and have them delivered to his room. His roommate, Clete Boyer, would fill their bathtub with ice and a couple of cases of beer. A lot of guys would come up to the room, and Roger would have a little party.

Once, they ordered three bushels of crabs instead of the usual two, meaning we had plenty left over. Then Roger went out for a while and returned with a live lobster. One of our trainers, Joe Soares, was known to have a couple of beers at night, and when you saw him, you knew he had made a pit stop at the bar. While Soares was out, we got a key to his room. Roger brought the lobster while Clete and I took the crabs to his room. We put the crab shells under the covers of Joe's bed and Roger dumped the lobster in the toilet. The place smelled something awful. We left the room, and nothing happened for a while. But about midnight, we heard this scream, and there was Joe running down the hallway, babbling about a lobster in his toilet. Apparently he had drunk too much to smell the crab shells.

"Roger liked a good time as much as anyone," said Clete Boyer. "But once he got going in 1961, he was under the gun all the time, and that was bound to change his personality. Roger was a country boy from Fargo, North Dakota. He never understood how great he was. And the guy was a great player. They like to say that 1961 was a fluke, but Roger hit 39 homers and was the American League MVP in 1960. Not too many stiffs become back-to-back MVPs. See, Roger thought he was a good ballplayer, a complete ballplayer. But he never thought of himself as a forty or sixty home run guy. In 1961 he got on this unbelievable roll, and the press made him out to be nothing but a home-run hitter. Roger knew he couldn't hit forty or fifty homers year after year, but he found himself in the position of trying to be something he was not. And there was the press, asking him about being another Babe Ruth. Then they made Mickey out to be the good guy and Roger the bad guy because it gave them good stories. What a bunch of crap. He was twenty-six, just a kid. Some guys say he didn't handle everything the best. Well, how could anyone handle it? Roger was like the rest of us. What he wanted to do the most was win. He wanted to get into the World Series for two reasons — the prestige and the check. Believe me, that eight-thousand-dollar World Series check came in handy every Christmas."

When I think of sixty-one, I first think of Roger Maris.

Roger Angell

Excerpt from
Several Stories with Sudden Endings: October 1977

Late Innings

. . . The Yankees, it may be recalled, had a little trouble along the way. Their relentlessly publicized off-the-field sulks and tiffs and rumorings and squabbles will not be re-examined here, if only because the daily turns of plot of a soap opera — "Churls' Way," perhaps — lose their edge when seen from a little distance. The trouble, of course, was a violent multiple clash of personalities, brought on by owner George Steinbrenner's intense ambition and his impatient, meddlesome need for total success; by Billy Martin's insecure ego, his dangerous temper and occasional deviousness, and his capacity for martyrdom; by Reggie Jackson's money and display of money, his love of the hottest part of the spotlight, and his actorish ways with the press; by Thurman Munson's brooding silences, his injured pride as a challenged leader, and his distaste for big-city maneuverings; and by the various and equally urgent wants and responses of a dozen other well-paid but fame-frazzled and (in the end) exhausted professional athletes, whose every word and gesture was recorded, from April to October, by enormous squads of local and national reporters and media people. I visited the Yankees after many games last summer, but I rarely stayed long, because it was the most joyless clubhouse I had ever been in. In time, I became sorry for them all, and it even occurred to me that this rich and favored team was terribly unlucky, because it didn't seem to have a true leader — one carefree or charismatic veteran star who could laugh at all this once in a while and thus suggest to the other players that they were young, after all, and that what they were engaged in was, for them if not their glum employers, still a game.

On the field, the Yanks never bored me. In hindsight any champion team acquires an aura of brilliance and inexorable success, but these Yankees did favor a highly melodramatic style of baseball, often seeming to wait for the big game, attended by the largest and most expectant audience, before coming up with the sudden astounding performance, the impossible play, the killing blow. In June, playing before a gigantic weekend home audience against the Red Sox, just a week after the Sox had humiliated them by belting out sixteen homers during a three-game sweep at Fenway Park, the Yankees took the opener when Roy White tied the game with a two-run, two-out homer in the ninth and Reggie Jackson hit a game-winning single in the eleventh. They won the next game, too, and the one after that — on a ninth-inning single by Paul Blair — to cut the Boston lead from five games to two. The Yankees probably began their pennant move on August 10th, when Reggie Jackson was at last moved to the cleanup spot in the order, but the upward path was a long and bumpy one. On August 16th, at the Stadium, the free-swinging White Sox, trailing by 9–4, erupted for six runs in the top half of the ninth against Ron Guidry and Sparky Lyle — and were immediately beaten in the bottom half on a two-run homer by Chris Chambliss. A couple of weeks later, with the club finally in first place, Chambliss came off the bench and hit a three-run homer in the eighth that whipped the Royals by 5–3. The Yankees won the next day, against the Mariners, on Mickey Rivers' homer in the eleventh, and the day after that on Graig Nettles' homer in the ninth. This kind of momentum, which requires a deep and talented lineup, makes everyone, including the manager, look nine feet tall, but once the Yankees began to make their headlines on the field instead of in the clubhouse, one could see at last that most of these expensive athletes were performing at superlative levels — not only the dangerous Jackson and Munson and Graig Nettles but outfielders Lou Piniella and Mickey Rivers (who batted .330 and .326 this year) and Willie Randolph, who had established himself as the best young second baseman in the league. Sparky Lyle won thirteen games and saved twenty-six more with his down-ducking slider; and Ron Guidry, an unknown left-hander, finished with an earned-run average of 2.82 — fourth best among the league's starting pitchers. The manager of such a club might seem to have the same responsibilities as a private chauffeur, but it is my conviction that Billy Martin in the late weeks of this season was the best on-the-field manager I have ever seen. From mid-August to mid-October, his shifts of the batting order, his selections from a roster of often ailing or unsound pitchers, his late-inning picks of pinch-hitters or relief hurlers (or his almost mystifying patience with an incumbent) must have left rival teams and managers at times with the feeling that they had been not only beaten up by the big-city slickers but somehow bamboozled as well. The pilot of a squad like the 1977 Yankees is often disparaged as a "push-button manager," but anyone who knows this game understands that there are a hundred different ways to push those buttons in every game, and many thousands of ways over the course of a season. The piano may be an easier instrument. Away from the field, Billy Martin often seems indifferent or depressed, and unable to shake off the pain of a lost game, which he takes as a deadly personal defeat. He also appears to be distracted by the office work of baseball — scouting reports, statistics, public relations — and this may be the real source of his difficulties with George Steinbrenner, who is a driving and unrelenting businessman. But up on the dugout step Martin is someone else altogether. His intensity is unique. Under the cap, his face is pale and tight, and he looks almost ill with concentration and hostility. His eyes are cold, moving constantly about the field and across the dark inner ranges of stratagem and intuition, in search of the sudden edge, the flicker of advantage, that will win again. It is the face of a man in a street fight, a man up an alley when the knives have just come out. It is win or die.

The Yankees won their pennant, we now know, by taking the first two games of a classic three-game series from the Red Sox at the Stadium in the middle of September. I think that many fans who were there may remember those games even more vividly than the Yanks' later triumphs in the play-offs and the World Series — the enormous crowds (the total of 164,852 spectators was the biggest three-game baseball audience since 1958), the oceans of sound, the weight of the ancient rivalry, the claustrophobic tension of the games themselves. The visitors, who came into the series a game and a half behind and only one game down in the lost column, were frightening at the plate. Their sluggers — Jim Rice, Carlton Fisk, Carl Yastrzemski, George Scott, Butch Hobson, and the rest — set or tied eighteen major-league home-run records this year. (Hobson alone hit thirty homers and batted in a hundred and twelve runs — fair work for an eighth-place hitter.) Against the Pinstripes now, they attacked the ball violently, as always, but the Yankee pitchers and the Yankee ballpark broke their hearts. Fisk and Rice and Hobson and Scott all whacked enormous drives that were pulled in at the last moment just in front of the distant fences. Carlton Fisk, I imagine, will sometimes start up in bed in the middle of the night this winter with the vision of Mickey Rivers at the base of some faraway blue wall gathering in yet another of his four-hundred-foot fly balls, firing the ball back, and then finishing the play with that odd little shiver of his arms and shoulders, like a man ridding himself of a bad thought. In the first game, Rivers also poled a first-pitch drive into the low bleachers, and skinny Ron Guidry fanned nine of the Sox' big swingers and won it, 4–2. In the next, Reggie Cleveland nailed Mickey Rivers in the back with his first delivery of the night (let's see you pull *that* pitch, Mick!) and then set down rows of Yankee hitters in disorderly but effective fashion while his teammates tried frantically to get on the scoreboard. But Reggie Jackson made two marvelous catches in right field, and in the fifth the Sox loaded the bases off Ed Figueroa with none out but failed to score (Lynn bounced into a home-to-first double play; Yaz ripped a sure single up the middle that collided with Figueroa's hip, and was thrown out), and the current of the game, one sensed, reversed direction. No ballplayer is more inflammable in this sort of situation than Reggie Jackson, who, with Thurman Munson aboard in the ninth inning, hit a splendid three-and-two slider by Reggie Cleveland deep into the right-field bleachers for the only runs of the game. The win put the Yankees ahead of the Red Sox by three and a half games (and two and a half ahead of the Orioles), and although the Sox won the following night and subsequently beat the Yankees twice more, up at Fenway Park, they were never able to close the gap. Boston and Baltimore ended the season in a tie for second place, two and a half games behind. . . .

The roily and momentous events of the two championship playoffs and the World Series have left such vivid pictures on our baseball consciousness that probably only the lightest burnishing is required to bring back the colors. The Yankees' six-game triumph over the Dodgers in the World Series, and Reggie Jackson's epochal feat (in this case, perhaps, hyperbole may be forgiven) of smashing those three successive home runs in the final game, should not let us forget how very close the Yankees came to missing the World Series altogether. Reggie saved baseball's crown jewels. Without him, this would have been another year in which the more brilliant and emotional October baseball came in the preliminary series. It is my guess that the Phillies and the Royals were great public favorites to win their playoffs, if only because both these attractive teams had been losers in the same event last fall and then had made the long summer journey back to win their divisional titles again, each of them with a deeper and far more confident lineup than in the year before. This time, each was eliminated on its own home turf, where it had every expectation of winning at last, and each was beaten under bitter and extraordinary circumstances. I cannot remember such a painful week of baseball.

The Yankees and the Royals began at Yankee Stadium, taking up their business, it seemed, exactly where they had left off last fall, when Chris Chambliss's ninth-inning homer broke up a tied game and a tied series. This time, however, the power hitting was by the team in the dusty-blue road uniforms: Kansas City, which had altered some batting strokes and batting attitudes this year to beef up its attack, racked up six runs in the first three innings and whipped the Yanks, 7–2, on homers by Hal McRae, John Mayberry, and Al Cowens. McRae's attack the next night was on the person of Willie Randolph, whom he upended violently at second base while breaking up a double play; the two ended up in a tangle, yards beyond the bag, with the ball on the ground and McRae, as he peered through the dust, waving urgently and then triumphantly to Freddie Patek, the base runner ahead of him, who scored the run that tied the game at 2–2. McRae's body block seemed legal but ill-advised; it affronted the Yankee hitters, who immediately responded with three runs in the bottom half of the inning. Their pitcher, Ron Guidry, allowed but one subsequent K.C. runner to reach first, and won by 6–2, on a three-hitter.

Pitching is nearly everything in a short series, and the Royals' admirable Dennis Leonard, a twenty-game winner this year, proved this adage in Game Three, with an effortless four-hit, 6–2 victory on his home field, to the ecstatic pleasure of the Kansas City rooters. I watched the game on television, enjoying (via some wonderful NBC camerawork) Leonard's laserlike deliveries and the Royals' eager, contact-hitting style of ball. By my calculation, the Yankees were now out of sound pitchers and out of luck, but I had somehow forgotten about the ever-available Sparky Lyle, who entered the next day's doings in the fourth inning — very early for him —

and, bearing down on the batters and on his gigantic chaw of tobacco, threw shutout two-hit ball for sixteen outs and the ballgame, which the Yanks won, 6–4.

Game Five: It began with a fistfight at third base between George Brett and Graig Nettles, and ended with Freddie Patek alone and in tears in the empty Kansas City dugout. The Yankees' comeback, last-inning victory, it might be noted, was the first break in a pattern of nine consecutive alternate wins and losses by these two courageous and uncompromising teams, beginning with their first playoff game last year. The rarity and satisfaction of this kind of competition can best be suggested in diagram:

NY KC NY KC NY KC NY KC NY NY

Here in Game Five (or Game Ten) Billy Martin, stretching his luck and risking his job, benched Reggie Jackson (who had looked bad at the plate and in the field) and put Paul Blair in his spot in right field, and got an essential hit out of both men — Jackson's was a pinch-hit single — late in the game. That's *managing!* The Royals led early, 3–1, but could not widen that lead. Looking back on it all now, I can't be sure whether it was the Yankees' resolution in putting their leadoff batters aboard in both the eighth and ninth innings that really won this game, or whether it was Mike Torrez's dogged work in relief of Ron Guidry, or whether Kansas City manager Whitey Herzog's somewhat precipitate derricking of Paul Splittorff lost it, or whether it wasn't really the Yankees' obstinate defense in the middle innings that made it all happen: a very deep running catch by Mickey Rivers in the fourth and, in the fifth, two dazzling plays by Willie Randolph and a great peg, nailing a base runner, by Thurman Munson. But never mind. The Kansas City fans, who fell into a shocked, incredulous silence in the eighth and ninth, as the Yankees caught up and then went ahead at last, will have all winter and all next summer to think about these doleful issues. Rivers tied it with a single, and Randolph hit the gamer — a sacrifice fly — and the Yankees won, 5–3. When it was over, I was nearly in despair myself, there in front of the set. I couldn't bear to have either team lose. . . .

Even before Reggie Jackson took matters in hand, this was a rousing World Series. The Dodgers hit nine home runs, setting a National League Series record, and if they had somehow been able to carry the action into a seventh game there is good reason to think they could have won it. By far the best game, it turned out, was the first, at Yankee Stadium, and the Yankees' coup was undoubtedly the three runs they scored off the suave and redoubtable Don Sutton. The visitors, it will be recalled, bravely tied the game with a run in the ninth, but then ran smack into Sparky Lyle; deep in the unstilly night, the Yanks won it, 4–3, on a twelfth-inning double by Randolph and a single by Paul Blair. The next evening, Catfish Hunter, who had suffered through a dreary season of injuries and illness, was badly manhandled by the Dodgers, who whacked four homers and won, 6–1. Hunter, a lighthearted hero of many previous Octobers, smiled and shrugged in response to the postgame questions. "The sun don't shine on the same dog's ass all the time," he said.

Out West, within the vast pastel conch of Dodger Stadium, the Yanks now captured two fine, extremely grudging games behind some stout pitching by Torrez and Guidry, who both went the full distance. The Dodgers, apparently determined to win on pure muscle, excited their multitudes with more downtowners, but the Yankees took the first game, 5–3, on two deflected infield singles, and the second, 4–2, on some modest wrong-field hits and a solo homer by Reggie Jackson. Thurman Munson hit a homer in Game Five, and so did Jackson (a homer to be more noticed later on), but only after the Dodgers had whanged out thirteen hits for Don Sutton, who coasted home in a 10–4 laugher.

With the Yankees leading the Series by three games to two, we came back to New York for the extraordinary conclusion. In this game, the Dodgers took an early 3–2 lead on

Reggie Smith's home run off Mike Torrez; it was the third
round-tripper for Smith, who was beginning to look like the
dominant figure in the Series. The other Reggie came up to
bat in the fourth inning (he had walked in the second) and
instantly pulled Burt Hooton's first delivery into the right-
field stands on a low, long parabola, scoring Munson ahead of
him and putting the Yankees ahead for the rest of the game
and the rest of the year. Jackson stepped up to the plate again
in the next inning (Elias Sosa was now pitching for the
Dodgers), with two out and Willie Randolph on first, and this
time I called the shot. "He's going to hit it out of here on the
first pitch," I announced to my neighbors in the press rows,
and so he did. It was a lower drive than the first and carried
only four or five rows into the same right-field sector, but it
was much more resoundingly hit; at first it looked like a
double, or even a loud single, but it stayed up there — a
swift white message flying out on an invisible wire — and
vanished into the turbulent darkness of the crowd.

My call was not pure divination. With the strange insect
gaze of his shining eyeglasses, with his ominous Boche-like
helmet pulled low, with his massive shoulders, his gauntleted
wrists, his high-held bat, and his enormously muscled legs
spread wide, Reggie Jackson makes a frightening figure at
bat. But he is not a great hitter. Perhaps he is not even a
good one. A chronic overstrider and overswinger, he swings
through a lot of pitches, and the unchecked flailing power of
his immense cut causes his whole body to drop down a foot
or more. He often concludes a trip to the plate (and a Yankee
inning) with his legs grotesquely twisted and his batting
helmet falling over his eyes — and with the ball, flipped
underhand by the departing catcher, rolling gently out to the
mound. It is this image, taken in conjunction with his salary
and his unending publicity in the sports pages, that seems to
enrage so many fans. "Munson!" they cry, like classicists
citing Aeschylus. "Now, you take Munson — *there's* a hitter!"
And they are right. But Reggie Jackson is streaky and
excitable. I have an inexpungeable memory of the two violent
doubles he hit for the Oakland A's against Tom Seaver in the

sixth game of the 1973 World Series, and of the homer he hit the next day against Jon Matlack to destroy the Mets. I remember the gargantuan, into-the-lights home run he hit in the All-Star Game of 1971 in Detroit. And so on. Reggie Jackson is the most emotional slugger I have ever seen. Late in a close big game — and with the deep, baying cries from the stands rolling across the field: "Reg-gie! Reg-gie! Reg-gie!" — he strides to the plate and taps it with his bat and settles his batting helmet and gets his feet right and turns his glittery regard toward the pitcher, and we suddenly know that it is a different hitter we are watching now, and a different man. Get *ready,* everybody — it's show time. And, besides, Reggie had been crushing the ball in batting practice and he had hit a homer in each of the last two games against the Dodgers. Hence (to sound very much like Howard Cosell) my call.

I did not call the third homer. One does not predict miracles. This one also came on the first ball pitched — a low and much more difficult pitch, I thought, from knuckleballer Charlie Hough. The ball flew out on a higher and slower trajectory — inviting wonder and incredulity — this time toward the unoccupied sector in faraway center field that forms the black background for the hitters at the plate, and even before it struck and caromed once out there and before the showers of paper and the explosions of shouting came out of the crowd, one could almost begin to realize how many things Reggie Jackson had altered on this night. The game was won, of course (it was 8–4 in the end), and the Yankees were world champions once again. It was their first championship since 1962, and their twenty-first in all. Jackson's five homers for the Series was a new record, and so were his ten runs and twenty-five total bases. The three home runs in a single Series game had been done before — by Babe Ruth, in 1926 and again in 1928, but neither of Ruth's splurges had come on consecutive at-bats, and neither had been conclusive. Reggie Jackson's homer in the previous game had been hit on his last trip to the plate, and his base on balls in the second inning had been on four straight pitches. This meant that he had hit four home runs on four consecutive swings of the bat — a deed apparently unique in the annals of the game. But Jackson's achievement, to be sure, cannot properly be measured against any of the famous *sustained* one-man performances in World Series history — by Brooks Robinson in 1970, for instance, or by Roberto Clemente in 1971. Reggie's night — a thunderclap — was both less and more. It was *hors concours*. Jackson, in any case, had won this game and this World Series, and he had also, in some extraordinary confirming fashion, won this entire season, reminding us all of its multiple themes and moods and pleasures, which were now culminated in one resounding and unimaginable final chord.

Beyond this — or to one side of it, perhaps — Reggie had at last secured his own fame. He had justified his gigantic salary, if it *could* be justified, and in all probability he had suddenly increased the number of players who will now decide to seek their fortunes as free agents in the next few years. More than that, he had arranged for them all to receive a great deal more money for their services. Even the flintiest traditionalists among the owners — and among the fans, too — must sense that a new time has arrived in baseball. We are in the Jacksonian Era.

This World Series was famous at the very end, but it was notorious all the time. Even while they were winning, the Yankees continued their off-the-field bickerings and grudges and complaints. During the Series, clubhouse reporters wrote that Thurman Munson hoped to play for Cleveland next year, that Mickey Rivers and Graig Nettles were also eager to be traded, that Ed Figueroa had almost jumped the team, and that Reggie Jackson was bitterly critical of Martin's use of Catfish Hunter in the second game. A news-magazine story claimed that in the middle of the season two Yankee players had asked George Steinbrenner to fire Billy Martin; Thurman Munson said that the story was a lie. A press conference was convened by the Yankees at which it was announced that the club was giving Billy Martin a new car and a bonus. Reggie Jackson, who is never at a loss for words, continued to grant startling interviews to great masses of media people. "I couldn't quit this summer, because of all the kids and the blacks and the little people who are pulling for me," he said at one point. "I represent both the underdog and the overdog in our society."

In the Dodger camp, the tone of the news, at least, was different. Manager Tom Lasorda, who did a remarkable job on the field this summer and this fall, attracted hundreds of reporters to pregame interviews, during which he told a lot of Vegas-style standup-comic jokes, and also declared his love for his country and his family and the Dodger organization. "During the national anthem," he said at one point, "a tear came to my eye — I'm not ashamed to admit that. It's the kind of guy I *am*." He made frequent mention of the Big Dodger in the Sky. One day, he confirmed to reporters that he and his wife had had dinner the night before with his good friend Frank Sinatra and *his* wife. Lasorda said that his friend Don Rickles had come to the clubhouse before the fourth game to invigorate his players with insults. "Our team is a big family," he said. "I *love* my players. They've got manners, they've got morals. They're outstanding human beings." The Dodger players, who are clean-shaven and neatly dressed and youthful in appearance, were friendly and cheerful with the press. (The Dodgers are instructed in public relations during spring training, and many of them who live in and around Los Angeles appear at community dinners and other Dodger-boosting functions during the off-season.) Steve Garvey, asked by a reporter what he thought about the Yankee Stadium fans, paused for a moment and then said, "Well, throwing things on the field is not my idea of a well-rounded human being."

I think I prefer the sour Yankee style to the Dodgers' sweetness, since it may bear a closer resemblance to the true state of morale on a professional ball team during the interminable season. It probably doesn't matter much either way. The outcome of this World Series suggests that neither of these contrasting public images had anything to do with what happened on the field. What we can be certain of is that none of this will go away. We live in an unprivate time, and the roar of personality and celebrity has almost drowned out the cheering in the stands. The ironic and most remarkable aspect of Reggie Jackson's feat is that for a moment there, on that littered, brilliant field, he — he, of all people — almost made us forget this. Suddenly he confirmed all our old, secret hopes. He reminded us why we had come there in the first place — for the game and not the news of the game, for the feat and not the feature. What he had done was so difficult and yet was done so well that it was inexplicable. He had become a hero.

Thomas Boswell

The Greatest Game
Ever Played

How Life Imitates the World Series

> I was trying to will the ball to stay up there and never come
> down.
> — Carlton Fisk on watching the Yastrzemski pop-up that
>   ended the Red Sox-Yankee playoff

A baseball game, at its best, can be like an elaborate and
breathlessly balanced house of cards. Tension and a sense of
crisis build with each inning. Each deed of the game, each
player, finds his supporting role. In 1978 that house of cards
was built not for one afternoon, but for an entire six-month
season. By closing day each player seemed to carry with him
a nimbus of symbols, an entire personal history like some
Athenian warrior whose exploits against Sparta were memo-
rized by an entire community.

In fact, one game — the playoff game between the Yankees and the Red Sox that decided the Eastern Division of
the American League — served as an almost perfect micro-
cosm of seventy-five years of baseball warfare between the
Apple and the Hub — a distillation of the game's richest and
longest rivalry.

In the history of baseball, only one other moment —
Bobby Thomson's home run to end the '51 playoff between

the New York Giants and the Brooklyn Dodgers — has provided such a monumental house of cards as the bottom of the ninth inning of this Yankee victory.

When that impossible distinction "best game ever" is being thrashed out in heaven, these games must be mentioned first. Perhaps they should each have a crown — best in the annals of their respective leagues.

The '51 playoff, marvelous for its fireworks and confetti, was the epitome of baseball's age of innocence, a game that any child could grasp.

The '78 playoff, however, pitted teams of darker and more complex personality in a far subtler game — a contest for the student of inside baseball. Is there any other kind?

The '51 classic ended in raw pandemonium; the '78 masterpiece in utter profound silence. Certainly, it is possible to prefer the latter in such a matter of taste.

It must not be held against this masterpiece that it merely ended a divisional race, that the Yanks still had to upend two more pretenders before they could keep their World Championship for a second consecutive year. New York needed just four games to eliminate Kansas City in the American League playoffs and only six to lick Los Angeles in the World Series. Neither joust reached a moment of primitive emotion.

To beat the Bosox, the Yankees bled for six months, only to find themselves tied after the 162nd and last game of the regular season. Their final margin of triumph — 5–4 in this one-day sudden-death showdown — was thin as smoke, a distinction almost without a difference between the two most powerful teams in the sport.

Even now, that concluding moment of delicious indeterminance remains as fresh as the crack of the first line drive of spring. Baseball returns. But the Yankee-Red Sox playoff of 1978 lasts.

The sun is warm in Winter Haven now, the Florida orange trees nod their full branches over the outfield fences of the Red Sox spring training retreat.

But for Carlton Fisk, and many another Sox and Yank, the

air still seems crisp, the sky a dazzling autumn azure and one solitary pop-up hangs high over Fenway Park.

The final split-seconds of that playoff afternoon are one of baseball's indelible frozen paintings. Let Fisk speak about the moment when the air burst from a balloon that had been blown ever larger for 163 games.

"I knew the season would be over as soon as Yastrzemski's pop-up came down," said the tall, patrician catcher with his hair parted in the middle like Henry Mencken. "It seemed like the ball stayed up forever, like everything was cranked down into slow motion. I was trying to will the ball to stay up there and never come down . . . what a dumb thing to have run through your mind. Even the crowd roar sounded like a movie projector at the wrong speed when everything gets gravelly and warped.

"After the last out, I looked around and the crowd was stunned. Nobody moved. They looked at each other like, "You mean it's over now? . . . It can't be over yet . . . oh, nuts. . . .

"It had only been going on for half a year, but it seemed like a crime for it to end."

The buildup to that final crescendo actually began more than twenty-four hours before. The great playoff of '78 was, in reality, two days of absolutely contrasting atmosphere and mood.

Boston's Fenway Park is normally best on the worst days, in raw, misty spring and foggy fall. The streets around the Fens are crowded, narrow, and damp. Taxis blow their horns at the herds of Soxers in Lansdowne Street. That's the way it was on the first day of October — the last day of the regular season. A healing rain caressed that ancient, indescribably delicious ballyard — a rain of balm and absolution. In that soft October drizzle the Sox of Boston were washed clean just as New England was ready to give up hope, the prayers of Red Sox fans were answered. On that final Sunday, Boston won and the New Yorkers, playing three hundred miles away in Yankee Stadium, lost.

The most spectacular and sustained pennant race in American League history had reached the only climax worthy of it — the two best teams in baseball each had 99 victories. One of them would have to win 100.

Just two weeks before, the Red Sox had finished one of the most ignominious collapses in history — losing 17½ games in the standings to the inexorable Yankees, blowing all of a 14-game lead, and falling 3½ games behind with only 14 to play.

If Cotton Mather had been alive, he would have been a Bosox fan. And he would have been mad.

In other towns, the incipient collapse of a beloved team might bring forth prayers and novenas, as Brooklyn once lit candles for the Dodgers. In fickle Fenway, however, the faithful reacted as though the Sox had deliberately knelt in the hallowed Fens and licked the Yankees' boots.

The Red Sox have long memories. It is their curse. They are an imaginative team — more's the pity — susceptible to hauntings and collective nervous breakdowns. They prove that those who cannot forget the past are also condemned to repeat it. The evil that the Bosox do lives after them. The good is oft interred with their moans. Somewhere it must be written that the Carmine Hose shall suffer. When the Sox are winning, every player is a minor deity. When the angels fall, they are consigned to the nether regions.

So, that final-day victory, Boston's eighth in a row and twelfth in 14 games over the last two weeks, was like an emotional reprieve from the gallows. The entire final week of the season was summarized in that final chilling Sunday. Each day Boston would throw an early lead on the scoreboard, hoping to shake the New Yorkers' faith in their tiny 1-game lead. And each day the Yankee dreadnought would send its message back via the radio waves with an answering victory. A new punishment had been found to fit the Sox felony of squandering a huge lead — torture by victory. A sense of fatality, or inexorable and well-deserved punishment, seemed to hang over the Sox. The Prayer to St. Jude, patron saint of lost causes, was tacked to their bulletin board.

Finally, the ghost was all but given up. Brave talk ceased. Predictions of a playoff were swallowed. During that Sunday morning batting practice, the Sox were grim. Then the spirit of mischief seemed to enter Fenway. Toronto's flaky outfielder Sam Ewing snuck through the open door in the scoreboard and posted a fictitious "8" next to the name of the Yankees' opponent — Cleveland. The early-arriving crowd went into a tizzy that did not stop for three hours. Bizarre echoing eruptions rumbled through the stands whenever word of the Yankee demise arrived by radio. All afternoon, Sox relief pitcher Bob ("Big Foot") Stanley kept a transistor radio to his ear in the bullpen, leaping to his feet to lead hundreds of fans in ovations for Cleveland's runs. Slowly, a ripple, and finally a roar would erupt from 32,000 people as, one-by-one, the blessed message was passed like a fire bucket. Before the game even ended — with Boston ahead, 5–0, and New York behind, 9–2 — the scoreboard exulted: "Next Red Sox Home Game Tomorrow."

This was the afternoon that made '78 unique in baseball's century.

Two other teams had suffered breakdowns comparable to Boston. The New York Giants of 1914 got the rubber bone for blowing a 15-game, Fourth of July lead to the Miracle Braves of Boston, and eventually losing by a craven 10½ games. And the '51 Dodgers had a 13-game lead on August 11, only to be tied on the last day of the season, then beaten. But no team had ever looked into the abyss of absolute self-betrayal and recovered from it, come back to finish the season — despite injuries — like a furious hurricane.

At their nadir, the Sox had lost 6 straight September meetings with the Yankees by a total score of 46–9. They were outhit, 84–29. "It was so lopsided," said Boston pitcher Mike Torrez, "that you wouldn't have believed it if it had happened to the original Mets."

The real victims of the Boston collapse were, in part, the Yankees. The Horrid Hose were so disgraceful that they drained the glory from the Yanks' great comeback. "Never sell the Yankees short," said Boston coach Johnny Pesky, who has hated pinstripes for forty years. "They played great the last three months [52–22]. They'll never play that well again as long as they have assholes."

While other teams are too tight to breathe in a crisis, the Yankees spit their tobacco and smooth the dirt with their spikes. The Yanks, with their almost unsinkable raw talent, their polished passion for the game once the contest begins, and their partial immunity to the pandemonium that swathes them, have gradually come to resemble a sort of Leviathan with hiccups.

In midseason the champions were hemorrhaging in Boston. There are other New England sharks than the mythical Jaws of Amity. The pearly white teeth snapping around them on those moon-bathed nights at Fenway were the healthy and rapacious Sox. "If Boston keeps playing like this," said New York's Reggie Jackson, "even Affirmed couldn't catch them. We'll need motorcycles. . . ."

Every day and every night in those final hours of troubled manager Billy Martin the scene around the Yankees was the same. The crowds in the hotel lobbies, at the ticket windows and outside the players' entrances were huge, pummeling the players with kisses and curses.

Meanwhile, the Sox read their press clippings. Everyone from Ted Williams to the cop in Yawkey Way said these Sox were the best edition since '01. What blighter would point out that the Fenway Chronicles show an almost inexorable baseball law: A Red Sox ship with a single leak will always find a way to sink. For documentation, see the Harvard Library. Doctoral theses are on file there.

In other seasons, the Sox self-immolation was a final act consonant with the team's public image for generations — a green wall at their backs, green bucks in their wallets, green apples in their throats. Red Sox fans had come to view their heroes with deep skepticism, searching for the tragic flaw. No team is worshipped with such a perverse sense of fatality. "Human, all too human," that's the Red Sox logo.

Ever since the day sixty years before when dastardly Harry Frazee sold Babe Ruth to the Yankees, fortune had forsaken the Sox. The axis of baseball power swung south with Ruth. Since Boston last raised a Series banner in 1918, the Yankees have been champions 22 times.

This grim heritage, however, was an unfair burden to the '78 Sox who were the antithesis of their predecessors. If the Sox had a critical flaw, an Achilles' heel, it was their excess of courage, their unquestioning obedience to the god of guts. This, they swore to a man, was the year for that eternally receding World Series Triumph. Let the '80s be damned.

The Sox scapegoat was easy to find — doughty little Manager Don Zimmer, the man with the metal plate in his head whom Bill Lee contemptuously called "the gerbil." Zimmer was publicly seen as a hard guy who was given a high-strung, high-octane Indy race car and kept the pedal to the metal as though he were driving an old dirt-track stocker. Naturally, the engine blew and the Sox coasted to a dead stop.

However, the Yankees also had catastrophic pitching problems, constant injuries for the first 100 games and a manager who had to be fired for his own health's sake.

Why were the Yankees so good at cutting their losses, while the Red Sox were so poor at minimizing theirs? Why did the Yankees have the restraint to let their injured heal in June, when the Sox were pummeling them, while the Sox exacerbated their miseries by going full throttle?

It's all tied up with history and that old Yankee fear. It's axiomatic in the Northeast that no Red Sox lead is safe. And it is cradle lore that no Boston team ever has faced up to a Yankee challenge in September. Therefore, Zimmer had little choice but to push his delicately balanced power plant until the black smoke poured from the exhaust. Mythology forced his hand. Only a 20-game lead would suffice.

The Sox pushed that lead to 14, but then the black flag waved the Sox into the pits, while the Yanks kept circling the track.

The hordes of invading Yankee fans even took to taunting

the Sox in their own lair. In the tunnel under the Fenway stands, Yankee fans set up a cheer each night as they passed the doors of the Boston locker room. "Three, three, three . . . two, two, two . . . one, one, one . . . ZERO, ZERO, ZERO," they counted down the dwindling Boston margin each night as the Yankees swept the famous 4-game series that will live in lore as The Boston Massacre.

As soon as the massacred Bostonians, the despair of eight states, threw in the towel, gave up the ghost, and tossed in the sponge, they pinned the Yankees' ears back in their seventh-and-last September meeting. That, of course, is the visceral clubhouse definition of choking. If you can't tie your shoelaces under pressure but play like a world-beater as soon as it's too late, that's worse in the dugout world than being a no-talent klutz. That is called taking the apple.

Even if Boston's sweet fruit of victory had a bitter pit of self-knowledge at its center, the hard swallow was medicinal. One day the Sox were pathetically cornering reporters, asking, "Tell me, what's wrong with us?" Soon, it seemed, they would be asking that sorrowful question of lampposts and parked cars. But a small thing like one victory over New York, even one that seemed meaningless, broke the grip of the curse.

So, when the Yankees arrived at Fenway on Playoff Day, they no longer came either as June victims or September conquerors. They came as October equals — very worried equals.

The house of cards was finally built. And it was monstrous. Which way it would fall no player claimed to know.

At baseball's showcase World Series games, the batting cage is as congenial as a Kiwanians convention. Teams arrive for fame and fun; no grudges fester. Before the playoff, the Yankees and Red Sox circled each other like lions and leopards around the same African watering hole. Their only words were taunting barbs disguised as light humor.

Some celestial handicapper must have written out the lineup cards. They were too symbolic to have been penned by mortals named Don Zimmer and Bob Lemon, the Yankees' caretaker manager.

Each team spotted the other a Golden Glover as both Dwight Evans and New York's Willie Randolph were sidelined. But far better for symmetry were the starting pitchers: Torrez against Ron Guidry, the man called "Lou'siana Lightnin'."

Just a year before, Torrez had been the Yankees' World Series pitching hero, winning 2 games. Then the Sox signed him at free agent auction for $2.7 million — their loud pronouncement that they would match the Yankee pocketbook. Just four days before, Torrez had emerged from the emotional low point of his career. If one player's failure epitomized the charge of gutlessness made against all the Sox, it was Torrez. For forty days down the stretch when he was desperately needed, he had not won a single game, while losing 6.

The Sox feelings about the great Guidry were simply summed up. "We have the home field. We have the momentum. They . . . " said shortstop Rick Burleson, pausing, "have Guidry."

Guidry's feelings were even more elemental. Asked if a mere 1-game playoff were fair, the left-handed executioner answered, "One's enough. I can only pitch one."

Discovering Guidry in the Yankee locker room is like stumbling over a dog in a cathouse. His story is the hidden moral kernel in the vain bluster of the Yankee saga. Imagine, if it can be done, a player amid these New Yorkers who has the innate confidence of an only child, the proud self-containment of a Lou'siana Cajun, and the strong silences of a small-town boy raised on hawk hunting and walking the railroad tracks.

No star player is so invisible on his own team, whether loping across the outfield or lounging in the dugout. But for this playoff, no player approached Guidry for being conspicuous. The reason was cogent — Guidry entered the game

with the best record of any 20-game winner in the history of
baseball: 24–3.

Every game needs a call to arms, but this one started with
trumpet blasts.

A brilliant fall light — a painter's vivid stark light — bathed
Fenway as Torrez began the day by throwing his first four
pitches to Mickey Rivers low, high inside, and outside. The
Yankee speedster waited only one pitch to steal second base.

"So that's it," the throng seemed to say by its sigh. It was
going to be just like last time, when New York jumped to
leads of 12–0, 13–0, 7–0, and 6–0 in four Fenway days. When
the long history of the Sox sorrows is written, those hor-
rific first innings in September would rank infernally high.
Each game came complete with the same chilling footnote:
"Ibid . . . for full details, see previous night's game."

Would it be so again? Always, it was Rivers beginning the
psychic unraveling, stealing second as though it had been left
to him in old Tom Yawkey's will. That sad lopsided spectacle
seemed under way again when Torrez made an egregious
error — throwing Reggie Jackson a fastball strike on an 0–2
pitch with 2 outs. The ball climbed to the level of the left-field
light towers, climbed until it seemed to look in the faces of
the teenagers, who had scrambled atop the Gilby's Gin sign
beyond the wall. The Yankees would lead, 2–0, Guidry would
breeze. The great day would be a dud. But the groaning
crowd had forgotten the Fenway winds.

Whenever the Sox and Yanks meet in Boston, the first
order of business is to inspect the flags. The Yankees, a
predominantly left-handed hitting team, desperately want
an inward breeze to enlarge the confines of the cozy Fens.
The Sox, designed along Brobdignagian lines, with seven
home-run hitters, would settle for dead calm. Only when
the flag points toward the plate do they droop. When the
Yanks arrived in early September, for four straight days
the Sox grumbled as the wind blew, sometimes thirty miles an
hour, straight in from left. Betrayed again, even by Fenway
Park.

So, when Jackson's blast was suddenly stymied by the wind and fell almost straight down, nearly scraping the wall as it fell into Carl Yastrzemski's glove, a marvelous sense of irony swept over the Boston dugout. The Yankees had been robbed by the same fates that had bedeviled Boston.

"That was no wind," said Lee later. "That was Mr. Yawkey's breath."

It is a unique quality of baseball that the season ticket holders who see all of a club's crucial games believe they can also read the minds of the players. Each team's season is like a traditional nineteenth-century novel, a heaping up of detail and incident about one large family. After 162 chapters of that tome, chapter 163 is riddled with the memories, implications, and foreshadowings of the thousands of previous pages. Any play that rises above the trivial sends a wave of emotion into that ocean-size novel of what has gone before. Since everyone is reading the same vast book, the sense of a collective baseball consciousness can become enormous. With each at bat, each pitch, there is an almost audible shuffling of mental pages as the pitcher, hitter, and catcher all sort through the mass of past information they have on one another. Just this sort of extended personal history existed between the Yankee star Guidry and the Boston captain Yastrzemski to begin the second inning. In a word, Yaz was harmless against Guidry when the left-hander was at, or even near, his best. So, when Yastrzemski rocked back on his heels on the second pitch of the second inning to thrash at a fastball in his wheelhouse (up-and-in), it should have been a feeble mistake. Instead, it was a home run — a hooking liner that curled around the right-field foul pole by less than a bat length. Yaz had turned the Lightnin' around.

Suddenly, the afternoon bristled with potential.

Guidry was at his weakest. Torrez, who was to strike out Yankee captain Thurman Munson three times with nibbling, teasing sliders, was at his best. In other words, they were even.

"When these teams play," Fisk had said two weeks before,

"it is like a gigantic will controls the whole game. And it's either all behind one team, or all behind the other."

But this day the forces of the game could not make up their minds. It was a beautiful ambivalence.

The crowd seemed to be in the grip of angina, the cheers caught in their nervous throats. The Keep Your Sox On faithful sat silent in their fireman caps decorated with the nicknames of their undependable deities: Boomer and Butch, Soup and Scooter, Rooster and Pudge, Eck and Louie, Big Foot and Spaceman, Dewey and Yaz. By the end of the fifth, the day's work more than half done, the ball park was so silent that those in the rooftop seats could hear Blair pleading to his Yankees, "Let's go, man. Let's go."

For this single afternoon to achieve permanence, it had to be a miniature of the entire season, a duplication of the same emotional roller coaster. So, in the sixth, the Sox scored again, Burleson lining a double over third and Jim Rice clipping an RBI single to center. As Rice's hit, his 406th total base of the season, bit into the turf, it seemed that the game, the year, and a Most Valuable Player duel between Rice and Guidry had all been decided on a single pitch.

More folly. Any historian knows that a 2–0 lead after the sixth is the quintessential Red Sox lead — just enough to merit euphoria; just enough to squander. After all, in the seventh game of the 1975 World Series Boston could taste its incipient upset over Cincinnati, leading 3–0. And that turned to dust.

Every seesaw needs a fulcrum, and Lou Piniella quickly provided one for this game.

A ground out and an intentional walk put men on first and second, 2 outs, and Fred Lynn at bat. When fragile Freddy yanked a Guidry slider into the right-field corner, every dugout mind had the same thought: "Two runs." Piniella, however, materialized directly in the path of the ball. He was so far out of normal Lynn position that he ought to have had a puff of magical smoke curling up behind him.

"It was a ridiculous place for him to be . . . about

twenty yards from where he normally plays me," said Lynn.

"I talked to Munson between innings," said Piniella afterward. "We agreed that Guidry's slider was more the speed of a curveball and that somebody could pull him." Even so, Piniella was stationed in a sort of private twilight zone.

"It was a hundred-to-one shot any way you look at it," said Lynn. "He plays hunches out there. The man's just a gambler."

At bat, Piniella says, "I've guessed on every pitch that was ever thrown to me . . . don't do too bad, do I?"

To those in the stands, the play looked routine, like so many in baseball: a blistering line drive directly at an outfielder standing a few feet in front of the fence. It was the hallmark of this game that its central plays reflected the true daily life of the inner sport. They were not flamboyant and egalitarian, but exclusive and subtle. Baseball's well-kept secret is that it has never been solely a democratic national pastime, but an elitist passion as well.

The Babe and the Iron Horse will never understand what happened next. Big Ed Barrow and Colonel Jacob Ruppert will take a lot of kidding in baseball heaven when tales are told of the tiny home-run hero of the Playoff. Since the roaring '20s, the diamond nine from New York that wore gray pinstripes has meant heartless hegemony, monolithic muscle. Bucky Dent, though he bats last in the Yank order, nonetheless is a symbol of power himself — the power of cash. For two seasons George Steinbrenner was obsessed with getting Dent away from the Chicago White Sox. Finally, a trade was made.

When Dent dragged his bat to home plate with 2 out and 2 men on base in the Yankee seventh, then fouled the second pitch off his foot, hopping out of the batter's box in pain, he looked as ineffectual and inconspicuous as a CIA agent with a bomb in his briefcase. Normally, the worrywart Fisk uses such delays to visit his pitcher with admonitions, or to demand warm-up pitches. "Fisk is out at the mound so much," needles Lynn, "that I've threatened to change the number of Carlton's position from '2' to '1½.'"

But for Dent, what's the worry?

As Dent was administered a pain-killing spray, on-deck hitter Rivers, who had forgotten his sunglasses and butchered a flyball earlier, suddenly became uncharacteristically observant. He saw a crack in Dent's bat and fetched him another one of the same style. Of such minutiae is history made. That and fastballs down the middle.

"After Dent hit it," said Fisk, "I let out a sigh of relief. I thought, 'We got away with that mistake pitch.' I almost screamed at Mike.

"Then I saw Yaz looking up and I said, 'Oh, God.'"

Several innings before, the wind had reversed and was blowing toward the left-field corner. Yastrzemski watched that boosting wind loft the ball barely over the wall, fair by thirty feet. As the 3-run homer nestled in the net, Yastrzemski's knees buckled as though he had been hammered over the head with a bat.

The Yankees erupted from the dugout like souls released from Hades. What followed seemed as inexorable as a shark eating the leg after it tastes the foot.

Quicker than you could say, "Rivers walks and steals second again," Torrez was leaving the game. Though he had fanned the next hitter — Munson — three times, Zimmer waved in Stanley. Naturally, Munson doubled to the wall for the inning's fourth run.

When Reggie Jackson, the Hester Prynne of sluggers who walks through the baseball world with a scarlet dollar sign on his chest, knocked a home run into the center-field bleachers in the eighth, it seemed like mere hot doggery. And when Jackson slapped hands with Steinbrenner in the box seats before greeting any of his mates to celebrate the 5–2 lead, it was just another of Reggie's compulsive theatrical gestures.

Little did the crowd suspect what all the players knew — that the war had not ceased.

Beyond the Fenway fences, the trees of New England were tinged with reds and oranges. They might as well have been tears.

This game, like the entire season, was about to be salvaged

by the sort of Red Sox rally against fate that had no historical precedent.

If Torrez and Guidry went down as the pitchers of record — the official loser and winner — then Stanley and that ornery Goose Gossage were the pitchers of memory.

In the eighth, Jerry Remy grounded a double over the first-base bag off Gossage and scored on Yastrzemski's crisp single to center. Yaz followed Remy home when Fisk and Lynn cracked singles, using their quick strokes to combat Gossage's numbing speed.

The bear trap was set for the Yanks — men on first and second with only 1 out, and the lead down to 5–4.

The great book of the season had, however, been turned to the wrong page to suit Boston.

Gossage mowed down Butch Hobson and George Scott — low-average sluggers with long, looping swings. Neither could get untangled quickly enough to handle his rising fastballs.

Never mind. The stage has been set for the bottom of the ninth with Gossage protecting his 5–4 lead.

From the press box, baseball is geometry and statistics. From the box seats, it is velocity, volume, and virtuosity. From above, Gossage is a relief pitcher. From ground level, eye-to-eye in his own world, he is a dragon.

Nevertheless, the brave Bosox started beating on Gossage's ninth-inning door. The feisty Burleson drew a 1-out walk.

Winning is an ancient Yankee story, a heritage of talent, mixed with an audacious self-confidence and an unnerving good fortune. Losing is an old sadness for the Sox, a lineage of self-doubt and misfortune. All those threads of history and baseball myths were about to come together in one play.

The 5-foot-6 Remy slashed a liner to right when the Goose's 0–2 fastball laid an egg. The assembled parishioners sang "Hallelujah," then groaned their eternal "Amen" as they saw the ball fly directly toward Piniella. Little did they, or Burleson on first, know that only one person in the park had no idea where Remy's liner was — Piniella.

"I never saw it," he said. "I just thought, 'Don't panic. Don't wave your damn arms and let the runner know you've lost it.'"

So Piniella the Gambler stood frozen, trusting, as he has so often, to luck. While Piniella waited for the streaking ball to hit at his feet or in his face, Burleson waited between bases, assuming Piniella had an easy play.

These Yankees, who seem to abolish chance with their poise, let luck fall about their shoulders like a seignoral cloak. "I never saw it until the ball hit about eight feet in front of me," said Piniella later, drenched with champagne. "It was just pure luck that I could get my glove on the ball and catch it before it went past me. If it had gone to the wall, those two scooters would still be running around the bases."

Had Burleson, after stopping in his tracks, tried to go first-to-third, he would have been a dead Rooster. Piniella's throw was a one-hop strike to the bag. Had Piniella not had the presence of mind to fake a catch, Burleson would have reached third easily. From there, he could have scored to tie the game on Rice's subsequent fly to Piniella. From second, he could only tag and go to third.

If Dent's homer has been discussed throughout America, then Piniella's two gambles — his out-of-position catch on Lynn and his blinded grab on Remy — are still being dissected in every major league dugout. "It's the play I'll always remember," said Graig Nettles.

Steinbrenner will never forget either. "I have a tape cassette of the whole game in my office," said the owner. "I don't know how many times I've watched that game. And I always stop at the Piniella play and run it over and over. What if Jackson had been out there? He's left-handed, so the glove's on his other hand, the ball gets by him, Remy has an inside-the-park homer, and we lose.

"It's annoyed me that our playoff game seems to have been overshadowed by us beating the Dodgers in the Series for the second year in a row," said Steinbrenner. "Don't people understand? Somebody wins the Series every year. There's only one game like that in a lifetime. I'd call it the greatest game in the history of American sports, because baseball is the best and oldest game, and that's sure as hell the best baseball game I ever saw."

If any game ever brought seventy-five years of animosity to a climax, this was it.

"When they had two on in the ninth with Rice and Yaz coming up," said New York's Roy White, "I was just holding my breath. You wanted to close your eyes and not see 'em swing. The wind was blowing out and I could feel that Green Monster creeping in closer."

"All I could think of was Bobby Thomson and that '51 playoff," said Nettles. "I figured if anybody was going to beat us, those were the guys."

This playoff lacked only one thing: a time machine. When Captain Carl, Boston cleanup man, stood at the plate facing Gossage with the tying run dancing off third and the winning run on first, that moment should have been frozen. The 32,925 standing fans, the poised runners, Yaz's high-held bat, Gossage's baleful glare: For once baseball had achieved a moment of genuine dramatic art — a situation that needed no resolution to be perfect. A game, a season, and an entire athletic heritage for two cities had been brought to razor's edge.

"I was in the on-deck circle, just like I was when Yaz flew out to end the '75 Series," said Fisk. "You know, they should have stopped the game right then and said, 'Okay, that's it. The season is over. You're both world champions. We can't decide between you, and neither of you should have to lose.'"

Sports' moments of epiphany are written on water. The spell of timelessness must be shattered, the house of cards collapse. Yaz cannot stand poised forever, waiting for the Goose. Art may aspire to fairness, but games cannot aim that high. They must settle for a final score.

"I was thinking, 'Pop him up,'" said Nettles. "Then, Yaz did pop it up and I said, 'Jeez, but not to me.'"

When the white speck had fallen into Nettles' glove, the Fenway fans stood in their places. For long minutes no one moved, as the baseball congregation drank in the cathartic sweetness of the silence. Proud police horses pranced on the infield, waiting to hold back a crowd that never charged. "They should have given both teams a standing ovation," said Nettles. But he was wrong. This was better.

Finally, the whir of a public address recording began. Gently, softly, the music of an old-fashioned melancholy carousel drifted through Fenway Park. The sun was going down, so we all went home, bearing with us canvases for a lifetime.

I WAS THE YANKEES

In his delicate reminiscence, "The Anxious Fields of Play," Richard Hugo reflects on a lonely boyhood during the Depression relieved only by the power of the imagination to turn a vacant lot into a ball park and allow a 10-year-old with a stick and a stone in his hands to declare, "I was the Yankees."

Who were the 10-year-olds who grew up and out of their imaginations to actually become Yankees? They were the Bambino, the Iron Horse, the Yankee Clipper, the Ol' Perfesser, the Switcher, Yogi; characters sprung, it seemed, as if from the greatest boy's book ever written — swashbucklers, knights-errant, prodigies, and clowns. Here we get a glimpse of them all, either through their own inimitable words, as with Casey and Yogi, or in profile by some of the best writers who ever cared to watch a ball game, including Red Smith on the Babe, James P. Dawson on Lou Gehrig, David Halberstam on Joe D., and George Vecsey on Mickey Mantle.

The excerpt from Jim Bouton's *Ball Four* marks a definite turning point in this section, as it did when it first came out in 1970, and in sports biographies in general — more humor, less modesty; more honesty, less romance. And the debunking age is fully upon us with the selections from Brendan C. Boyd and Fred C. Harris's *Great American Baseball Card Flipping, Trading and Bubble Gum Book*.

It's hard to imagine Gehrig or DiMaggio ever actually saying, "I was the Yankees," but surely, with the next five offerings here, we find players who, with the invaluable contributions of their own personal Boswells (and we don't mean Thomas), do not shrink from the first person singular. It's difficult to believe there's a crisis of literacy in the land when we have so many jocks moonlighting as authors. But here we have it — I was the Yankees — Sparky Lyle (with Peter Golenbock), Dock Ellis (whose *I* is filtered through the narrative of Donald Hall), Graig Nettles (with Peter Golenbock), Catfish Hunter (with Armen Keteyian), and Reggie (with Mike Lupica).

The section ends with a return to humility — Thomas Boswell on Don Mattingly. In the '90s he is the Yankees.

Richard Hugo

The Anxious Fields of Play

By the mid-'30s, when I was 10 or 11, baseball had become such an obsession that I imagined ball parks everywhere. In the country, I visualized games in progress on the real grass cattle were eating. In the city as I rode down Fourth Avenue on the bus, the walls of warehouses became outfield fences with dramatic doubles and triples booming off them. Hitting was important in my fantasies. Pitching meant little except as a service necessary for some long drive far beyond the outfielders. I kept the parks small in my mind so home runs wouldn't be too difficult to hit.

The lot across the street from my grandparents' house was vacant and whenever I could get enough neighborhood friends to join me we'd have a game there. In center field a high board fence bounded the west side of the Noraines' backyard. It was about 100 feet from the worn spot we called home plate. The right field fence, a good 40 feet away at the imagined foul line, ran east and bordered the north side of the Brockerman's yard. "Over the fence," I yelled, "is a home run." "Over the fence," said Mr. Brockerman from his yard, hoping to keep his windows intact, "is out." "It's our game and we can make the rules, and besides you can't even get a job," I yelled back. It was a cruel remark. The depression was on and my grandfather was the only man in the neighborhood who had steady work. A few years later when I was old enough to realize the hopeless state of things for men during the depression, I wanted to apologize to Mr. Brockerman, but he had long since moved away. No left field fence. Just some trees and the ground of the Burns' yard, looking more trampled than the ferns and grass of the vacant lot.

One evening the men in the neighborhood joined us for a game. I was so excited, I bubbled. Growing up with my grandparents, I missed the vitality of a young father. I ran about the field loudly picking all the men for my team. My hopes for a dynasty were shattered when a grown-up explained that we might have a better game if we chose even sides. Days after, I trudged about the neighborhood asking the fathers if they would play ball again, but no luck.

When my grandparents had the basement put in, a concrete full-sized basement replacing the small dirt cave where Grandmother had kept her preserves, a pile of gravel was left on the north side of the house. Our house was the only house on that side of the block and in my mind the woods to the north became a baseball field. The rocks — smooth, round, averaging about the size of a quarter — were perfect for my purpose.

I fashioned a bat by carving a handle on a one-by-four and I played out entire nine-inning games, throwing the rocks up and swatting them into and over the trees. Third base was a willow tree. Second base was (I knew exactly in my mind) just beyond the honeysuckle and the giant hollow stump that usually held a pool of rainwater inside its slick mossed walls. Many times that pool reflected the world and my face back at me in solitary moments. First base, not really important because I seldom hit rocks that way, was vaguely a clump of alders.

I knew exactly how far a rock had to sail to be a home run. It had to clear a fence I dreamed beyond the woods. My games were always dramatic and ended with a home run, bases loaded, three runs down, two out, the count three and two, bottom of the ninth. How did I manage that? It was easy. I could control my hits well enough to hit three singles to load the bases because my notion of what constituted a single was flexible. Then I'd select a rock whose size and shape indicated it might sail well, and clobber it. If, for some reason, it didn't sail far enough to be a home run, I simply tried again.

Inning after inning, I swatted rock outs, rock singles, rock doubles, rock triples, and rock home runs. I was the Yankees and also my opponents, the Giants. The only major league ball I heard was the World Series. It was carried on the radio and the Yankees were usually playing. The Yankees also had the most glamorous stars. Sometimes I played out the entire series, all seven, letting the Giants win three. The score mounted. The lead changed hands. Then the last of the ninth, when Babe Ruth, Lou Gehrig, or Joe DiMaggio broke it up. I don't remember now if Ruth still played with New York when DiMaggio joined the team but on my Yankees they were teammates.

One game, the dramatic situation in the ninth, a strong wind was blowing, as usual from the south. I tossed a flat round stone, perfect for sailing and caught it just right. I still can see it climb and feel my disbelief. It soared out over the trees, turned over once, and started to climb like a determined bird. I couldn't have imagined I'd ever hit one that far. It was lovely. It rose and rose. I thought it might never stop riding that high wind north. It crossed the imaginary left field fence before its flight became an aesthetic matter, and it disappeared, a dot, still climbing, somewhere over Rossner's store on the corner of 16th and Barton. I believe that rock traveled about two blocks. Why not? Joe DiMaggio had hit it.

I couldn't see the neighborhood beyond the trees. I simply drove the rocks out over the woods and imagined the rest, though sometimes I heard doubles rattle off the sides and roof of the community hall in center field just beyond the woods. A few years later I realized how dangerous my Yankees had been, spraying stones about the neighborhood. During my absence in World War II, the woods were wiped out by new housing.

Red Smith

One of a Kind

Grantland Rice, the prince of sportswriters, used to do a weekly radio interview with some sporting figure. Frequently, in the interest of spontaneity, he would type out questions and answers in advance. One night his guest was Babe Ruth.

"Well, you know, Granny," the Babe read in response to the question, "Duke Ellington said the Battle of Waterloo was won on the playing fields of Elkton."

"Babe," Granny said after the show, "Duke Ellington for the Duke of Wellington I can understand. But how did you ever read Eton as Elkton? That's in Maryland, isn't it?"

"I married my first wife there," Babe said, "and I always hated the gawdam place." He was cheerily unruffled. In the uncomplicated world of George Herman Ruth, errors were part of the game.

Babe Ruth died 25 years ago but his ample ghost has been with us all summer and he seems to grow more insistently alive every time Henry Aaron hits a baseball over the fence. What, people under 50 keep asking, what was this creature of myth and legend like in real life? If he were around today, how would he react when Aaron at last broke his hallowed record of 714 home runs? The first question may be impossible to answer fully; the second is easy.

"Well, what d'you know!" he would have said when the

record got away. "Baby loses another! Come on, have another beer."

To paraphrase Abraham Lincoln's remark about another deity, Ruth must have admired records because he created so many of them. Yet he was sublimely aware that he transcended records and his place in the American scene was no mere matter of statistics. It wasn't just that he hit more home runs than anybody else, he hit them better, higher, farther, with more theatrical timing and a more flamboyant flourish. Nobody could strike out like Babe Ruth. Nobody circled the bases with the same pigeon-toed, mincing majesty.

"He was one of a kind," says Waite Hoyt, a Yankee pitcher in the years of Ruthian splendor. "If he had never played ball, if you had never heard of him and passed him on Broadway, you'd turn around and look."

Looking, you would have seen a barrel swaddled in a wrap-around camel-hair topcoat with a flat camel-hair cap on the round head. Thus arrayed he was instantly recognizable not only on Broadway in New York but also on the Ginza in Tokyo. "Baby Roos! Baby Roos!" cried excited crowds, following through the streets when he visited Japan with an all-star team in the early nineteen-thirties.

The camel-hair coat and cap are part of my last memory of the man. It must have been in the spring training season of 1948 when the Babe and everybody else knew he was dying of throat cancer. "This is the last time around," he had told Frank Stevens that winter when the head of the H. M. Stevens catering firm visited him in French Hospital on West 30th Street, "but before I go I'm gonna get out of here and have some fun."

He did get out, but touring the Florida training camps surrounded by a gaggle of admen, hustlers and promoters, he didn't look like a man having fun. It was a hot day when he arrived in St. Petersburg but the camel-hair collar was turned up about the wounded throat. By this time, Al Lang Stadium had replaced old Waterfront Park where he had drawn crowds when the Yankees trained in St. Pete.

"What do you remember best about this place?" asked Francis Stann of *The Washington Star.*

Babe gestured toward the West Coast Inn, an old frame building a city block beyond the right-field fence. "The day I hit the adjectival ball against the adjectival hotel." The voice was a hoarse stage whisper; the adjective was one often printed these days, but not here.

"Wow!" Francis Stann said. "Pretty good belt."

"But don't forget," Babe said, "the adjectival park was a block back this way then."

Ruth was not noted for a good memory. In fact, the inability to remember names is part of his legend. Yet he needed no record books to remind him of his own special feats. There was, for example, the time he visited Philadelphia as a "coach" with the Brooklyn Dodgers. (His coachly duties consisted of hitting home runs in batting practice.) This was in the late nineteen-thirties when National League games in Philadelphia were played in Shibe Park, the American League grounds where Babe had performed. I asked him what memories stirred on his return.

"The time I hit one into Opal Street," he said.

Now, a baseball hit over Shibe Park's right-field fence landed in 20th Street. Opal is the next street east, just a wide alley one block long. There may not be 500 Philadelphians who know it by name, but Babe Ruth knew it.

Another time, during a chat in Hollywood, where he was an actor in the film *Pride of the Yankees,* one of us mentioned Rube Walberg, a good left-handed pitcher with the Philadelphia Athletics through the Ruth era. To some left-handed batters there is no dirtier word than the name of a good left-handed pitcher, but the Babe spoke fondly:

"Rube Walberg! What a pigeon! I hit 23 home runs off him." Or whatever the figure was. It isn't in the record book but it was in Ruth's memory.

Obviously it is not true that he couldn't even remember the names of his teammates. It was only that the names he remembered were not always those bestowed in the baptismal font. To him Urban Shocker, a Yankee pitcher, was Rubber Belly. Pat Collins, the catcher, was Horse Nose. All redcaps at railroad stations were Stinkweed, and everybody else was Kid. One day Jim Cahn, covering the Yankees for *The New York Sun,* watched two players board a train with a porter toting the luggage.

"There go Rubber Belly, Horse Nose and Stinkweed," Jim said.

Don Heffner joined the Yankees in 1934, Ruth's last year with the team. Playing second base through spring training, Heffner was stationed directly in the line of vision of Ruth, the right fielder. Breaking camp, the Yankees stopped in Jacksonville on a night when the Baltimore Orioles of the International League were also in town. A young reporter on *The Baltimore Sun* seized the opportunity to interview Ruth.

"How is Heffner looking?" he asked, because the second baseman had been a star with the Orioles in 1933.

"Who the hell is Heffner?" the Babe demanded. The reporter should, of course, have asked about the kid at second.

Jacksonville was the first stop that year on the barnstorming trip that would last two or three weeks and take the team to Yankee Stadium by a meandering route through the American bush. There, as everywhere, Ruth moved among crowds. Whether the Yankees played in Memphis or New Orleans or Selma, Ala., the park was almost always filled, the hotel overrun if the team used a hotel, the railroad depot thronged. In a town of 5,000, perhaps 7,500 would see the game. Mostly the players lived in Pullmans and somehow word always went ahead when the Yankees' train was coming through. At every stop at any hour of the night there would be a cluster of men on the platform, maybe the stationmaster and telegrapher, a section gang and the baggage agent watching the dark sleeping cars for the glimpse of a Yankee, possibly even the Babe.

It was said in those days, probably truly, that receipts from the pre-season exhibitions more than paid Ruth's salary for the year, even when he was getting $80,000, which was substantially more than any other player earned, or any manager or baseball executive. It was more than President Herbert Hoover received, but if this was ever pointed out to Ruth he almost surely did not reply, as the story goes: "I had a better year than he did." He would have been correct, but the Babe was not that well informed on national affairs.

Crowds were to Ruth as water to a fish. Probably the only time on record when he sought to avert a mob scene was the day of his second marriage. The ceremony was scheduled for 6 A.M. on the theory that people wouldn't be abroad then, but when he arrived at St. Gregory's in West 90th Street, the church was filled and hundreds were waiting outside.

A reception followed in Babe's apartment on Riverside Drive, where the 18th Amendment did not apply. It was opening day of the baseball season but the weather intervened on behalf of the happy couple. The party went on and on, with entertainment by Peter de Rose, composer-pianist, and May Singhi Breen, who played the ukulele and sang.

Rain abated in time for a game next day. For the first time, Claire Ruth watched from a box near the Yankees' dugout, as she still does on ceremonial occasions. Naturally, the bridegroom hit a home run. Rounding the bases, he halted at second and swept off his cap in a courtly bow to his bride. This was typical of him. There are a hundred stories illustrating his sense of theater — how he opened Yankee Stadium (The House That Ruth Built) with a home run against the Red Sox, how at the age of 40 he closed out his career as a player by hitting three mighty shots out of spacious Forbes Field in Pittsburgh, stories about the times he promised to hit a home run for some kid in a hospital and made good, and of course the one about calling his shot in a World Series.

That either did or did not happen in Chicago's Wrigley Field on Oct. 1, 1932. I was there but I have never been dead sure of what I saw.

The Yankees had won the first two games and the score of the third was 4–4 when Ruth went to bat in the fifth inning

with the bases empty and Charley Root pitching for the Cubs.
Ruth had staked the Yankees to a three-run lead in the first
inning by hitting Root for a home run with two on base. Now
Root threw a strike. Ruth stepped back and lifted a finger.
"One." A second strike, a second upraised finger. "Two."
Then Ruth made some sort of sign with his bat. Some said,
and their version has become gospel, that he aimed it like a
rifle at the bleachers in right center field. That's where he hit
the next pitch. That made the score 5–4. Lou Gehrig followed
with a home run and the Yankees won, 7–5, ending the series
the next day.

All the Yankees, and Ruth in particular, had been riding the
Cubs unmercifully through every game, deriding them as
cheapskates because in cutting up their World Series money
the Chicago players had voted only one-fourth of a share to
Mark Koenig, the former New York shortstop who had joined
them in August and batted .353 in the last month of the
pennant race. With all the dialogue and pantomime that went
on, there was no telling what Ruth was saying to Root. When
the papers reported that he had called his shot, he didn't deny
it.

He almost never quibbled about anything that was written.
During the 1934 World Series between the Cardinals and
Detroit Tigers, the *St. Louis Post-Dispatch* assigned its Washington correspondent, Paul Y. Anderson, to write features.
His seat in the auxiliary press box was next to Ruth, a member of the sweaty literati whose observations on the games
would be converted into suitably wooden prose by a syndi-
cate ghost-writer. Babe was companionable as usual.

"You see the series here in '28?" he asked.

"No," Anderson said, "was it a good one?"

"That was when I hit three outta here in the last game."

"Gee," Anderson said, "a good day for you, eh?"

"Yeah," Babe said, "I had a good day. But don't forget, the
fans had a hell of a day, too."

Paul Anderson was at ease with men as dissimilar as Huey
Long, John L. Lewis and Franklin D. Roosevelt but he had

never encountered anyone quite like this child of nature. He devoted his story to the bumptious bundle of vanity seated beside him. To his discomfort, a press-box neighbor asked Ruth the next day whether he had read the story. Ruth said sure, though he probably hadn't. "What did you think of it?" the other persisted while Anderson squirmed.

"Hell," Babe said, "the newspaper guys always been great to me."

A person familiar with Ruth only through photographs and records could hardly be blamed for assuming that he was a blubbery freak whose ability to hit balls across county lines was all that kept him in the big leagues. The truth is that he was the complete ballplayer, certainly one of the greatest and maybe the one best of all time.

As a left-handed pitcher with the Boston Red Sox, he won 18 games in his rookie season, 23 the next year and 24 the next before Ed Barrow assigned him to the outfield to keep him in the batting order every day. His record of pitching 29⅔ consecutive scoreless innings in World Series stood 43 years before Whitey Ford broke it.

He was an accomplished outfielder with astonishing range for his bulk, a powerful arm and keen baseball sense. It was said that he never made a mental error like throwing to the wrong base.

He recognized his role as public entertainer and understood it. In the 1946 World Series the Cardinals made a radical shift in their defense against Ted Williams, packing the right side of the field and leaving the left virtually unprotected. "They did that to me in the American League one year," Ruth told the columnist, Frank Graham. "I coulda hit .600 that year slicing singles to left."

"Why didn't you?" Frank asked.

"That wasn't what the fans came out to see."

Thirteen years after Ruth's death, when another right-fielder for the Yankees, Roger Maris, was threatening the season record of 60 home runs that Babe had set 34 years earlier, I made a small sentimental pilgrimage in Baltimore where the Yankees happened to be playing. The first stop was the row house where Babe was born. A gracious woman showed visitors through the small rooms. Next came a drink in the neighborhood saloon Babe's father ran when Babe was a boy. Nobody ever came in who remembered the Ruth family, the bartender said. The tour ended at St. Mary's Industrial School, which the wrecker's big iron ball was knocking down.

St. Mary's was Babe's home through most of his boyhood because his parents weren't interested in rearing him. He left the home on Feb. 27, 1914, three weeks after his 19th birthday, to pitch for the Baltimore Orioles of the International League. Jack Dunn, the owner, paid him $600 and sold him late that summer to the Red Sox for $2,900. He was 6-foot-2 and an athlete, thick-chested but not fat. "A big, lummockin' sort of fella," said a waiter in Toots Shor's who had worked in a restaurant near the Red Sox park where young Ruth got sweet on one of the waitresses.

When his hard-pressed employers sold him to the Yankees, he was still a trim young ballplayer who had hit 29 of the Boston club's 32 home runs that season of 1919. He hit an unthinkable 54 in his first New York summer, 59 in his second, and became a god. His waistline grew with his fame, until the legs that nobody had considered spindly began to look like matchsticks and his feet seemed grotesquely small.

He changed the rules, the equipment and the strategy of baseball. Reasoning that if one Babe Ruth could fill a park, 16 would fill all the parks, the owners instructed the manufacturers to produce a livelier ball that would make every man a home-run king. As a further aid to batters, trick pitching deliveries like the spitball, the emery ball, the shine ball and the mud ball were forbidden.

The home run, an occasional phenomenon when a team hit a total of 20 in a season, came to be regarded as the ultimate offensive weapon. Shortstops inclined to swoon at the sight of blood had their bats made with all the wood up in the big end, gripped the slender handle at the very hilt and swung from the heels.

None of these devices produced another Ruth, of course,

because Ruth was one of a kind. He recognized this as the simple truth and conducted himself accordingly. Even before they were married and Claire began to accompany him on the road, he always occupied the drawing room on the team's Pullman; he seldom shared his revels after dark with other players, although one year he did take a fancy to a worshipful rookie named Jimmy Reese and made him a companion until management intervened; if friends were not on hand with transportation, he usually took a taxi by himself to hotel or ball park or railroad station. Unlike other players, Ruth was never seen in the hotel dining room or sitting in the lobby waiting for some passerby to discard a newspaper.

St. Louis was one town where he was always met. When the team left St. Louis, his friends would deliver him to the station along with a laundry basket full of barbecued ribs and tubs of home brew. Then anybody — player, coach or press — was welcome in the drawing room to munch ribs, swill the yeasty beer and laugh at the Babe's favorite record on the Babe's portable phonograph. He would play Moran & Mack's talking record, "Two Black Crows," a hundred times and howl at the hundredth repetition: "How come the black horses ate more'n the white horses?" "Search me, 'cept we had more black horses than white horses."

Roistering was a way of life, yet Ruth was no boozer. Three drinks of hard liquor left him fuzzy. He could consume great quantities of beer, was a prodigious eater and his prowess with women was legendary. Sleep was something he got when other appetites were sated. He arose when he chose and almost invariably was the last to arrive in the clubhouse, where Doc Woods, the Yankees' trainer, always had bicarbonate of soda ready. Before changing clothes, the Babe would measure out a mound of bicarb smaller than the Pyramid of Cheops, mix and gulp it down.

"Then," Jim Cahn says, "he would belch. And all the loose water in the showers would fall down."

The man was a boy, simple, artless, genuine and unabashed. This explains his rapport with children, whom he met as intellectual equals. Probably his natural liking for people communicated itself to the public to help make him an idol.

He was buried on a sweltering day in August, 1948. In the pallbearers' pew, Waite Hoyt sat beside Joe Dugan, the third baseman. "I'd give a hundred dollars for a cold beer," Dugan whispered. "So would the Babe," Hoyt said.

In packed St. Patrick's Cathedral, Francis Cardinal Spellman celebrated requiem mass and out in Fifth Avenue thousands and thousands waited to say good-by to the waif from Baltimore whose parents didn't want him.

"Some 20 years ago," says Tommy Holmes, the great baseball writer, "I stopped talking about the Babe for the simple reason that I realized that those who had never seen him didn't believe me."

James P. Dawson

2,130: Lou Gehrig Takes Himself Out

New York Times, May 2, 1939

Lou Gehrig's matchless record of uninterrupted play in American League championship games, stretched over fifteen years and through 2,130 straight contests, came to an end today.

The mighty iron man, who at his peak hit 49 home runs in a single season five years ago, took himself out of action before the Yanks marched on Briggs Stadium for their first game against the Tigers this year.

With the consent of Manager Joe McCarthy, Gehrig removed himself because he, better than anybody else perhaps, recognized his competitive decline and was frankly aware of the fact he was doing the Yankees no good defensively or on the attack. He last played Sunday in New York against the Senators.

When Gehrig will start another game is undetermined. He will not be used as a pinch hitter. The present plan is to keep him on the bench. He may swing into action in the hot weather, which should have a beneficial effect upon his tired muscles.

Meanwhile Ellsworth (Babe) Dahlgren, until today baseball's greatest figure of frustration, will continue at first base. Dahlgren had been awaiting the summons for three years.

It was coincidental that Gehrig's string was broken almost in the presence of the man he succeeded as Yankee first baseman. At that time Wally Pipp, now a business man of Grand Rapids, Mich., was benched by the late Miller Huggins to make room for the strapping youth fresh from the Hartford Eastern League club to which the Yankees had farmed him for two seasons, following his departure from Columbia University. Pipp was in the lobby of the Book Cadillac Hotel at noon when the withdrawal of Gehrig was effected.

"I don't feel equal to getting back in there," Pipp said on June 2, 1925, the day Lou replaced him at first. Lou had started his phenomenal streak the day before as a pinch hitter for Pee Wee Wanninger, then the Yankee shortstop.

The latest momentous development in baseball was not unexpected. There had been signs for the past two years that Gehrig was slowing up. Even when a sick man, however, he gamely stuck to his chores, not particularly in pursuit of his all-time record of consecutive play but out of a driving desire to help the Yankees, always his first consideration.

What Lou had thought was lumbago last year when he suffered pains in the back that more than once forced his early withdrawal from games was diagnosed later as a gall bladder condition for which Gehrig underwent treatment all last winter.

The signs of his approaching fade-out were unmistakable this spring at St. Petersburg, Fla., yet the announcement from Manager McCarthy was something of a shock. It came at the end of a conference Gehrig arranged immediately after McCarthy's arrival by plane from his native Buffalo.

"Lou just told me he felt it would be best for the club if he took himself out of the lineup," McCarthy said. "I asked him if he really felt that way. He told me he was serious. He feels blue. He is dejected.

"I told him it would be as he wished. Like everybody else I'm sorry to see it happen. I told him not to worry. Maybe the warm weather will bring him around.

"He's been a great ballplayer. Fellows like him come along

once in a hundred years. I told him that. More than that, he's been a vital part of the Yankee club since he started with it. He's always been a perfect gentleman, a credit to baseball.

"We'll miss him. You can't escape that fact. But I think he's doing the proper thing."

Gehrig, visibly affected, explained his decision frankly.

"I decided last Sunday night on this move," said Lou. "I haven't been a bit of good to the team since the season started. It would not be fair to the boys, to Joe or to the baseball public for me to try going on. In fact, it would not be fair to myself.

"It's tough to see your mates on base, have a chance to win a ball game, and not be able to do anything about it. McCarthy has been swell about it all the time. He'd let me go until the cows came home, he is that considerate of my feelings, but I knew in Sunday's game that I should get out of there.

"I went up there four times with men on base. Once there were two there. A hit would have won the game for the Yankees, but I missed, leaving five stranded. Maybe a rest will do me some good. Maybe it won't. Who knows? Who can tell? I'm just hoping."

Gehrig's withdrawal from today's game does not necessarily mean the end of his playing career, although that seems not far distant. When the day comes Gehrig can sit back and enjoy the fortune he has accumulated as a ballplayer. He is estimated to have saved $200,000 from his earnings, which touched a high in 1938, when he collected $39,000 as his Yankee salary.

When Gehrig performed his duties as Yankee captain today, appearing at the plate to give the batting order, announcement was made through the amplifiers of his voluntary withdrawal. A deafening cheer resounded as Lou walked to the dugout, doffed his cap and disappeared in a corner of the bench.

Open expressions of regret came from the Yankees and the Tigers. Lefty Vernon Gomez expressed the Yankees' feelings when he said:

"It's tough to see this thing happen, even though you know it must come to us all. Lou's a great guy and he's always been a great baseball figure. I hope he'll be back in there."

Hank Greenberg, who might have been playing first for the Yanks instead of the Tigers but for Gehrig, said, "Lou's doing the right thing. He's got to use his head now instead of his legs. Maybe that Yankee dynasty is beginning to crumble."

Everett Scott, the shortstop who held the record of 1,307 consecutive games until Gehrig broke it, ended his streak on May 6, 1925, while he was a member of the Yankees. Scott began his string, once considered unapproachable, with the Red Sox. By a strange coincidence, Scott gave way to Wanninger, the player for whom Gehrig batted to start his great record.

With only one run batted in this year and a batting average of .143 representing four singles in twenty-eight times at bat, Lou has fallen far below his record achievements of previous seasons, during five of which he led the league in runs driven home.

David Halberstam

From *Summer of '49*

Joe DiMaggio was the most famous athlete in America. In fact, he seemed to stand above *all* other celebrities. Soon after he retired as a player, he returned with a group of friends to the Stadium to watch a prize fight. He was with Edward Bennett Williams, the famed trial lawyer, Toots Shor, the saloon-keeper, Averell Harriman, the politician-diplomat, and Ernest and Mary Hemingway. Suddenly an immense mob gathered. Hundreds of kids, a giant crowd within a crowd, descended on DiMaggio demanding autographs. One kid took a look at Hemingway, whose distinctive face had graced countless magazine covers. "Hey," the kid said, "you're probably somebody too, right?" Hemingway said without pause, "Yeah, I'm his doctor." For even Hemingway, then at the height of his fame, could not compete with DiMaggio. Endless magazines sought DiMaggio's cooperation to place his picture on their covers. Already two hit songs celebrated his deeds and fame: a light ditty about "Joltin' Joe DiMaggio," commemorating his 1941 hitting streak ("Who started base-ball's famous streak / That's got us all aglow? / He's just a man and not a freak / Joltin' Joe DiMaggio . . ."); and "Bloody Mary" from the 1949 hit musical *South Pacific* ("Her skin is tender as DiMaggio's glove . . ."). Still to come was a generous mention in Hemingway's *The Old Man and the Sea:* Manolin fears the Indians of Cleveland, but Santiago, the older man, reassures him: "Have faith in the Yankees my son. Think of the great DiMaggio."

His deeds remain like a beacon to those who saw him play. More than thirty years after DiMaggio retired, Stephen Jay Gould of Harvard, one of the most distinguished anthropologists in the United States, was still fascinated by him. He had first seen him play in 1949, when Gould was seven. Opening Day, he wrote in an essay for *The New York Times,* is not merely a day of annual renewal, "it evokes the bittersweet passage of our own lives — as I take my son to the game and remember when I held my father's hand and wondered whether DiMag would hit .350 that year."

Gould discovered that another Harvard professor, Edward Mills Purcell, a Nobel physicist, was also fascinated by DiMaggio. Purcell had run most of the great baseball records through his computer looking for any statistical truths they might produce. The computer responded that all but one were within the range of mathematical probability: that someone (Babe Ruth) would hit 714 home runs, that someone (Roger Maris) would one day come along and hit 61 home runs in one season, and that even in modern times a player (Ted Williams) might on occasion bat .406. But the one record that defied all of Purcell's and his computer's expectations was DiMaggio's 56-game hitting streak in 1941. A .400 hitter, after all, could have a bad day and compensate the day after. But to hit in 56 straight games challenged probability, Purcell noted, because of the difficulty of hitting a small round ball traveling at a great speed with a wooden cylinder — "and where if you are off one eighth of an inch a hit becomes a pop-up."

Purcell's description of the difficulty of batting was strikingly similar to one that DiMaggio himself gave after a game in St. Louis. "You know," he told Red Patterson, the traveling secretary, as they rode to the train station, "they always talk about this being a game of fractions of an inch. Today proved it. I should have had three home runs today. I knew I was going to get fastballs and I got them and I was ready each time. But I didn't get up on the ball — I hit it *down* by that much [he held his thumb and index finger about an eighth of an inch apart and then touched them just above the center of the ball]. If I got under them that much [he lowered his fingers just slightly *below* the middle of the ball], I get three home runs."

DiMaggio had size, power, and speed. McCarthy, his longtime manager, liked to say that DiMaggio might have stolen 60 bases a season if he had given him the green light. Stengel, his new manager, was equally impressed, and when DiMaggio was on base he would point to him as an example of the perfect base runner. "Look at him," Stengel would say as DiMaggio ran out a base hit, "he's always watching the ball. He isn't watching second base. He isn't watching third base. He knows they haven't been moved. He isn't watching the ground, because he knows they haven't built a canal or a swimming pool since he was last there. He's watching the ball and the outfielder, which is the one thing that is different on every play."

Center field was his territory — right center and left center too — for most of his career. The other outfielders moved into his domain with caution. At the tail end of the 1948 season Hank Bauer was brought up from the minors and he chased, called for, and caught a ball in deep-right center field. Between innings in the dugout, Bauer noticed DiMaggio eyeing him curiously. "Joe, did I do something wrong?" the nervous rookie asked. "No, you didn't do anything wrong, but you're the first son of a bitch who ever invaded my territory," DiMaggio said. It was not a rebuke, but Bauer deeded over more of right center in the future.

DiMaggio complemented his natural athletic ability with astonishing physical grace. He played the outfield, he ran the bases, and he batted not just effectively but with rare style. He would glide rather than run, it seemed, always smooth, always ending up where he wanted to be just when he wanted to be there. If he appeared to play effortlessly, his teammates knew otherwise. In his first season as a Yankee, Gene

Woodling, who played left field, was struck by the sound of DiMaggio chasing a fly ball. He sounded like a giant truck horse on the loose, Woodling thought, his feet thudding down hard on the grass. The great, clear noises in the open space enabled Woodling to measure the distance between them without looking.

He was the perfect Hemingway hero, for Hemingway in his novels romanticized the man who exhibited grace under pressure, who withheld any emotion lest it soil the purer statement of his deeds. DiMaggio was that kind of hero; his grace and skills were always on display, his emotions always concealed. This stoic grace was not achieved without a terrible price: DiMaggio was a man wound tight. He suffered from insomnia and ulcers. When he sat and watched the game he chain-smoked and drank endless cups of coffee. He was ever conscious of his obligation to play well. Late in his career, when his legs were bothering him and the Yankees had a comfortable lead in a pennant race, a friend of his, columnist Jimmy Cannon, asked him why he played so hard — the games, after all, no longer meant so much. "Because there might be somebody out there who's never seen me play before," he answered.

To DiMaggio, how people perceived him was terribly important. In 1948 during a Boston–New York game, Tex Hughson, who liked to pitch him tight, drilled him with a fastball in the chest. It was obvious to everyone in both dugouts that the pitch really hurt. Even as he was hit, Joe McCarthy, by then the Boston manager, turned to his own players and said, "Watch him, he won't show any pain." Nor did he.

During the 1947 World Series, in a rare outburst of emotion, he kicked the ground near second base after a Brooklyn player named Al Gionfriddo made a spectacular catch, robbing him of a three-run home run. The next day while he was dressing, a photographer who had taken a picture of him kicking the ground asked him to sign a blowup of it. At first DiMaggio demurred and suggested that the photographer get Gionfriddo's signature. "He's the guy who made the play," DiMaggio said. But the photographer persisted, and so reluctantly DiMaggio signed it. Then he turned to a small group of reporters sitting by him. "Don't write this in the paper," he said, "but the truth is, if he had been playing me right, he would have made it look easy."

Ted Williams, himself caught in endless comparisons with DiMaggio, once said that the difference between the two of them was that DiMaggio did everything so elegantly. "DiMaggio even looks good striking out," Williams said.

Theirs was a rivalry that existed in the minds of their fans, in the minds of their teammates, and, though never admitted by either of them, in their own minds. Williams was, perhaps, the more generous of the two. Clif Keane, the Boston sportswriter, once went to New York in the late forties to cover a fight. He was staying at the Edison Hotel, which was DiMaggio's residence. Traveling with him was a friend who was a great fan of DiMaggio. Keane called DiMaggio and asked if they could come up. DiMaggio said yes. "Joe," asked Keane's friend almost as soon as they were inside the room, "What do you think of Ted Williams?" "Greatest left-handed hitter I've ever seen," DiMaggio answered. "I know that," said the man, "but what do you think of him as a *ballplayer?*" "Greatest left-handed hitter I've ever seen," repeated DiMaggio.

Unsure of his social skills and uncomfortable in any conversation that strayed far from baseball, DiMaggio was wary of moving into a situation in which he might feel or reveal his limitations. He did not push against certain New York doors that would have readily opened for him in those years. Some of his close friends thought the reason for his behavior was his sensitivity about being an Italian immigrant's son in an age when ethnic prejudice was far more powerful than it is today. In 1939, *Life* magazine did a piece on him that its editors thought sympathetic but which said, among other things, "Italians, bad at war, are well suited for milder competition, and the number of top-notched Italian prize fighters, golfers

and baseball players is out of all proportion to the population."
Life found the young DiMaggio to be better groomed than
expected for someone who was not a Wasp: "Instead of olive
oil or smelly bear grease, he keeps his hair slick with water.
He never reeks of garlic and prefers chicken chow mein to
spaghetti . . ." In fact, he was meticulous about his appearance, and unlike most of his teammates, who dressed casually
in sports clothes, he almost always came to the ball park in a
custom-tailored dark-blue suit, with a white shirt and tie. His
overcoats were tailored as well, and he even took his army
uniforms to be tailored during World War II.

He was spared the normal, crude byplay of the locker
room. The other players were aware that he did not like it,
and they did not dare risk displeasing him. (About the only
person who could tease DiMaggio was Pete Sheehy, the
clubhouse man, who seemed to be as much a part of the
Yankee scene as the Stadium itself. Once when DiMaggio had
been examining a red mark on his butt, he yelled over to
Sheehy, "Hey, Pete, take a look at this. Is there a bruise
there?" "Sure there is, Joe, it's from all those people kissing
your ass," Sheehy answered.)

DiMaggio's sensitivity to being embarrassed never diminished. He carried for no short length of time a grudge against
Casey Stengel because Stengel, during the 1950 season,
dropped him in the batting order from the cleanup position to
the number-five slot, and told him to play first base, a position
where he was not comfortable. His teammate Tommy Henrich noticed that when DiMaggio came into the dugout from
first base near the end of the game, his uniform was soaked
with sweat. Henrich knew immediately that it was not the
physical exhaustion that had caused the sweat — it was
caused by tension from the fear of embarrassing himself.

After a game he would always linger in the locker room for
two or three hours, in order to avoid the crowd of fans who
waited outside the players' entrance. He simply needed to sit
in front of his locker, catch his breath, drink a beer, and relax.
Once he was sure there were no outsiders around, he would

conduct an informal seminar on the game just played. In those moments he was absolutely relaxed and unthreatened. He might turn to Shea. "Spec," he would say to the young pitcher, "you have to stay with the game plan when you go after the hitters. If you say you're going outside, stay outside, don't cross us up. Otherwise we're going to end up with a big gap out there. The other thing you were doing today is you were goosing the ball. Not really throwing it. Pushing it. Just throw it next time." "Phil," he might tell Rizzuto, "you didn't get over quite quickly enough on that grounder in the third inning. I know you made the play, but that isn't what worries me. What worries me is you getting hurt. If you get hurt, this team is in trouble. We can't afford it."

When he was sure that most of the crowd at the players' entrance was gone, he would get ready to leave. The call would come down to the gate people: "Joe's ready to go." A taxi would be called and a group of attendants would form a flying wedge so that he could get out with as little harassment as possible.

Although DiMaggio was largely suspicious of newspapermen and reserved with most of them, his relationships with them were actually rather good. The last line of the last column of the greatest sportswriter of two eras, Red Smith, concluded: "I told myself not to worry: Someday there would be another DiMaggio." The writers were, of course, wired to DiMaggio. They treated him as the White House press corps might treat a wildly popular president. They understood the phenomenon, what caused it and what made it work, and they were delighted to be part of it, mostly because their readers wanted to know all about DiMaggio. Besides, the writers respected DiMaggio; for many of them he was the best all-around player they had ever seen. He frequently carried the team and he always did it modestly.

If DiMaggio wanted them at a distance, they readily accepted that. For one thing, even if he might not have been the perfect interviewee (when he first came up, he was so unsophisticated, he liked to recall, that when the sportswriters asked him for a quote, he thought they were talking about a soft drink), he was a gent. As he took his own dignity seriously, he generally accorded the writers theirs. On questions about *baseball,* he was generally candid. He was also aware of the uses of good publicity, and he was, if anything, closer to some of the writers, particularly the columnists, than he was to his teammates. He understood that if he gave too little of himself, the press would rebel. He never upbraided a reporter who transgressed, as Williams did, but he was, in his own way, just as tough. If a reporter displeased him, even slightly, DiMaggio would ruthlessly cut him off.

W. C. Heinz, one of the best writers of that era, thought that his colleagues were different with DiMaggio from the way they were with other athletes. As they entered the Yankee locker room, they were cocky, brash, and filled with self-importance. Then, as they approached DiMaggio's locker, they began to change from men to boys. They became reverential, almost apologetic for even asking questions. You could, Heinz thought, hear the rustle of the paper in their notebooks as they steeled their courage to ask him how he felt.

DiMaggio had good reason for being suspicious of the press. In his first two seasons as a Yankee, he had been nothing less than brilliant, leading New York back to the pennant after a hiatus of three years. In his second season he hit .346 and 46 home runs, and knocked in 167 runs. He had been paid only $8,000 for his first year, and for his second, $15,000 plus, of course, his World Series checks, which Yankee management viewed as part of his salary. For the third year he decided to ask for $40,000. The Yankees offered him $25,000. Ed Barrow, the general manager, told him that $40,000 was more than the great Lou Gehrig made. "Then Mr. Gehrig is a badly underpaid player," DiMaggio answered. The Yankee management turned its full firepower on him. This was the Depression, and, typically, the ownership did not view the question in relation to how much money the Yankees had made, or to how many millions Colonel Ruppert was worth, but rather to DiMaggio's salary as measured against the wages of the average American.

The assault was surprisingly harsh. He was privileged and spoiled. "DiMaggio is an ungrateful young man and is very unfair to his teammates to say the least," Colonel Ruppert said. "As far as I'm concerned that's all he's worth to the ball club, and if he doesn't sign we'll win the pennant without him." Then Ruppert added: "Is it fair for him to remain home while the other boys are training down South? No! Absolutely no!" DiMaggio himself remained adamant, which made Ruppert angrier. As the holdout progressed he added, "I have nothing new on DiMaggio. I've forgotten all about him. Presidents go into eclipse, kings have their thrones moved from under them, business leaders go into retirement, great ballplayers pass on, but still everything moves in its accustomed stride." Why, said the Colonel, if you included World Series checks, DiMaggio had averaged *$20,000* a year since he came up.

Soon Joe McCarthy joined in: The Yankees, he said, could win without DiMaggio. No one came to DiMaggio's defense, not even the writers. The beat reporters, who had coveted his goodwill in the past, proved to be toadies to management. They helped turn the fans against him — he was often booed that year — and he learned the limits of his bargaining power the hard way. Finally, on April 20, with no leverage of his own, DiMaggio surrendered. He would come back at the salary he had been offered. The Yankees even tightened the screw: DiMaggio would have to get back into condition at his own expense and the Yankees would deduct $167 a day, his per diem salary, from his pay until he did. "I hope the young man has learned his lesson," Colonel Ruppert said.

Gradually the scar from the press's treatment of him during that holdout healed. Something of a pecking order developed in the way he treated writers: The beat reporters respected him, but except for Lou Effrat were not his pals; the grander figures of the time — such columnists and magazine writers as Jimmy Cannon, Tom Meany, and Milton Gross — might pal around with him. There was no danger that DiMaggio would cut off Jimmy Cannon. Cannon was at the height of his fame. He was forty years old and a columnist for the *New York Post.* In the late 1940s he was probably the most influential sports columnist in New York. He and DiMaggio were pals. Unlike the genteel Red Smith, who wrote for the *Herald Tribune,* an upper-middle-class paper favored by Wall Street executives, Cannon was passionate. It was easy reading him, to know who were the good guys and who were the bad guys. The *Post* was blue-collar liberal, and its readers were baseball-obsessed. Cannon was the New York street kid as columnist — salty, blunt, with a style not unaffected by Hemingway. He loved being a sportswriter, he once told Jerome Holtzman of the *Chicago Tribune,* because "[he] spent most of [his] life at glad events as a sportswriter, amid friendly multitudes gathered for the purpose of pleasure." Sportswriting, he also told Holtzman, could be either the best writing or the worst writing in the paper. How do you know when it's bad? Holtzman asked him. "You feel the clink," he answered.

The son of a minor Tammany politician, Cannon grew up in a cold-water flat alongside the docks on the west side of Greenwich Village. He went to high school for one year, never attended college at all, but was a voracious reader, so much so that his family warned him he would damage his eyes. A wonderful sense of the city, the sharpness and edginess of its life, ran through his writing. He loved Damon Runyon, always dapper, with his wonderful collection of suits, and his three carnations — one red, one white, one blue — which were delivered every day. He emulated him, eventually becoming Runyon's hand-picked successor as a chronicler of the raffish side of the city. Indeed, he loved to quote Runyon about a mutual friend: "He's out hustling, doing the best he can. It's a very overcrowded profession now." Runyon had once been a heavy drinker, and he had taught Cannon, the latter said, to drink a bottle of brandy a day. Eventually Runyon stopped drinking and warned his protégé that if he did not stop "you're going to end up a rumpot." For a long time Cannon did not heed that advice. As far as he was concerned he did not have a drinking problem because he did not drink in the morning. That was the dividing line.

By the late forties, though, Cannon did stop, and in his own words, "When I quit I took the title with me." Home, for much of his life, was two rooms in the Edison Hotel. Restless at night, his work done, he often made the rounds with Leonard Lyons, the *Post*'s gossip columnist. Lyons had a proscribed route: Shor's to "21" to Palm Court, and Cannon knew where he would be at all times. It was better than going to bed. Cannon and DiMaggio shared a special palship because they had a lot in common. Both of them were lonely, without family. They were both insomniacs, and they both liked to make the New York scene, Cannon with his regular date, the actress Joan Blondell, DiMaggio with some show girl. Cannon loved the moment they entered a nightclub, when everyone there gawked to get a look at this baseball god.

He wrote often and well about DiMaggio, and in the process he helped create not just the legend of DiMaggio as the great athlete but, even more significant, DiMaggio as the Hemingway hero, as elegant off the field as on it. Cannon was in awe of his friend, and he lovingly passed that on to his readers. The view he provided of DiMaggio was an uncommon blend of genuine intimacy and pseudo intimacy. Only the better qualities were worthy of mention, of course — those allowed near the star knew what to write and what not to write. Lou Effrat once was invited to spend a week with DiMaggio in Florida during the winter. It was a pleasant interlude, but near the end of his stay Effrat asked DiMaggio a question about his contract for the next year. "What are you doing, turning writer on me?" DiMaggio asked him. That ended the subject of contracts.

DiMaggio was not a man who boasted, but once, late in his career, he talked with a group of younger reporters and mentioned, almost shyly, that when he first came to the

Yankees in 1936 the local newspapers were constantly criti-
cizing McCarthy for finishing second. "Then we won three
times in a row, and four times out of five," he said. He paused
for a moment before adding, "I had something to do with
that." It was a rare moment, thought Leonard Koppett, then
a young sportswriter. DiMaggio had almost dared to be
candid about his own abilities, wary as he always was of
appearing to boast.

DiMaggio was aware that he was often a virtual prisoner of
his own shyness. Some of his friends thought this was due to
his fear of embarrassing himself. But it was also an innate
reserve.

Once, early in his career, he was sitting with a few writers
at Toots Shor's when his friend Lefty Gomez, the most
gregarious Yankee of that era, dropped by. Gomez did not
join the table but stood and told a few stories, all of which
delighted his listeners. DiMaggio watched him leave and then
said, "What I'd give to be like that."

On another occasion at Shor's, he told Lou Effrat to stick
around. "I've got a date," he said, "and I need company."
DiMaggio's date turned out to be a young actress. After
Shor's they went to "21" and then on to a few other places.
Around three A.M. Effrat finally got away. The next day he
asked DiMaggio why he had insisted that he stay around.
"Ah, Lou, you know me," DiMaggio answered, "until mid-
night with girls I'm speechless."

The stories of DiMaggio's reserve were legendary. When
he first joined the Yankees, he drove from California to
Florida with Tony Lazzeri and Frank Crosetti, two veterans,
neither famous for being talkative. They passed the first two
days of the trip without talking at all, and then Lazzeri asked
DiMaggio if he wanted to drive. Only then did DiMaggio say
he did not know how to drive. It was simply not a subject that
had come up before.

The three of them hung out together a fair amount that
year, and Jack Mahon, a reporter for the old INS, ran into
them while they were sitting in the lobby of the Chase Hotel

in St. Louis. The three, according to Mahon, were watching the other guests come and go. "I bought a paper and sat down near them and after a while became aware of the fact that none of them had a word to say to the others. Just for fun I timed them to see how long they would maintain their silence. Believe it or not, they didn't speak for an hour and twenty minutes. At the end of the time DiMaggio cleared his throat. Crosetti looked at him and said: 'What did you say?' And Lazzeri said, 'Shut up. He didn't say nothing.' They lapsed into silence and at the end of ten more minutes I got up and left. I couldn't stand it anymore."

His teammates did not resent DiMaggio's need to be private. Watching him play day after day, often under immensely difficult circumstances, they became the true advocates of his greatness. Some forty years later, Henrich, a proud, unsentimental man, would point out that when fans asked him to compare the Mantle and DiMaggio outfields, he always said that DiMaggio's was better "because we had the better center fielder." Then Henrich would point out an astonishing and revealing statistic about DiMaggio: By and large, such power hitters as DiMaggio have a high strikeout ratio. It is in the nature of the big swing. Reggie Jackson, for example, has almost four and a half strikeouts for each home run. Even Hank Aaron, a marvelous line-drive hitter whose power came from his wrists, struck out twice for every home run. Ted Williams, whose eyesight was as legendary as his concentration, struck out 709 times against 521 home runs. But Joe DiMaggio, Henrich pointed out, hit 361 home runs and struck out 369 times.

His teammates understood that he put extra pressure on himself to live up to the expectations of the media and the fans. They knew that he pushed himself to his limits both physically and emotionally to carry the team. That being the case, they appreciated that he was different, that he worked things out for himself. Once when he was going through a prolonged slump, Bill Dickey, by then the hitting coach, explained to Mel Allen, the broadcaster, what he thought

DiMaggio was doing wrong. "How does Joe react to what you've just said?" Allen asked. "Oh, I haven't spoken to Joe yet," Dickey answered. "Why not?" Allen pursued. "A player like Joe, when he's in a slump, you don't go to him. You wait until he comes to you. First he tries to work it out himself. Then if he doesn't he'll let you know he's ready," Dickey answered.

DiMaggio rarely dined with the other players on the road, even Keller and Henrich, with whose names his was inextricably linked in a thousand box scores. He led the league, his teammate Eddie Lopat once shrewdly noted, in room-service. He sought out dark restaurants, where he would sit in the back, in a corner, so that he would not be recognized. If DiMaggio palled around with anyone on the team, it was usually the newer or more vulnerable players who hero-worshiped him and ran favors for him: there was Joe Page, the relief pitcher, whose behavior was erratic enough so that his place on the team was rarely secure; then, for a time, there was Clarence Marshall, the handsome young pitcher; and finally, at the end of his career, DiMaggio palled around with Billy Martin. Martin began his friendship with DiMaggio by violating the most sacred rule of Yankee etiquette: *He* asked DiMaggio out for dinner, "Hey Joe, let's go to dinner tonight," a statement so startling, a presumption so great, that his teammates long remembered it. DiMaggio was so amused by him that he assented, and the two became friends.

Some DiMaggio hangers-on were known as his Boboes, the phrase then popular for caddies. One who was proud to be known as a DiMaggio Bobo was Lou Effrat, the *Times*'s baseball writer. On occasion, Effrat would come in late to Toots Shor's, the main wateringhole of baseball men and sportswriters, to be told by Shor himself that his presence was requested. "The Daig [for "Dago," DiMaggio's nickname] wants you," Shor would say to Effrat. "What does he want?" Effrat would ask. "He wants to go to a midnight movie." Effrat knew the drill. He would finish his meal, give his wife ten dollars to get home, and join DiMaggio for a late movie. Mrs. Effrat was not invited. Women, particularly wives, never were.

DiMaggio himself squired a series of beautiful show girls, but he was very discreet about it. He never participated in the endless locker-room discussions about women. He made it very clear to his friends in the press that he wanted nothing written about this part of his life, and so nothing was written.

There was a contradiction to DiMaggio's shyness: He wanted to touch the bright lights of the city, but not be burned by them. When he made the scene, he was often seen with the most unlikely of his buddies — a man named George Solotaire. Solotaire, for a time, was his roommate and closest friend as well as a golfer. He ran his errands, took care of his clothes, and made sure that if DiMaggio did not want to go out to eat, sandwiches were brought in. Solotaire specialized in knowing where the action and the pretty girls were. He was also one of the city's top Broadway ticket brokers; he liked to boast that he had once supplied J. P. Morgan with a choice ticket for the same show for seven Saturdays in a row because he assumed that Morgan liked one of the show girls. Solotaire was forty-six years old, short, and stocky, and he spoke in his own Broadway shorthand: If he was out of money, he was in Brokesville; a boring show was Dullsville; a divorce was Splitsville; if he had to leave New York, he would tell friends he had to go camping for a few days; when he returned he would say that it was good to be back in the United States. He at one time wanted to be a songwriter, and wrote two-line jingles for the *Hollywood Reporter* that were, in effect, reviews of shows. Of a show with Ethel Merman he wrote: "The show is infirm / but it's still got the Merm." Of *Fiddler on the Roof* he wrote: "Have no fear about *Fiddler* / This is a triple-A honest diddler." Writing these couplets, he said, was better than sitting around all day with Freddy or Gladys (tickets for rows F and G).

Solotaire was absolutely awed by his friendship with Di-Maggio, and they became the odd couple. Those who thought they knew Solotaire well were often surprised to find out there was a Mrs. Solotaire, who apparently considered herself happily married and was the mother of their son. Instead, friends remembered Solotaire with DiMaggio, sitting at dinner in the Stage Delicatessen, an unlikely father-son act, the meal passing but no words spoken. Once Solotaire called up a young woman named Ruth Cosgrove and suggested that she be part of a foursome for dinner with the Yankee star. When she arrived at dinner she was pleasantly surprised to find that Solotaire, whose manners were not exactly exquisite, was pulling back a chair for her to sit down. Then she realized that Solotaire was not holding the chair for her, he was holding it for DiMaggio.

Dining with Joe DiMaggio, Ms. Cosgrove felt, gave her a remarkable insight into the male animal. The entire restaurant came to a halt for two hours. The chair of every man was angled so that its occupant could keep an eye on her date. Each one, she noted, seemed to come up with an excuse for passing their table at least once. As for DiMaggio himself, she thought him kind and almost unbearably shy. He asked her out again, and she, who knew nothing about baseball, cemented their friendship by asking early in the evening, "Joe, what's an error?" With that he was finally able to talk.

The possible loss of DiMaggio for the season put a considerable chill on the Yankees as they headed north. They were hardly a one-man team, but it was comforting to know that in big games Joe DiMaggio would hit in the cleanup slot and play center field. Tommy Henrich thought his very presence gave the Yankees a considerable edge.

Years later Charlie Keller could still see DiMaggio batting against the best pitcher in the league, Bob Feller. DiMaggio seemed to summon extra adrenaline for such moments: the best against the best. You could actually see the veins and muscles in DiMaggio's neck stand out, Keller remembered. They were like taut red cords. His whole body was tensed. Bobby Brown recalled that on certain occasions when the Yankees really needed a run, DiMaggio would hit a ball that was not quite going to make the gap between the outfielders. Not much of a chance for a double on that one, Brown would think. Then he would watch DiMaggio go into overdrive, legs extended, going for two bases from the very start. He always made it. There might have been players in the league who were faster going to first base, but there was no player in those days who went from home to second or from first to third or from second to home faster, and no one could better calibrate the odds than DiMaggio. Years later, Frank Crosetti, who coached at third for much of DiMaggio's career, said that DiMaggio had never been thrown out going from first to third. . . .

Senate Testimony of Casey Stengel

On July 9, 1958, hearings were held in Washington by the Subcommittee on Anti-trust and Monopoly of the Committee of the Judiciary of the United States Senate. The subcommittee was considering H.R. 10378 and S. 4070: to limit anti-trust laws so as to exempt professional baseball, football, basketball and hockey. The chief witness: Charles Dillon Stengel. Following are excerpts of his testimony:

Senator Estes Kefauver: Mr. Stengel, you are the manager of the New York Yankees. Will you give us very briefly your background and your views about this legislation?

Mr. Stengel: Well, I started in professional ball in 1910. I have been in professional ball, I would say, for 48 years. I have been employed by numerous ball clubs in the majors and in the minor leagues.

I started in the minor leagues with Kansas City. I played as low as Class D ball, which was at Shelbyville, Kentucky, and also Class C ball and Class A ball, and I have advanced in baseball as a ballplayer.

I had many years that I was not so successful as a ballplayer, as it is a game of skill. And then I was no doubt discharged by baseball in which I had to go back to the minor leagues as a manager, and after being in the minor leagues as a manager, I became a major league manager in several cities and was discharged, we call it discharged because there is no question I had to leave. (Laughter.)

And I returned to the minor leagues at Milwaukee, Kansas City and Oakland, California, and then returned to the major leagues.

In the last 10 years, naturally, in major league baseball with the New York Yankees, the New York Yankees have had tremendous success and while I am not a ballplayer who does the work, I have no doubt worked for a ball club that is very capable in the office.

I have been up and down the ladder. I know there are some things in baseball 35 to 50 years ago that are better now than they were in those days. In those days, my goodness, you could not transfer a ball club in the minor leagues, class D, class C ball, class A ball.

How could you transfer a ball club when you did not have a highway? How could you transfer a ball club when the railroads then would take you to a town you got off and then you had to wait and sit up five hours to go to another ball club?

How could you run baseball then without night ball?

You had to have night ball to improve the proceeds, to pay larger salaries, and I went to work, the first year I received $135 a month.

I thought that was amazing. I had to put away enough money to go to dental college. I found out it was not better in dentistry. I stayed in baseball.

Any other questions you would like to ask me?

Senator Kefauver: Mr. Stengel, are you prepared to answer particularly why baseball wants this bill passed?

Mr. Stengel: Well, I would have to say at the present time, I think that baseball has advanced in this respect for the player help. That is an amazing statement for me to make, because you can retire with an annuity at 50 and what organization in America allows you to retire at 50 and receive money?

Now the second thing about baseball that I think is very interesting to the public or to all of us that it is the owner's own fault if he does not improve his club, along with the officials in the ball club and the players.

Now what causes that?

If I am going to go on the road and we are a traveling ball club and you know the cost of transportation now — we travel sometimes with three Pullman coaches, the New York Yankees, and I am just a salaried man and do not own stock in the New York Yankees, I found out that in traveling with the New York Yankees on the road and all, that it is the best, and we have broken records in Washington this year, we have broken them in every city but New York and we have lost two clubs that have gone out of the city of New York.

Of course, we have had some bad weather, I would say that they are mad at us in Chicago, we fill the parks.

They have come out to see good material. I will say they are mad at us in Kansas City, but we broke their attendance record.

Now on the road we only get possibly 27 cents. I am not positive of these figures, as I am not an official.

If you go back 15 years or if I owned stock in the club, I would give them to you.

Senator Kefauver: Mr. Stengel, I am not sure that I made my question clear. (Laughter.)

Mr. Stengel: Yes, sir. Well, that is all right. I am not sure I am going to answer yours perfectly, either. (Laughter.)

Senator Joseph C. O'Mahoney: How many minor leagues were there in baseball when you began?

Mr. Stengel: Well, there were not so many at that time because of the fact: Anybody to go into baseball at that time with the educational schools that we had were small, while you were probably thoroughly educated at school, you had to be — we had only small cities that you could put a team in and they would go defunct.

Why, I remember the first year I was at Kankakee, Illinois, and a bank offered me $550 if I would let them have a little notice. I left there and took a uniform because they owed me two weeks' pay. But I either had to quit but I didn't have enough money to go to dental college so I had to go with the manager down to Kentucky.

What happened there was if you got by July, that was the

big date. You did not play night ball and you did not play Sundays in half of the cities on account of a Sunday observance, so in those days when things were tough, and all of it was, I mean to say, why they just closed up July 4 and there you were sitting there in the depot.

You could go to work some place else, but that was it.

So I got out of Kankakee, Illinois, and I just go there for the visit now. (Laughter.)

Senator John A. Carroll: The question Senator Kefauver asked you was what, in your honest opinion, with your 48 years of experience, is the need for this legislation in view of the fact that baseball has not been subject to anti-trust laws?

Mr. Stengel: No.

Senator Carroll: I had a conference with one of the attorneys representing not only baseball but all of the sports, and I listened to your explanation to Senator Kefauver. It seemed to me it had some clarity. I asked the attorney this question: What was the need for this legislation? I wonder if you would accept his definition. He said they didn't want to be subjected to the *ipse dixit* of the Federal Government because they would throw a lot of damage suits on the *ad damnum* clause. He said, in the first place, the Toolson case was *sui generis*, it was *de minimus non curat lex.*

Do you call that a clear expression?

Mr. Stengel: Well, you are going to get me there for about two hours.

Senator Kefauver: Thank you, very much, Mr. Stengel. We appreciate your presence here.

Mr. Mickey Mantle, will you come around?

Mr. Mantle, do you have any observations with reference to the application of the anti-trust laws to baseball?

Mr. Mantle: My views are just about the same as Casey's.

George Vecsey

Mickey Mantle: It's All Over

The retirement of a player as great as Mickey Mantle should inspire only a recitation of great deeds and enjoyable moments, yet his story must include frustration and unfulfillment along with the glory. Mantle never enjoyed his 18 years in New York the way many other stars have enjoyed their careers, and injuries and personal struggles were equally responsible.

For many years he seemed on the verge of becoming a happy, healthy star — he was certainly a hero to millions of fans — but injuries and temper delayed that process. Then in the closing years, after he had achieved many great things on the field and developed a relative maturity to appreciate them, he was cheered every time he poked his head out of the dugout.

However, Mantle understood that the cheers were for him as a descending star and he had never wished to be the central figure in a tragic-opera situation. When fans in Houston gave him a standing ovation last summer after he had struck out in the All-Star Game, he talked of being "tired" and retiring. The one glorious year of being whole and happy had never quite come.

The intermingling of pain and joy began in Mantle's first season in the major leagues. Born in Spavinaw, Oklahoma, on October 20, 1931, he needed only two years in the minor leagues before joining the Yankees in 1951 — a powerful, fleet young man who could not miss being a star if a boyhood case of osteomyelitis, a bone disease, remained arrested.

That first season saw him twist his right knee on a drain pipe while playing right field in the second game of the World Series. For the rest of the Series he was in the hospital — in a bed next to his father, who was suffering from Hodgkin's disease, which would eventually kill him.

The records show that Mantle's best years were in 1956–57, when the Yankees won pennants as usual and he was twice voted Most Valuable Player. He batted .353 in 1956, hit 52 home runs and drove in 130 runs, leading the league in all three categories, the so-called "triple crown." In 1957, he batted .365 with 34 homers and 94 runs batted in. When the Giants took Willie Mays to San Francisco after 1957, Mantle was clearly New York's biggest sports hero.

But Mantle never was at home in New York, preferring to settle in Dallas with his wife and four sons and rent homes or live in hotels during the season. And even in the best of summers, New York was not his scene. The fans saw him heave his batting helmet in disgust when he struck out and he heard as many boos as cheers.

"Me and the fans really had a go-around those first couple of years," he recalled recently. "I didn't like them and they didn't like me. But it's gotten better since then."

When fans did approach Mantle, he often did not seem to know how to react. Whereas many stars would chat with their fans — while trotting toward the sanctuary of the clubhouse — Mantle would often bolt frozen-faced through them, occasionally scattering youngsters like the halfback he wished he had been. And Mantle's reaction to the press was inconsistent and occasionally rude, although he was a funny and loyal friend to his teammates, who liked and respected him.

After the first decade, Mantle began to cope with many things, running bases, playing center field and swinging the bat with a new understanding, coupling wisdom with his physical skills.

"It seemed like I was finally getting the hang of it," he once said.

Then the injuries struck again. He tried to play the 1961 World Series with an abscess on his right buttock that oozed blood through his uniform, visible to players and fans. In 1962 he pulled a right-thigh muscle while running to first base and fell to the ground "as if he had been shot," as one reporter described it. Mantle recovered in a month from the hamstring, but he had bruised his left knee in the fall and he wound up playing only 123 games that year. Yet the Yankees won the pennant and he was voted Most Valuable Player for the third time.

The games diminished to 65 in 1963 as he broke his foot when his spikes caught in a wire fence in Baltimore. He also had knee cartilage removed in the off-season.

By 1964 it was commonly accepted by players and fans that Mantle was playing mostly on courage. Players saw him pull himself up stairways using his powerful arms to supplement his wobbly knees, and they marveled that he could play at all.

"Every time he misses, he grunts in pain," one opposing catcher said. "You think he's going to fall down."

In 1965, as the Yankees fell from first to sixth place, Mantle suffered back and neck spasms, shoulder and elbow aches and he pulled his left hamstring and missed 21 games. He had a chip removed from his right shoulder before the 1966 season, yet he insisted on opening the season in left field — to minimize his throwing. He later strained a hamstring and bruised his left hand.

By 1967, Mantle moved to first base and played 144 games, suffering only minor aches. His average fell to .245 and his pride was hurt, but he did not quit.

"I need the money," he sometimes said, laughing as if it were a joke. But friends whispered that he needed his $100,000 salary because of poor investments, so he played on. Last year he appeared in 144 games again, this time batting only .237.

As he grew older, Mantle became extremely popular with the New York fans and he had always been adulated by fans in other cities. Last year many clubs asked if they could honor Mantle on the Yankees' final appearance in their town, just in case it was his final performance. Mantle usually said he did not want a fuss made over him and he refused the honors. He still will be honored many times, of course, but as a retired hero rather than a future hero or a declining one, two roles he never thoroughly enjoyed.

Yogi Berra with Tom Horton

Sayings

Yogi: It Ain't Over . . .

"90 percent of putts that are short don't go in" — did Yogi Berra say that? I don't know if I have said 90 percent of what I am supposed to have said, or even 10 percent. I really don't. I don't think it is possible I will ever know. Carmen would say it is possible that no one cares. The subtitle of this book — "It ain't over until it's over" — is supposed to be the best thing I ever said. I hope not. (And I try to say: "It *isn't* over until it's over.") I said it, but I am amazed to this day that somebody didn't claim that Rocky Bridges said it first. I mean I'm amazed that some reporter didn't look back after I got credit and find out that Rocky or Clint Courtney said it first.

Rocky played for the Dodgers and the Reds and some other teams. He and Courtney, who played one game for the Yankees and a lot more for the Washington Senators, were great talkers. Clint managed in the minors. One time when his team lost by a lot of runs and because of a lot of errors, he told the lone reporter, "We may lose again tomorrow, but not with the same guys." Another time Rocky was in the same spot and said, "If you don't catch the ball, you catch the bus."

The other thing about the "it isn't over . . ." saying is that I said it in 1973. The way the Mets were bouncing around in the standings that year, it was true. We won the National League division by winning 82 games and losing 79. That was a 50.9% average, and it meant it isn't over until it is over, or until the team is in first place after the last game.

Sometimes it is over before it begins — if I fought Joe Louis in his prime, it would be over before it began. But in 1973 what I said made sense. When I think back on that year, I get a little mad, but I will save that until later. Let me just say this much. A lot of writers said it was awful that the Mets won with such a lousy percentage. But when the Yankees later would clinch their division by September 1, those same guys would say, "Break up the Yankees."

You have to give 100 percent in the first half of the game. If that isn't enough, in the second half, you have to give what is left. The first time I said that is right here.

When I was watching a Steve McQueen movie on TV, I said that he "must have made that before he died." I said the same thing about Jeff Chandler and some other actors, too, I am sure. It seemed to make sense at the time.

When I went to the mayor's mansion in New York City on a hot day, Mayor Lindsay's wife, Mary, said to me, "You look nice and cool, Yogi." I answered, "You don't look so hot yourself." I didn't mean for it to sound that way, and Mrs. Lindsay knew what I meant.

This next one happened when a lot of reporters were asking questions, trying to get me to say something. I almost think this was one I worked at. The question was, "What would you do if you found a million dollars?" I said, "If the guy was poor, I would give it back." I was a manager when I said that. Now it seems like such a dumb thing to have said that maybe I say I worked at it so I'll feel better. Maybe it was the way the question was asked. It made sense at the time, that's all I can say.

Another one I did say, and am sort of proud of, was when some of the guys wanted me to see a dirty movie. I didn't want to go. I really didn't want to go, but I have never been good at saying no. I kept saying, "I want to see *Airport.*" (This all happened before I got the movie critic job; now I could say, "I have to see *Airport.*") Anyway, I got tired of saying "No, let's go see *Airport,*" so I said "Okay, who's in it?" People seem to think that response is great, and it may be. I am just happy that they know I don't like going to dirty movies.

"Baseball is 90 percent mental; the other half is physical." I have seen this written as: "Baseball is 50 percent mental and the other 90 percent is physical." Either way, the writer will say something like: "Yogi may think fine, but he can't add." It may be 95 percent or it may be only 80, but anybody who plays golf, tennis, or any other sport knows what I mean.

One day last year, three guys in our dressing room put on conehead caps. I saw them at the other end of the clubhouse and said to Matt Galante, "Those guys make a pair." The funny thing was that Matt went to St. John's for four years, and he didn't even say anything about it until at least an hour later. Well, maybe it wasn't an hour, but it was almost an hour.

"You can see a lot just by observing" is the way I felt when I said it. I don't know when that was. I think I would say it the same way today. I don't think it is that bad. Like when Ken Boswell, an infielder with the Mets, told me he was hitting up, undercutting the ball, I told him, "Swing down." Do you think that should be in the newspapers? Don't get me *right,* I'm just asking.

"If you come to a fork in the road, take it." I really don't know about that one. The commencement speaker at Arizona State used that in his speech last year. Somebody sent me the student newspaper. The Dartmouth College student newspaper called a big meeting on campus "A Yogi Berra Affair." The reason I thought it was funny is that I didn't finish high school, and now college people use something I said, or maybe never said, to make a point. The Dartmouth story was about a long meeting. That was not a cheap shot, but I don't think it was a good shot. Maybe I should say it this way. If the Dartmouth reporter wants to use my name in the headline of a story about a long meeting, that's fine. I think it is like reaching for a pitch out of the strike zone. But it was sort of fun to see it, and they didn't try to make me look bad.

A writer for the *Wall Street Journal* once said, "Yogi Berra, on the other hand, is a figure of mirth, or — to use the technical term — a dummy." I thought that was a bad and cheap shot. The story had a good headline, "You can hear a lotta Yogi-isms just by listening." I thought that was nice.

I think headline writers are like bullpen catchers; they do very good things, and most people don't give them enough credit. I like a good headline, and the one I would put in a headline writers' Hall of Fame is the one the *New York Daily News* used after a Red Sox–Yankee game: "Sox cop two — Ted poles pair." Even when the Red Sox beat you twice and Ted hits two home runs and your team has lost two, when you see that headline the next morning you just have to smile. Not for long, but you have to admire the guy who wrote that. I never met a guy who wrote headlines.

The college mentions would be enough to make you feel good, but when then–Vice President Bush used "wrong mistake" in a debate and said that I said it, I not only got a thrill (I guess I have to use that word), I also am not going to say I didn't say it. He not only went to college, he went to Yale and is a Phi Beta Kappa. (Maybe I am supposed to say *was* a Phi Beta Kappa?) He is a baseball fan and played first base for Yale. He threw out the first ball at an Astro game when he was making a swing through Texas when he was running for President. The late Herbert Walker, who used to own part of the New York Mets, is related to George Bush. Vice President Bush said, "Mrs. Walker is still living in the same house in Connecticut and watches the Mets on WWOR." The *W* in George W. Bush is for Walker. I think it may have something to do with the Walker Cup in golf. Anyway, he said, "I wish Herbie could see me now." I really felt good for him when he said that. It was the way I felt when I wished my mom could see me do well, and if you run for the President's job, you *are* doing well. It was a nice thing for him to lean over and say that to me, and I hope he doesn't mind my telling it here.

I also have to tell the rest of the story. Vice President Bush was leaving the dugout because the game was about to start, and I said something about good luck. He said, "Yogi, Texas is very, very important." He said it as though I was sitting next to George Will on that Sunday morning TV show. I said, "I know, Texas has a lot of electrical votes." He didn't smile because he knew what I meant. I don't know who told the press, but I bet it wasn't George Walker Bush.

So many people claim that they have asked me what time it was and I said, "Do you mean now?" that if I listed them all, this would be a very fat book. Not many people ask me what time it is anymore, and if they do, I don't answer. I thought my answer made sense when I said it. I will admit that when the waitress asked if I wanted my pizza cut into four or eight slices and I said, "Four, I don't think I can eat eight," I knew she was going to laugh and write it down. I was with my son, Tim. He knew what I meant, but I know why she didn't.

Twenty questions is a game. If you know it, I don't need to explain it; and if you don't it really isn't worth it. One time when we were playing on a train trip, I asked the question, "Is he living?" Then, without thinking, I asked, "Is he living now?" I got a lot of heat about that one. But one time when I was playing with Del Webb, who was part owner of the Yankees, driving from Minneapolis to Rochester, Minnesota, Webb asked a question way down the list, maybe number 17 or even 18. After we had gone through bread box and all that, he asked, "Is he short and fat?" Nobody laughed or said anything. I guess if you are an owner, you can get away with that. I just said, "Is he alive now," without thinking. I know Webb was thinking when he asked his question because it was the only one he asked. Later on we let Webb win a game so he could be "it." Nobody came close to guessing his secret. It turned out to be the clubhouse man for the Philadelphia Phillies. He was short and fat.

I am not going to say I didn't ask, "What kind of bird is a cyst?" I asked that question of Joe Page when he told me he had been hunting with Enos Slaughter, and Enos had been jumping in and out of the bushes so much looking for quail that he got a cyst on his back. I don't hunt, and I thought it was a good question. People have asked me dumber questions. Lots dumber.

When Carmen and I went to see the opera *Tosca* at La Scala, I really liked it. I told somebody I did and added, "Even the music was nice." That was true, and so was a story I still think is funny — a story about Venetian blinds. We were going to have some of ours repaired, only I didn't know it. I was upstairs when our son Larry called out, "The man is here for the Venetian blinds." I told him to look in my pants pocket and give him five bucks. Numbers are not big with me. That may come as a surprise to some people, but when somebody asked me if I take a nap before a night game, I said, "I usually take a two-hour nap from one to four."

When I said, "He is a big clog in their machine," like Tony Perez with the Reds, or Ted Williams, I meant to say "cog." But it didn't come out right, and they didn't let me forget it. Other times I don't understand as much as I would like. Once I bought a lot of insurance and was getting some heat from a guy in the clubhouse. He was a selfish player and selfish in other ways. He would buy a new car before his wife had a washer. He was the kind of guy who would be happy if he did well but we lost. I got a little hot when he said I was foolish and what good would all that money do me and I said, I will get it when I die. I didn't understand as much as I should, but I understood that a young father should have insurance — some kind of insurance. I am still not sure what the best kind is, but none is bad.

"Contract lens" is easy for anybody to say, and I hope you have, or something like it. One of my friends calls those low-slung German dogs "Datsuns." I can't prove it, but I bet he tells people he got it from me. I know some people say I told them, "When I was young and green behind the ears . . ." and "Never answer an anonymous letter." I didn't, but the anonymous letter idea is a good one.

"Why buy good luggage? You only use it when you travel."

I did say that. I thought that made sense when I said it, but I don't think so any more. The good stuff lasts longer and looks better, too.

I didn't say about a sick friend that he was in "Mt. Sinus Hospital," but I could have. I could also have said, "We've had enough trowles and tribulations," if I knew what it meant. I don't, but it has been written that I said it.

I did say "It gets late early out there." I said that when I missed a ball in the sun. I was playing left field in the World Series. It was 1961, against the Reds. What I meant was that because of the shadows in Yankee Stadium at that time of year, it was tough to see the ball even early in the game. Baseball parks are all very different. I played right field, left field, and third base. Once a reporter asked me which field I liked the best. I said, "Chicago." He thought it was funny, but I thought I answered his question. If he had asked me which ballpark I liked best for hitting, I would have said, "Detroit."

In 1973 the Reds beat the Mets in the play-offs. Pete Rose won the game in the twelfth inning with a home run. A reporter asked me if I had been apprehensive. I said, "No, but I was scared." I missed that one.

I don't remember which year GM stopped making the Corvair, but that year I told a friend I was going to miss the car because it had the engine in the rear. It was great in the snow. I said, "They are not going to make them next year, so I am going to buy a Volkswagen or a foreign car."

Another car story that came back to haunt me is one that Frank Scott, an old friend, likes to tell. He can make it last 15 or 20 minutes. Frank came to our house once with a big dog in the back of his car. He said, "What do you think of my daughter's Afghan?" I said, "Looks nice. I am thinking about a Vega." I have seen several versions of that story. The name of the dog is the same in all of them, but the name of the car changes.

I used to work with Yoo-Hoo. It is a soft drink with a chocolate flavor. It used to be good. I haven't had any for a long time, so I don't know anymore. It was not a real big company when I started to work with them, and that is one reason I liked it. One time I was in the office and the phone rang when no one else was around. I always answer a ringing phone, so I did. The woman who was calling asked if Yoo-Hoo was hyphenated. I said, "No ma'am, it's not even carbonated." I've forgotten what she said. It may have been better than what I said because she was from a library. One of the reasons I liked the product was that I thought it was good and might even be good for you. At least it was better than some of the other stuff people drank.

I hope that I have gotten over this much. I don't mind people making up things I have said. I don't know what is true and what is not, and I don't spend time wondering what is and what is not. I do wonder about this next story — wonder in the way you used to when you watched the TV show *Twilight Zone*.

Big league teams stay in good hotels. In San Diego, the Astros stay in a garden hotel, the Town and Country. It has walk-ways and several pools. One day when I was out for a walk a truck that goes around to construction sites pulled up. You know, the kind that brings coffee and sandwiches to the crew. This was a little ways from the hotel. I asked the guy if he had Reese's Peanut Butter Cups. He said no. Then I swear he said, "When we don't have them, nobody wants them." It would be an even better story if he had recognized me and had said something like, "I sound like you." But he didn't. And as you know, I am not one to make something up.

Something I have said to a lot of people that I have never seen in print yet is that "If the world were perfect, it wouldn't be." I don't know if that's a good thing to say or a bad thing. But I believe it, and since this is the chapter where I am going to put down all the things I said and didn't say, I wanted to mention it. As I have said, I believe you have to have some ups and downs or you don't know what up is. Also, and I know this has been said better and long ago, I feel that you have to make the best of every day. Life is a train trip and you can't expect to find a rainbow at the end; it's the trip that counts. I thought that fit in here, and I am going to hear a lot of chug-chug-chugging and "the Berra Special is coming" in the Houston clubhouse as soon as this book comes out.

Two people in the Houston clubhouse are Mark Hill and Gene Clines. Mark Hill was a catcher for the Giants and White Sox, and Gene played with the Pirates. I see a lot of them during the season, and we get along well. I get along well with everybody. The reason I mention Clines and Hill is that one day last spring we were driving to a golf course. I was in the back seat, which meant that I couldn't see too well, and all at once it began to rain. I said, "Where is that coming from?" Count 'em — five words. Those two guys couldn't get over what I had said. They tried to find a phone so they could call the networks.

We did play golf, and on the first hole I asked them what they were shooting. Gene said, "Ultra 2," Mark said, "Top Flight 2," and I said, "Then I will use a Molitor 3." They thought that was worth slapping their knees over.

I hope you realize I am not bad-mouthing Hill and Clines. If I can say hello and it makes somebody feel good, fine. I also know that over the years I have said some funny things. Some of them have been said on the golf course. I was playing in a scramble one time, and I really have heard so many versions of this story that I have forgotten who was in the foursome. Let's say it was Mickey Mantle, Whitey Ford, and Billy Martin, although I don't remember ever playing with Billy. I am sure it was Mickey and Whitey, and the fourth one really doesn't matter. I have heard the story at banquets and seen it in books, and the foursome goes from George Jessel and Don Knotts to Dave Winfield and Harry Carey. It doesn't matter.

You know that in a scramble all four players hit, and then you pick the best ball. You all hit that, and again pick the best ball. If the golfers are any good at all they come in 15 or 16 under par. After playing seven or eight holes, a Berra drive had not been used. On the next hole I got off a good one, but the other three said they did not want to use mine — it didn't have a good lie. Mickey's ball had a better angle to the green, or whatever you want to come up with. I got mad and said, "If I was playing alone, I would use my ball." Boy, was that funny!

This may not be funny to the Jiffy Lube people, but when I finished making their commercial, someone asked me where I had been. I said that I had been doing a commercial for Linseed Oil. Funny thing, no one said anything about that at the time. It hit me later. Carmen was in the ad. She had one line. All she had to say was, "And a free cup of coffee." It took her 21 takes. When I was doing movie reviews, she liked to sit in the background and laugh whenever I said "Ducactus." Now she knows what it's like.

The kind of Yogi Berra story I like is one that Robert Merrill, the opera star, likes, too. At least I've heard him tell it four or five times. He always tells it exactly the same way. Maybe that is because he was trained. I didn't think of that before. He had a rabbi friend who was the brightest Harvard graduate of all time. At least that's the way Merrill tells it. He and the rabbi come to the clubhouse, and the Rabbi tells me about the way he teaches his Hebrew students the *Ja* sound. Let me stop and say Robert Merrill is an opera star, and when he makes the *Ja* sound, it is low and you can almost start to dance to it. The rabbi, as played by Robert Merrill, goes on: "So, Yogi, I have them learn the *Ja* sound by saying 'Yogi, YOOGI, Ja and YOOGI.'" Merrill goes on with this, and after a time he says, "And Yogi said, 'Rabbi, does it work?'"

I think I listen better than a lot of people. Ira Berkow, a *New York Times* writer, did a column about my first spring with the Astros. It was a nice story and I read all of it. He said that while I was signing autographs, a woman said, "Hey, Yogi, do you have a minute?" I said, "For what?" At least that is the way he wrote it, and I am sure it happened. He also said that she blushed and I did, too. I am pleased — pleased that at my age I can still blush. I am glad that when I go to the movies to do my reviews it's dark because some of the new movies could make a donkey blush.

Not listening can make you look bad. One time I came out of the dressing room. I think it was during spring training with the Yankees. During that time you could have forty or fifty or even sixty players in camp. When you have been around as long as I have, you know how important it is to speak to everybody. No matter what is on your mind, you have to look at the other players and speak or nod. You don't want anyone to think you are high hat. Not only because you aren't but it could upset them, and you are a Yankee and these guys are teammates. It is part of winning. Not a big part, but most of the winning parts are not big. Anyway, I came out into the parking lot and saw this kid. I knew he was on the team and I said, "Who ya waiting for?" He said, "Bo Derek." I said, "I haven't seen him." He was kidding me and I ended up getting kidded.

Another time in spring training I was that young player, and the clubhouse man asked me what size hat I wore. I told him I was not in shape yet.

I said somewhere in this book that I really don't work at trying to say something funny, and I think maybe I should have added that if I do try, it doesn't work. When I was a coach with the Yankees, Joe Altobelli had a birthday. It was number 50. I told him that now he was an "Italian scallion."

When I said that a nickel wasn't worth a dime anymore, it was true. It's not anymore. I didn't say, "It's déjà vu all over again," and I didn't say, "always go to other people's funerals; otherwise, they won't go to yours." But I did get a phone call from William Safire, the *New York Times* columnist, asking if I had. He didn't seem disappointed when I told him no. That made me like him even though we had never met. Carmen got on the upstairs phone and they had a nice chat. She told him some things I had said and maybe some more for all I know. I didn't listen to all of it. I was watching the Giants and the Redskins.

By the time Johnny Bench broke my record, most home runs by a catcher, I had the reputation I have now. They sent him a telegram and said, "Congratulations. I knew the record would stand until it was broken." I don't know who the "they" was, but it was signed Yogi Berra. It was a public relations stunt.

I don't know if you think I have been too critical of sportswriters. I don't think I have. I know they have a job to do. While I am on the subject of what I said and didn't say, I can bring up one writer who thought about the truth. The truth and not another Berra-ism. Murray Chass, a *New York Times* writer, spent part of a column telling what really happened. If I could, I would pretend I was Paul Harvey and say, "And now, the rest of the story." I can't and the rest of his stories — at least the ones I've heard — are about important things. This isn't.

Chass said a writer thought he heard me say about Craig Biggio, a young Astro catcher, "If we didn't want to bring him up, we might as well have let him stay down." Not bad. Chass said the other writer was not listening closely. We had had to use Biggio every day because our other catchers were hurt. It was hard on him, but it had to be done. What I actually said was, "If we didn't want to use him every day, we might as well have let him stay down."

I have said a lot of times that I don't mind people making up things I said and didn't say. It has helped keep my name in the public. That is not all bad. It is not all good, but it is not all bad. It is nice to see a story like the Chass story and that's why it's here.

Oh, I don't want to forget. George Will — and if you don't know who he is, I didn't either so don't feel bad — said, "Yogi Berra, the syndicated movie critic, confused Glenn Close, the actress, with Glen Cove, a suburb." I don't want to start a fight, but when I was asked if I really did confuse the two, I said, "A little bit." I am not sure that is a good answer, but it is my story and I am sticking with it.

Jack Buck has been broadcasting games in St. Louis for so many years he has become a fixture. He asked me to be a guest on his radio show many years ago, and I said I would. After the show he gave me a check for $25.00 made out to "Bearer." I would have done the show as a favor, and I know that is going to get some comments but it's true. As I walked away, I looked at the check. Then I went right back to Jack and said, "How long have you known me and you still can't spell my name?"

Jack Buck swears that one time he saw me during a World Series, and I asked him what time his plane got in. When he said, "About 1 A.M." I asked what time he got to the hotel. "About 2 A.M." Then Jack said I asked him, "Was that local time?" If I did, I didn't mean to. I don't think I did. I think he needed some filler for dull games.

Another mix-up in words happened, they said, when I went to see a writer and said, "I went three for four yesterday and your paper said I was two for four." The writer said, "It was a typographical error." "Like hell it was. It was a clean single to right." Nice story. It never happened.

At least once a week someone will yell from the stands, "What time is it?" The answer I am supposed to have given to everyone from Tom Thumb to Tom Seaver is, "Do you mean now?" I did say, "Do you mean now?" but it was when Rube Walker, the Mets' pitching coach, asked me what time it was. We were flying from New York to Los Angeles. We may have been over Kansas or Nebraska, and I said, "Do you mean now?" I didn't know then and I don't know now. At least one flight attendant said the same thing happens to them even when they fly all the time. They get turned around on the time zones. I don't know what time it is in Nebraska right now. I probably should have said so, but if I had, Rube wouldn't have had a good story to tell on me and maybe I wouldn't have gotten a call from Stove Top Stuffing to do a commercial.

Our son Dale played in the Baltimore system last season, and they won the Governor's Cup. They played Tidewater and were getting ready to play Indianapolis. They used to call it the little World Series. I wanted to call him to wish him good luck. I know that your kids can misunderstand a phone call like that, and they can misunderstand a phone call you don't make. I made the call. Dale was pleased, and I am glad

I did. The reason I mention it is if your name is Yogi Berra and you make a person-to-person call to your son in the dressing room, the telephone operator may say something like "Are you the real Yogi Berra?" I don't know what to say to that. Then when you are asked to tell a Berra-ism while the clubhouse man looks for your son, you have to say something like "I don't do them on the phone" or "I am fresh out." No matter what you say you know the operator is going to feel short-changed.

I feel the best about having said something that people repeat when someone I like says, "I wouldn't say it that way, but that is good," or "that is a great way to say it." That happened to me with Nolan Ryan just last season. We were talking about the 1969 Mets. We were both on that team, and I said that we were "overwhelming underdogs." Nolan is not only a great pitcher, he is a smart one. He really liked the way I put it. He said that is *exactly* what we were. He said if I had gone to college, they would have made me talk clearer, but not better.

Jim Bouton

November 15

Ball Four

I signed my contract today to play for the Seattle Pilots at a
salary of $22,000 and it was a letdown because I didn't have
to bargain. There was no struggle, none of the give and take
that I look forward to every year. Most players don't like to
haggle. They just want to get it over with. With me signing a
contract has been a yearly adventure.

The reason for no adventure this year is the way I pitched
last year. It ranged from awful to terrible to pretty good.
When it was terrible, and I had a record of 0 and 7, or 2 and 7
maybe, I had to do some serious thinking about whether it
was all over for me. I was pitching for the Seattle Angels of
the Pacific Coast League. The next year, 1969, under expansion, the club would become the Seattle Pilots of the American League. The New York Yankees had sold me to Seattle
for $20,000 and were so eager to get rid of me they paid
$8,000 of my $22,000 salary. This means I was actually sold
for $12,000, less than half the waiver price. Makes a man
think.

In the middle of August I went to see Marvin Milkes, the
general manager of the Seattle Angels. I told him that I
wanted some kind of guarantee from him about next year.
There were some businesses with long-range potential I
could go into over the winter and I would if I was certain I
wasn't going to be playing ball.

"What I would like," I told him, "is an understanding that no matter what kind of contract you give me, major league or minor league, that it will be for a certain amount. Now, I realize you don't know how much value I will be for you since you haven't gone through the expansion draft and don't know the kind of players you'll have. So I'm not asking for a major-league contract, but just a certain minimum amount of money."

"How much money are you talking about?" Milkes said shrewdly.

"I talked it over with my wife and we arrived at a figure of $15 or $16,000. That's the minimum I could afford to play for, majors or minors. Otherwise I got to go to work."

To this Milkes said simply, "No."

I couldn't say I blamed him.

It was right about then, though, that the knuckleball I'd been experimenting with for a couple of months began to do things. I won two games in five days, going all the way, giving up only two or three hits. I was really doing a good job and everyone was kind of shocked. As the season drew to a close I did better and better. The last five days of the season I finished with a flurry, and my earned-run average throwing the knuckleball was 1.90, which is very good.

The last day of the season I was in the clubhouse and Milkes said he wanted to see me for a minute. I went up to his office and he said, "We're going to give you the same contract for next year. We'll guarantee you $22,000." This means if I didn't get released I'd be getting it even if I was sent down to the minors. I felt like kissing him on both cheeks. I also felt like I had a new lease on life. A knuckleball had to be pretty impressive to impress a general manager $7,000 worth. Don't ever think $7,000 isn't a lot of money in baseball. I've had huge arguments over a lot less.

When I started out in 1959 I was ready to love the baseball establishment. In fact I thought big business had all the answers to any question I could ask. As far as I was concerned clubowners were benevolent old men who wanted to hang around the locker room and were willing to pay a price for it, so there would never be any problem about getting paid decently. I suppose I got that way reading Arthur Daley in *The New York Times*. And reading about those big salaries. I read that Ted Williams was making $125,000 and figured that Billy Goodman made $60,000. That was, of course, a mistake.

I signed my first major-league contract at Yankee Stadium fifteen minutes before they played "The Star-Spangled Banner" on opening day, 1962. That's because my making the team was a surprise. But I'd had a hell of a spring. Just before the game was about to start Roy Hamey, the general manager, came into the clubhouse and shoved a contract under my nose. "Here's your contract," he said. "Sign it. Everybody gets $7,000 their first year."

Hamey had a voice like B. S. Pully's, only louder. I signed. It wasn't a bad contract. I'd gotten $3,000 for playing all summer in Amarillo, Texas, the year before.

I finished the season with a 7–7 record and we won the pennant and the World Series, so I collected another $10,000, which was nice. I was much better toward the end of the season than at the beginning. Like I was 4–7 early but then won three in a row, and Ralph Houk, the manager, listed me as one of his six pitchers for the stretch pennant race and the Series.

All winter I thought about what I should ask for and finally decided to demand $12,000 and settle for $11,000. This seemed to me an eminently reasonable figure. When I reported to spring training in Ft. Lauderdale — a bit late because I'd spent six months in the army — Dan Topping, Jr., son of the owner, and the guy who was supposed to sign all the lower-echelon players like me, handed me a contract and said, "Just sign here, on the bottom line."

I unfolder the contract and it was for $9,000 — if I made the team. I'd get $7,000 if I didn't.

If I made the team?

"Don't forget you get a World Series share," Topping said.

He had a boarding-school accent that always made me feel like my fly was open or something. "You can always count on that."

"Fine," I said. "I'll sign a contract that guarantees me $10,000 more at the end of the season if we don't win the pennant."

He was shocked. "Oh, we can't do that."

"Then what advantage is it to me to take less money?"

"That's what we're offering."

"I can't sign it."

"Then you'll have to go home."

"All right, I'll go home."

"Well, give me a call in the morning, before you leave."

I called him the next morning and he said to come over and see him. "I'll tell you what we're going to do," he said. "We don't usually do this, but we'll make a big concession. I talked with my dad, with Hamey, and we've decided to eliminate the contingency clause — you get $9,000 whether you make the club or not."

"Wow!" I said. Then I said no.

"That's our final offer, take it or leave it. You know, people don't usually do this. You're the first holdout we've had in I don't know how many years."

I said I was sorry. I hated to mess up Yankee tradition, but I wasn't going to sign for a $2,000 raise. And I got up to go.

"Before you go, let me call Hamey," Topping said. He told Hamey I was going home and Hamey said he wanted to talk to me. I held the phone four inches from my ear. If you were within a mile of him, Hamey really didn't need a telephone. "Lookit, son," he yelled. "You better sign that contract, that's all there's gonna be. That's it. You don't sign that contract you're making the biggest mistake of your life."

I was twenty-four years old. And scared. Also stubborn. I said I wouldn't sign and hung up.

"All right," Topping said, "how much do you want?"

"I was thinking about $12,000," I said, but not with much conviction.

"Out of the question," Topping said. "Tell you what. We'll give you $10,000."

My heart jumped. "Make it ten-five," I said.

"All right," he said. "Ten-five."

The bastards really fight you.

For my ten-five that year I won 21 games and lost only 7. I had a 2.53 earned-run average. I couldn't wait to see my next contract.

By contract time Yogi Berra was the manager and Houk had been promoted to general manager. I decided to let Houk off easy. I'd ask for $25,000 and settle for $20,000, and I'd be worth every nickel of it. Houk offered me $15,500. Houk can look as sincere as hell with those big blue eyes of his and when he calls you "podner" it's hard to argue with him. He said the reason he was willing to give me such a big raise right off was that he didn't want to haggle, he just wanted to give me a top salary, more than any second-year pitcher had ever made with the Yankees, and forget about it.

"How many guys have you had who won 21 games in their second year?" I asked him.

He said he didn't know. And, despite all the "podners," I didn't sign.

This was around January 15. I didn't hear from Houk again until two weeks before spring training, when he came up another thousand, to $16,500. This was definitely final. He'd talked to Topping, called him on his boat, ship to shore. Very definitely final.

I said it wasn't final for me, I wanted $20,000.

"Well, you can't make twenty," Houk said. "We never double contracts. It's a rule."

It's a rule he made up right there, I'd bet. And a silly one anyway, because it wouldn't mean anything to a guy making $40,000, only to somebody like me, who was making very little to start with.

The day before spring training began he went up another two thousand to $18,500. After all-night consultations with Topping, of course. "Ralph," I said, real friendly, "under ordinary circumstances I might have signed this contract. If you had come with it sooner, and if I hadn't had the problem I had last year trying to get $3,000 out of Dan Topping, Jr. But I can't, because it's become a matter of principle."

He has his rules, I have my principles.

Now I'm a holdout again. Two weeks into spring training and I was enjoying every minute of it. The phone never stopped ringing and I was having a good time. Of course, the Yankees weren't too happy. One reason is that they knew they were being unfair and they didn't want anybody to know it. But I was giving out straight figures, telling everybody exactly what I'd made and what they were offering and the trouble I'd had with Dan Topping, Jr.

One time Houk called and said, "Why are you telling everybody what you're making?"

"If I don't tell them, Ralph," I said, "maybe they'll think I'm asking for ridiculous figures. They might even think I asked for $15,000 last year and that I'm asking for thirty now. I just want them to know I'm being reasonable."

And Houk said something that sounded like: *"Rowror-rowrowrr."* You ever hear a lion grumble?

You know, players are always told that they're not to discuss salaries with each other. They want to keep us dumb. Because if Joe Pepitone knows what Tom Tresh is making and Tresh knows what Phil Linz is making, then we can all bargain better, based on what we all know. If one of us makes a breakthrough, then we can all take advantage of it. But they want to keep us ignorant, and it works. Most ballplayers in the big leagues do not know what their teammates are making. And they think you're strange if you tell. (Tom Tresh, Joe Pepitone, Phil Linz and I agreed, as rookies, to always tell. After a while only Phil and I told.)

Anyway, on March 8, my birthday, Houk called me and said he was going to deduct $100 a day from his offer for every day I held out beyond March 10. It amounted to a fine for not signing, no matter what Houk said. What he said was, "Oh no, it's not a fine. I don't believe in fining people." And

I'm sure it never occurred to him just how unfair a tactic this was. Baseball people are so used to having their own way and not getting any argument that they just don't think they can be unfair. When I called Joe Cronin, president of the league, to ask if Houk could, legally, fine me, he said, "Walk around the block, then go back in and talk some more."

After walking around the block and talking it over with my dad, I chickened out. Sorry about that. I called Houk and said, "Okay, you win. I'm on my way down." I salved my wounds with the thought that if I had any kind of a year this time I'd really sock it to him.

Still, if I knew then what I know now, I wouldn't have signed. I'd have called him back and said, "Okay, Ralph, I'm having a press conference of my own to announce that for every day you don't meet my demand of $25,000 it will cost you $500 a day. Think that one over."

Maybe I wouldn't have gotten $25,000, but I bet I would've gotten more than eighteen-five. I could tell from the negative reaction Ralph got in the press. And I got a lot of letters from distinguished citizens and season-ticket holders, all of them expressing outrage at Houk. That's when I realized I should have held out. It was also when Ralph Houk, I think, started to hate me.

The real kicker came the following year. I had won eighteen games and two in the World Series. Call from Houk:

"Well, what do you want?"

"Ordinarily, I'd say winning eighteen and two in the Series would be worth about an $8,000 raise."

"Good, I'll send you a contract calling for twenty-six-five."

"But in view of what's happened, last year and the year before that, it will have to be more."

"How much more?"

"At least thirty."

"We couldn't do that. It's out of the question."

A couple of days later he called again. "Does $28,000 sound fair to you?"

"Yes it does, very fair. In fact there are a lot of fair figures.

Twenty-eight, twenty-nine, thirty, thirty-two. I'd say thirty-three would be too high and twenty-seven on down would be unfair on your part."

"So you're prepared to sign now."

"Not yet. I haven't decided."

A week later he called again and said he'd sent me the contract I wanted — $28,000.

"Now, wait a minute. I didn't say I'd sign for that."

"But you said it was a fair figure."

"I said there were a lot of fair figures in there. I said thirty-two was fair too."

"You going back on your word? You trying to pull a fast one on me?"

"I'm not trying to pull anything on you. I just haven't decided what I'm going to sign for. I just know that twenty-eight isn't it."

By now he's shouting. "Goddammit, you're trying to renege on a deal."

So I shouted back. "Who the hell do you people think you are, trying to bully people around? You have a goddam one-way contract, and you won't let a guy negotiate. You bulldozed me into a contract my first year when I didn't know any better, you tried to fine me for not signing last year, and now you're trying to catch me in a lie. Why don't you just be decent about it? What's an extra thousand or two to the New York Yankees? You wonder why you get bad publicity. Well, here it is. As soon as the people find out the kind of numbers you're talking about they realize how mean and stupid you are."

"All right. Okay. Okay. No use getting all hot about it."

When the contract came it was like he said, $28,000. I called and told him I wouldn't sign it. I told him I wouldn't play unless I got thirty.

"No deal," he said, and hung up.

Moments later the phone rang. Houk: "Okay, you get your thirty. Under one condition. That you don't tell anybody you're getting it."

"Ralph, I can't do that. I've told everybody the numbers before. I can't stop now."

Softly. "Well, I wish you wouldn't."

Just as softly. "Well, maybe I won't."

When the newspaper guys got to me I felt like a jerk. I also felt I owed Ralph a little something. So when they said, "Did you get what you wanted?" I said, "Yeah." And when they said, "What did you want?" I said, "Thirty." But I said it very low.

Now, I think, Ralph really hated my guts. Not so much because I told about the thirty but because he thought I went back on my word.

Four years later Ralph Houk was still angry. By this time I had started up a little real-estate business in New Jersey. A few friends, relatives and I pooled our money, bought some older houses in good neighborhoods, fixed them up and rented them to executives who come to New York on temporary assignment. Houses like that are hard to find and Houk, who lives in Florida, needed one for the '69 season. After a long search he found exactly what he wanted. Then he found out I owned it. He didn't take it. Too bad, it might have been kind of fun to be his landlord.

Of course, I may misunderstand the whole thing. It's easy to misunderstand things around a baseball club. Else how do you explain my friend Elston Howard? We both live in New Jersey and during my salary fights we'd work out a bit together. And he always told me, "Stick to your guns. Don't let them push you around." Then he'd go down to spring training and he'd say to the other guys, "That Bouton is really something. Who does he think he is holding out every year? How are we gonna win a pennant if the guys don't get in shape? He should be down here helping the club."

I didn't help the club much in 1965, which was the year the Yankees stopped winning pennants. I always had a big overhand motion and people said that it looked, on every pitch, as though my arm was going to fall off with my cap. I used to laugh, because I didn't know what they meant. In

1965 I figured it out. It was my first sore arm. It was my only sore arm. And it made me what I am today, an aging knuckleballer.

My record that year was 4–15, and we finished sixth. It wasn't all my fault. I needed lots of help and got it. Nevertheless my spirits were high waiting for my contract because of something Houk had said. He'd been painted into a corner with Roger Maris. There was a story around that after Maris hit the 61 home runs he got a five-year, no-cut contract. But he'd had a series of bad years and should have been cut. So to take himself off the hook with Maris, Houk said that anybody who had a poor year because of injuries would not be cut. Fabulous, man, I thought. That's me.

When I got my contract it called for $23,000, a $7,000 cut.

"But, Ralph, I was injured and you said . . ."

"You weren't injured."

"The hell I wasn't."

"Then how come you pitched 150 innings?"

"I was trying to do what I could, build my arm up, trying to help the team."

Somehow he remained unmoved. I guessed it was my turn to be humble. "Look, Ralph, I know that people think you lost the battle with me last year and I know some of the players are upset that I got $30,000. So I know there are reasons you have to cut me. Tell you what. Even though I could stand firm on the injury thing if I wanted to, I'll make a deal with you. Cut me $3,000 and we can both be happy." He said okay.

After that, it was all downhill. Which is how come I was happy to be making $22,000 with the Seattle Pilots.

Brendan C. Boyd and Fred C. Harris

From *The Great American Baseball Card Flipping, Trading and Bubble Gum Book*

Tex Clevenger

If the camera indeed does not lie then what are we to make of all this.

Tex Clevenger could never seem to shake this lingering and nagging self-doubt which plagued him throughout his career. Given his record, of course, this was readily understandable. But couldn't he have tried a little harder to cover it up? In this picture he seems to be saying to himself, "Geez, maybe I should get out of this racket."

Geez Tex, maybe you should.

But in the meantime stop picking your fingernails.

Phil Linz

Phil Linz gained a certain notoriety during the early sixties for four distinct, if dubious, accomplishments, none of which had anything to do with his baseball career.

First was his partnership in the New York dating bar, Bachelors Three.

Second was his close friendship with, and emulation of, the noted Alabama social critic and cultural historian, Joe Namath.

TEX
CLEVENGER
NEW YORK YANKEES

YANKEES

PHIL LINZ   inf-of

Third was the impression engendered in the hearts of all true Yankee-haters everywhere, by his mere presence in the New York lineup, that the end of the Yankee Golden Era had finally arrived.

And fourth, but certainly not least, was his harmonica-playing wizardry, which, when engaged in on the back of the Yankee team bus after a particularly galling New York defeat, so infuriated General Manager Ralph Houk that he was moved not only to fine Linz quite heavily but also to threaten to tear him limb from limb were he ever faced with a recurrence of such spontaneous musical virtuosity.

Phil, of course, cooled it immediately and went on to hit a staunch .207 that year before being traded to the Phillies for a bag of broken bats and a pop-up toaster. Philly manager Gene Mauch was rumored to have a soft spot in his heart for musically inclined second basemen. Phil pined for the bright lights of Broadway though, and his career, such as it was, languished. By 1968 he had played himself out of baseball entirely.

Frank Leja

We all make mistakes. Branch Rickey once touted Marvin Rackley as the "new Paul Waner." Rogers Hornsby thought Jim Rivera would burn up the major leagues. Joe McCarthy thought that Jack Phillips had the potential to be better than Marty Marion. The Yankee management called Jim Brideweser the greatest shortstop since Honus Wagner. And Leo Durocher predicted year after year that Gail Henley would become the best hitter in the majors. The young major league baseball prospect has a way of losing the bloom off his rose faster almost than you would think humanly possible. Like all those ingenues in the late forties' musicals who sink faster than a bowl of stale Wheat Chex.

Featuring Harvey Keck and Mary Louise Lovely. Introducing Terry Tide and Jennifer Jennerette.

The fifties had its share of unqualified duds. Tom Umphlett was supposed to make us forget about DiMaggio, Roger

Repoz had it all over Tris Speaker. And Clint Hartung — the Hondo Hurricane — was a prospect of such fabled potential that Tom Meany thought he shouldn't even bother to stop at the Polo Grounds but should report straight to Cooperstown instead. They didn't call Clint "Floppy" for nothing.

Frank Leja was a massive young power-hitting first baseman whom the Yankees signed for a huge bonus in 1953. According to the publicity releases, he could hit like Johnny Mize and field like Dick Sisler. As it turned out, he hit like Casey Wise and fielded like Dick Stuart.

Dear Ma, I'll probably be home some time next week. They're starting to throw me the curve ball.

Ryne Duren

Ryne Duren was a relief pitcher for the Yankees for three years in the late fifties. He was what the sportscasters like to refer to as a fireballing right-hander, a real flamethrower, an aspareen chucker. In other words he could really bring it. He also annually led the league in bad eyesight. He wore milk-bottle-thick, tinted glasses and he used to warm up before each inning by throwing a series of particularly nasty overhand fast balls into the ground in front of home plate, over the catcher's head, against the backstop, and into the stands. Not exactly the type of behavior likely to instill confidence in the hearts of prospective batters. Unfortunately, like most hard-throwing relief pitchers — Joe Black, Joe Page, Dick Radatz, et al. — his arm began to give out shortly after he learned to control his fast ball, and he spent his last few years in baseball trying to hang on with a succession of mediocre teams in both leagues.

Charlie Silvera

Some players play in the wrong era. Some players play with the wrong team. Some players play the wrong position. Charlie Silvera somehow managed all three. Charlie Silvera played nine years for the Yankees in the fifties, during which time they won seven American League pennants. This en-

abled him to cash quite a few World Series checks, but it sure didn't help to get him into the lineup. Charlie twice led the Pacific Coast League in catching defense, had a .283 lifetime batting average, and hit .315 the only year he was up more than 100 times. But he had about as much chance of ousting Yogi Berra and Elston Howard from the starting Yankee roster as I do of replacing Prince Ranier. In ten years in the majors he was up 482 times. It isn't enough just to be good at what you do.

You also got to know how to pick your spots.

Bob Cerv

No, Bob Cerv is not trying to knock himself unconscious with a fungo bat.

And that is not a blue felt gravy boat he is wearing either.

Every player is required to have two pictures taken of him for his baseball card. One with, and one without, a baseball cap. Just in case, God forbid, he should be traded. This accounts for Bob Cerv's subtly counterfeited headgear in this picture, although it in no way accounts for his Yankee uniform.

Don't laugh. Somebody had to take five years of John Nagy art lessons to learn how to do airbrushing like that.

Hector Lopez

In 1959 some sad-souled individuals of my acquaintance who have the calamitous and double-pronged ill fortune of living in Bay Shore, Long Island, New York, while being at the same time inveterate Yankee fans, had a fairly good-sized pool going amongst themselves, the object of which was to determine the precise number of games it would require for Hector Lopez, the suicidally inept Yankee third baseman, to seriously maim, cripple, or otherwise disfigure himself while patrolling the hot corner at Yankee Stadium.

Now, it is not necessary for me to declare that Hector Lopez was the worst fielding third baseman in the history of baseball. Everyone knows that. It is more or less a matter of public record. But I do feel called upon somehow to try and

hector lopez

KANSAS CITY ATHLETICS
SECOND BASE—THIRD BASE

ELI GRBA
Pitcher

Los Angeles
Angels

indicate, if only for the historical archivists among us, the sheer depths of his innovative barbarousness. Hector Lopez was quite literally a butcher. Pure and simple. A butcher. His range was about one step to either side, his hands seemed to be made of concrete, and his defensive attitude was so cavalier and so arbitrary as to hardly constitute an attitude at all. Hector did not simply field a ground ball, he attacked it. Like a farmer trying to kill a snake with a stick. And his mishandling of routine infield flies was the sort of thing of which legends are made. Hector Lopez was not just a bad fielder for a third baseman. In fact, Hector Lopez was not just a bad fielder for a baseball player. Hector Lopez was, when every factor has been taken into consideration, a bad fielder for a human being. The stands are full of obnoxious leather-lunged cretins who insist they can play better than most major leaguers. Well, in Hector's case they could have been right. I would like to go on record right here and now as declaring Hector Lopez the all-time worst fielding major league ballplayer.

That's quite a responsibility there, Hector, but I have every confidence you'll be able to live up to it.

Eli Grba

Rollie Sheldon, Johnny Kucks, Duke Maas, Jim Coates, Hal Reniff, Fred Talbot, and Dooley Womack to the contrary, you knew the Yankee pitching staff had really hit rock bottom when Eli Grba managed to slither his way into the starting rotation. In addition to having the hardest name to pronounce in the big leagues he also had just about the worst stuff. This is not an easy combination for any manager to bear and so Eli was cut adrift in the first expansion draft to the Los Angeles Angels. Here he joined Ted Bowsfield, Ron Kline, Ryne Duren, and Art Fowler to make up what must have been the most totally and unredeemedly washed up pitching staff of all time.

YANKEES

JIM BOUTON   pitcher

BILL
SKOWRON
LOS ANGELES DODGERS   1B

Jim Bouton

Jim Bouton is a big mouth.

Bill Skowron

Bill Skowron was, unless you count Norm Siebern (which I don't think anybody does), the last really good Yankee first baseman. Before him came Lou Gehrig, Hal Chase, and Johnny Mize. After him came Buddy Barker, Joe Pepitone, and Harry Bright. So you can see quality does tend to fall off here quite a bit.

Skowron was called Moose because he looked like . . . well, a moose. He was the only one of the many modern-day athletes who have had this nickname incidentally who actually deserved it. He was also the only man I have ever seen who had muscles in his nose. Bill Skowron was in fact muscle-bound. This curious malady, which most of us have heard about without actually believing in, probably prevented him from achieving anything approaching his true potential. His iambix was forever interlocking with his metatarsis and throwing his digitalis out of whack. But it didn't stop him from turning in twelve solid years with the Yankees and one or two more with various and sundry National League teams.

Another thing about Skowron that has always stuck in my mind is that despite the fact that he played in New York he lived, for some reason or other, in New Jersey, a curious circumstance which seemed to my eleven-year-old way of looking at things (and guided by my highly underdeveloped sense of geography) the very height of urban athletic sophistication.

Don Larsen

In the seventy-five or so years that the World Series has been in existence there have been perhaps 1,200 pitchers who have pitched in it. Of these, Don Larsen is the only one to have pitched a perfect game. Like Sophia Loren's marriage to Carlo Ponti, the continuing popularity of Danny Thomas,

and the political career of Spiro Agnew, there is no rational explanation for this. It just is.

Tom Tresh

But if you want to talk about a guy whose career just seemed to disintegrate, to come apart at the seams and unravel — slowly, methodically, almost geometrically — like a $35 polyester suit, then Tommy Tresh is definitely your man. In 1962 Tommy was one of the best rookies in the American League. He hit .286, had 20 home runs, 93 RBIs and played both shortstop and the outfield competently, if not spectacularly, for a pennant-winning New York Yankee ball club. He was a college graduate, the son of a former major leaguer, a minor league all-star, twenty-five years old, clean cut, a Yankee, and with a name like Tom Tresh can anybody possibly doubt that he was the very epitome of the all-American boy? Well, just to show you that things don't always go by the book, from 1962 to 1968 Tom Tresh's batting average declined almost 100 points from its peak — from .286 to .269 to .246 to .233 to .219 to .195, a neat 20 points a year — and his home-run output fell off from a high of 27 to a low of 11. Now, not even a young Yankee with a name like a movie star and a face like a choirboy can get by on a .195 batting average, even if he is a switch hitter. In 1962 Tom Tresh had everything. He loved the world and the world certainly loved him. By 1968 he didn't have much of anything. He was thirty-one years old; New York was in ninth place (two spots behind the Washington Senators); he was playing in an infield which consisted of Joe Pepitone, Ruben Amaro, and Bobby Cox (the catcher was the immortal Jake Gibbs); he had completely forgotten how to hit; the Yankees were desperately trying to trade him for just about anything. He was even beginning to get crow's feet. All that red-hot potential had turned as cold as a Harry M. Stevens hot dog. Tommy, baby, maybe they made the pants too long.

Tuesday, April 4, Fort Lauderdale

The Bronx Zoo

Some of the New York writers and a few of the guys were remarking that I haven't been my usual crazed self. I have a reputation of playing practical jokes, but since I've gotten down here my mind is preoccupied with this contract thing, and I haven't been in the right mood to fool around.

I pulled a good one on our trainer, Gene Monahan, during spring training last year. It was April first. I went in to pitch in one of the exhibition games, and just before I went out to the mound, I told Tidrow, "Make sure Monahan is watching me." It was something I had decided to do on the spur of the moment. I threw a warm-up pitch, and after I followed through I grabbed my pitching arm. I was bent over, grimacing, acting like I was in real pain. Monahan comes out to the mound immediately, and he's saying, "What's wrong?" I'm groaning and moaning, and I say, "I think I blew my elbow out." I'm going on and on, "Fuck, does it hurt!" and he's being real concerned and he's saying, "Christ, let's go in," and real gently he takes me by the other arm and starts to lead me to the dugout. I take a couple of steps and I yell, "April Fool." Ooh, he was mad. He says, "Why, you son of a bitch," and he picks up the resin bag and fires it down. Nettles, who's standing there with us, said to Gene, "You could hurt your arm throwing like that." That was it. Away he went.

Another time a few years ago I went to see a doctor friend of mine in Fort Lauderdale. I thought it would be terrific if he could fit me with a full body cast, but that would have taken almost a half a day to put on, so instead he put a cast on my pitching arm and another cast on one of my legs. Mary drove me to the ball park, where I went onto the field with these casts, walking on crutches.

When I got onto the field, I was watching Bill Virdon. He looked over, and he did a double take, as if to say, "Oh Jesus, what is this?" I had him for a second. I could see it. Virdon told the press, "Nah, he didn't fool me. Once I saw it was Lyle, I knew he wasn't hurt."

The funny part of that prank was at the doctor's office. I had gotten the casts on and I was walking out with my crutches, and it's hard to walk on those things, so when we got outside, I asked Mary to go and get the car and pick me up. There was a crowd of people standing out there watching me, and in front of all these people, she says, "Nah, you can walk to the car." *She* knew I didn't need the crutches, but the people didn't, and they're looking at her like, "What a nasty woman she must be. Here she's going to make this poor, crippled guy walk all the way to the car. He's hurting, and she's telling him, 'Screw you, buddy, I'm not picking you up.'"

Until the press ruined it for me, the thing I enjoyed more than anything was sitting on cakes. I used to do it all the time. It started when I was playing with Boston. Kenny Harrelson had a birthday party, and he had a lemon meringue pie, and he hit me in the face with it. I told Kenny, "I'm going to get you back for this."

Later someone sent him a great big cake that was Kelly green and shaped like Fenway Park. It was beautiful. Harrelson just loved it, and he didn't want anything to happen to it. So before batting practice ended, I went into the clubhouse, took off all my clothes, and waited for him. When he came in, I yelled, "Hey Kenny," and I did a half-gainer and sat right on top of the damned cake. Really squashed it good.

From that day on, every time somebody had a birthday,

the guys would start yelling that so-and-so has a birthday cake. For a little fun, I'd take my clothes off and go and sit on it.

When I was traded to the Yankees, a few of the guys knew I had been doing this. I was in New York about two weeks, and sure enough, someone got a cake, and Thurman, who knew about me, said, "Hey, Sparky, a cake." I took my clothes off and went and sat on the cake, and the other players absolutely couldn't believe it. They were saying, "Boy, that takes balls," and I couldn't understand what the big deal was. The big deal was that it turned out to be manager Ralph Houk's cake! I just about died. I figured, "Syracuse, here we come." But, no. Houk sort of growled, but he took it the right way. And as time went by, I sat on more and more cakes. Our pitching coach, Jim Turner, a really nice man, loved cake. I told him that the only way he was going to get a piece of the Yankee cakes was to cut a piece out before I got there to sit on them. I had warned him fair and square. Well, from that day on, you should have seen Turner. As soon as a cake would come in, the players would start hollering for me, and Turner would run and get a knife and try to get some of the guys to hold me back while he got to the cake. Poor Jim, he never beat me to the cake. Not once.

Then the media took that fun away from me when they started writing about it. There was a full-page story in the *Los Angeles Times* about me sitting on cakes. After that article, I said to myself, enough. I figured that some idiot would put a needle in the cake.

I remember one writer came up to me very seriously and he asked, "Why do you do that?" I said, "Did you ever sit on a cake bare-assed?" He said no. I said, "Number one, I strive for leaving a perfect ass print on the cake after I sit on it. If the icing goes right up in that little point where your ass cracks, then you've done it right. And it takes practice to do that." I'm going on and on, and this guy is writing all this down. I couldn't believe it.

Donald Hall with Dock Ellis

Billy's Boys

Dock Ellis in the Country of Baseball

Dock went to the Yankees for the 1976 season in the trade that brought Doc Medich to the Pirates and Willie Randolph to the Yankees, where Randolph remains a fixture at second base twelve years later. ("I told Willie he would be there forever; he is.") In retrospect, it was not a good trade for Pittsburgh, but Dock had to be traded because of his insubordination in Cincinnati, August, 1975. It was good luck for him that he was tossed into the deal. He enjoyed Yankee Stadium with its deep fences that extend the careers of aging fastballers, and when a toss-in wins seventeen games, his new club has lucked out. The resurgent Yankees of 1976 under Billy Martin's management were lively and aggressive; Dock never enjoyed playing professional baseball so much as he did that year. "We did everything together. Billy's Boys: *We didn't take no shit!*" It was not only a happy year, it was successful. Seventeen and eight was his second best record. (He went nineteen and nine in 1971.) Brains made the difference, and Yankee bats, and Billy Martin — but conditioning was probably most important of all. Earlier he had slipped from nineteen wins to fifteen, to twelve apiece in 1973 and 1974; 1975 was poor, eight and nine for a division winner.

Dock relished Billy Martin and the violent competitiveness of this Yankee club. "You had to be *good* to be on the team. Billy was going to run his horses into the *ground.*" This team could not stand to lose one game; when they lost they fought with each other. "I never saw guys fight among themselves the way they did. Fistfights. I mean *fights!* The first game, Catfish opened up in Milwaukee. We got beat; somebody hit a home run in the ninth inning or something. I go into the locker room and I say, 'Man, what is going *on* in here?' They are fighting. Man, they are throwing *blows*. I took a shower and got on out of there.

"Sometimes they argued about pitch selection, sometimes about a ball that should have been caught, or a ball that should have been hit. . . . They made it *interesting!* Then they made a few trades. Holtzman came over. Rudy May was there with me, whom I knew around L.A. . . . To watch Billy Martin, the way he maneuvered, was something. He knew the game!" Dock mimics Billy saying, "'I'm the smartest mother-fucker in the game! I know this game!' He was a good motivator. We balked at first — too many veterans. Then he begged. . . . He didn't really *beg*, he said, 'Let's do it my way, Goddamn it.'

"'All right, Billy, fuck you, we'll do it your way.' Then we kicked everybody's ass."

Dock remembers Martin's fights with his pitchers Ken Holtzman and Doyle Alexander. "Something was *always* going on," and of course Billy was always at the storm's center. Dock had been used to getting the attention himself. It was a relief when Billy told him: "You let *me* have the press." For once Dock stayed out of the newspapers. At the All-Star break, when Dock was passed over although his stats were good, he made the headlines for not making headlines. DOCK ELLIS DOES NOT COMPLAIN.

One night as they drank together in a bar, Billy spoke of Rudy May as gutless, which didn't sit too well with Dock — who then told Billy that Billy didn't run the team: Catfish did; which annoyed Billy as it was doubtless intended to. "Catfish has our *respect*," Dock told Billy. It was possible that Dock was not entirely lucid: "We were both drunk," says Dock, with a wave of dismissal. He told Billy, "Catfish *runs* the team; the players *respect* him," while Billy became more and more agitated: "What do you mean? What do you mean? *I* run the team." Finally Billy positioned himself by the door, asserted, "Don't you forget! I run the fucking team!" — and bolted out of the bar before Dock could contradict him.

It was a happy season, spoiled only by the World Series loss to Cincinnati. "I have to credit Thurman Munson. We had a smart catcher!" Of course, there were bad days even that year. "One day they were hitting *rockets* off me. Nettles — Nettles is crazy! — came over to me and said, 'Man! Get them to hit the ball the *other* way! You're going to get me killed out here!'"

(Ah, the conference on the mound in the country of baseball. The tall black pitcher does not show evidence of his accustomed skill. The third baseman, astute student of the game, approaches his teammate judiciously. "Excuse me, Mr. Ellis," he says. "Forgive my impertinence, but as I perceive your mechanics from my point of vantage, it seems possible that you are releasing the ball too quickly, if I do not mistake myself; or possibly, though I may be in error, you do not follow through with the vigorous extension we are accustomed to admire in your manner of delivery." The tall figure nods his head: "Thank you indeed, Mr. Nettles, I suspect that your observation is accurate and I will endeavor to rectify my errors.")

"'Man,'" I said, 'kiss my ass!'"

In Los Angeles in 1987 Dock laughs remembering 1976. "They were good dudes. They understood I didn't have shit that day. Billy came out to the mound and asked Thurman, 'What does he have?' Thurman said, 'He don't have shit.'" As he left the mound, Dock looked back to see Nettles hiding behind his glove, miming huge sighs of relief. "Kiss my ass!" Dock yelled back to Nettles. A week later, Nettles approached Dock and suggested that he speak to Munson, saying, "Thurman thinks you don't like him because he told

Billy you didn't have shit. When you were screaming at *me*, he thought you were screaming at *him*." Armed with this insight Dock, who *thought* that Munson was avoiding him, took his customary direct approach: "'Thurman, what's going *on?* Puff' — that's what I called Nettles — 'told me you thought I was cursing and screaming at you because you told Billy I didn't have shit.' Munson said, 'Weren't you?' I said, 'No! Man, I was cursing at *him*, because he was talking shit about how I was going to get him *killed*.'"

As Dock says, "That helped my relationship with Munson. He thought I was one of those guys that get mad if you tell them that they don't have shit." Dock shakes his head admiring his late batterymate. "He worked me through games when I didn't have much — switching up on guys, switching pitches. He was a *good dude*."

In New York the fans know the game. (The dumbest crowds are Philadelphia and Milwaukee.) "Even when you get shelled, they would say, 'It was a good *selection:* You just didn't have it in the right *place*.'

"I used to ask Thurman, 'Were you telling that little old lady what you were going to call? Have you got a *signal* for her?' She's screaming every pitch I'm throwing. She's saying, 'Come on, Dock! Throw him that sinkerball! I say, 'What in *hell* is going on? That little old lady back there . . . '"

Back when I spent seasons with Dock in the National League, he spoke with condescension about "the Little League" in which he would pitch for the Yankees. Despite his happy memories of New York, he holds to his old view: "The American League is slower," he says. "They don't even walk on and off the field in the same way. The games are longer. The umpires aren't so sure of themselves. The strike zone is all screwed up. The mannerisms of the ballplayers are not the same. In the National League they're more cocky, more aggressive; and the pitching is more aggressive. American League is trick pitch; I became a trick pitcher over there — more behind-in-the count curveballs instead of going after them. Catfish used to try to get me to change speed on *all* my pitches. I said, 'I'm not going to get *killed* out there!' I said, 'I'm going to go down throwing hard. I'm not going to lose my head out there! Only thing I'm going to take off with is the change-up — and I'm going to *know* I threw that: *And* I'm going to be ducking . . . because I didn't throw that good of a change-up.'"

There was a bad patch when he started getting hit. "I was all fucked up, thought I knew the American League, thought I was getting smart." He had come to know Bob Lemon, but as a National Leaguer from way back he was ignorant of Lemon's history with the Cleveland Indians. During the bad patch Lemon thought Dock was throwing too much junk. "Meat, come here!" said the old right-hander. "What's this shit? You don't want to throw them sliders and sinkers. I won two hundred and seven games throwing the same shit you throw! I had a bullshit change-up just like you."

"I said, 'You won *what?* I thought you were a third baseman.'

"'Aw, Meat,' said Bob Lemon. 'I won two hundred and seven games.'"

Dock went back to his old stuff, which included sinkers and sliders but relied on the fastball and on location. He went back to winning. "Everything down and away," he remembers, like all of us who forget from time to time the most important things we have learned in our lifetimes. "Everything down and away — how can you lose?"

The best thing about the Yankees was their single-mindedness. They continually talked about The Game. In the clubhouse, right after each game, the Yankees that year talked the game through play by play, distributing praise and blame. "I liked that! With the Pirates, only the Latin American ballplayers did that; on the Yankees *everybody* talked about the game. I liked that!"

Family feeling was strong, and families come together, of course, not only in love of each other but in hatred of other

families. When Dock hit Baltimore's Reggie Jackson in the
face, late in 1976, he found in his locker an anonymous
donation of new twenty-dollar bills. "Somebody didn't like
him! He was *supposed* to get hit!"

This incident, like everything profound, derived from old
roots and new causes, history and provocation. "I owed him
one," Dock recalls, "for the way he hit the home-run ball off
me in the All-Star Game." Dock was losing pitcher for the
National League in the 1971 All-Star Game when Reggie
Jackson pinch-hit a home run, Luis Aparicio on board, in the
third inning. It was a *long* one, hitting the light tower over the
upper deck in right field. Dock owed Jackson not so much for
the home run as for the hotdog gestures made while he
circled the bases.

In 1976 Reggie was coming out of the dugout late in the
game while Dock was pitching to the frail shortstop Mark
Belanger. "I'm losing three to one, and Cy-or-Cry is pitching
against me, so I know I'm going to lose." (Later Dock supplies
a gloss: "'Cy-or-Cry' is Jim Palmer. If he doesn't win it, he's
going to cry about it.") "You know I have to change balls
because my hands are so small?" When a ball felt too big, he
tossed it to his catcher, time out, and the umpire supplied him
with another. "I exchanged balls while Belanger was in the
box with his head down. The ball sailed, so I said to Belanger, 'Duck down.' Reggie was coming out of the dugout and
he saw Belanger duck. We are leading the league by about fifteen games in September; Baltimore doesn't stand a chance;
there is nobody in the stadium, about three or four hundred people, right? — so Reggie screams: 'Why don't you
hit a big motherfucker like me?'" Dock's mimicking voice rises
high into a street-whine.

That day, Dock remembers, he was "high as a Georgia
pine" on greenies. "I hear this little echo. Thurman runs out
to the mound: 'Did you hear your brother-man over there?'"
Dock laughs remembering Thurman Munson. "'Your brother-
man says why don't you hit a big motherfucker like him? What
are you going to do, Babe?'

"I said, 'You get your ass back there behind homeplate, and don't give me no signals.'

"The first pitch I threw him one of those sinkerballs away, and he swung like he always swings. Then I threw it up in there, to back him back. Threw another one inside, he swings and misses. Now he thinks I'm going to in-and-out him, right? So he's *sitting* on the pitch, right?"

After a suitable pause Dock makes the onomatopoetic sound of a baseball striking a cheekbone.

"Glass from his glasses comes out to the mound. I'm running over there, looking: I say, 'Is he dead?' The umpire grabbed me and threw me out of there."

Later in the game, as Dock remembers, Palmer hit Mickey Rivers with a change-up in retaliation. Little else resulted, except that "certain guys bought me drinks the rest of the year. There was that money in my locker." A newspaper quoted Reggie as saying that Dock should have called him to see how he was doing. In 1987, remembering, Dock shakes his head: "I was *embarrassed.* I didn't hurt him; I didn't break his cheekbone or *nothing.*"

His happy year with the Yankees ended in anticlimax. During the playoffs with Kansas City, Dock won one and lost one; he pitched poorly in the World Series and the Yanks lost to Cincinnati. "The team had a defeatist attitude going into the playoffs, which pissed me off. When we beat Kansas City, some of them had their cars packed early. They were satisfied with winning the league championship. 'No way we're going to beat Cincinnati.' I know that contradicts what I said about them being ready to *win* . . . but they had never been there; the majority of them had never been in any postseason play. . . . I got shelled. I think I was overreacting, trying to do *more,* because of the attitude. . . ."

Looking back, it is Martin's shrewd judgment of players and his wily manipulation that Dock admires. "Billy Martin was the *smartest* manager I ever worked for. One guy, if Billy didn't smell whiskey on his breath, he didn't play. When he had a hangover — really *loud,* red-eyed, still staggering — Billy would say, 'You're in there, big guy.' He'd get three or four hits." And Billy was forthright. If somebody complained about not playing, Billy would tell him, "You can't hit the guy, that's why you're not playing. You're scared of him."

Feeling mildly critical, I observe that Billy seems obsessed with manliness; he's always finding somebody gutless. Dock nods with approval.

"Yeah," he says, "he can really pick that up . . . "

Graig Nettles and Peter Golenbock

From *Balls*

There is nothing to replace intelligent defense. More than any other aspect of this game, intelligent defense is something that never shows up in the box score. The other players on the team understand and appreciate what it means to the team, but to really understand that, you have to play the game. That's why the writers don't understand it. I'm making the plays like I've always done, but the *Post* won't give me a break.

We were playing Oakland, and their right fielder, Mike Davis, tried to steal third. He overslid the base, rolling past it. At the same time the batter hit a fly ball to center field. Davis jumped back up and ran back to second to try to keep from getting doubled up.

Now I'm not saying this to blow my own horn, but merely to explain how intelligent defense can win you a ballgame. As he was stealing third, I saw both that he had a good jump and that the ball was hit in the air out toward center field. When I went over to cover third, I faked like there was a throw coming from the catcher. I knew that the Oakland players run with their heads down, without looking back at the hitter, so they are very easy to decoy, so I gave him the decoy, and he slid into the base and ended up over in foul territory, and I saw their coach, Clete Boyer, grab Davis and yell, "Get back to second." If the umpire had seen Clete touch the runner, he should have called him out right away. But he didn't call that.

But what I knew the umpire did see was that he didn't retouch third base going back to second. As the ball was being thrown in, and he was running back to second, I said to the umpire, "I hope you saw him not touch third base." And the umpire can't say a thing to me, but I could tell by the stony look he gave me that he saw he hadn't touched third. So when I did call for the ball and touched third, he called him out, and there was no argument from Oakland. It was late in a one to nothing game, and it kept them from scoring.

When we played Oakland back in New York, Willie Randolph, who has been the best second baseman in the league for years, suggested a play that won us a game. They had men on first and second, with Henderson the runner on second, and we made a pitching change. Randolph came to the mound and said to Wynegar, "If they're going to pull a double steal, there's no way to throw Henderson out at third. Let's throw it through to second base." Henderson got a great jump and stole third, and Butch threw to Willie at second and got the runner coming in by seven or eight feet. That's the only way to defense against that. That was good heads-up play by Randolph for suggesting it to Wynegar. It saved us another game.

I guess I take my ability to dive for balls and come up with the throw for granted. I often wonder why most of the other third basemen don't dive the way I do, and I really don't have an answer. When you dive through the air, your first thought is catching the ball, and then when you've caught it, your next thought is to get up immediately and make the throw as quickly as possible. Some guys can dive, but they get up slowly and then plant their feet and miss the runner by two steps. When I hit the ground, I want to try to bounce up as quickly as possible and throw the ball from down low. I don't want to have to stand straight up to throw it. That wastes too much time.

I can do it, so to me it's no big deal. Some guys just cannot do it. Maybe in the back of their minds they are afraid of getting hurt.

There's no trick to it. It's just a knack. You can't practice it. I never dive for balls in practice, because if you go after balls a hundred percent in practice, you end up hurting yourself. It's not a play to practice, and I would never advise anyone to practice it.

I've seen Ozzie Smith of the Cardinals. He dives, and he bounces up like he's on a trampoline and makes the throw. He doesn't have a strong, strong arm, but he gets up quick and gets rid of the ball quick.

I never saw Clete Boyer play, but I've been told he would dive for balls and throw runners out from his knees. I've tried that a few times this year, and a couple of times got the guy out. I prefer to get up and throw. Boyer's arm was much stronger than mine, but I feel if I can get up quickly, I'll make the out, because I've always been very accurate.

To make the dive down the line, you have to have good anticipation. I anticipate that every ball is going to be hit either to one side of me or to the other. I envision it in my mind before every pitch. I picture the ball being hit, both ten feet to the left and ten feet to the right. I never expect the ball to be hit right at me. As the pitcher winds up, I see the batter hitting the ball over the bag or into the hole and me diving for it. I'm ready to go either way. I'll have already rehearsed it in my mind, so it doesn't surprise me when it happens.

I know that some players envision the ball hit at them, and they are ready for that, but they don't envision it hit ten feet to either side. As a result, they don't get a good jump on it.

One of the events I remember vividly from '78 is Reggie's deliberately defying Billy by bunting when Billy ordered him not to. Dick Howser, the third-base coach, had walked down the line and told him, "The man wants you to hit away," and then Reggie came back to the plate and tried to sacrifice. It was hard to believe I was sitting in the dugout of a major league team. It was like Reggie was saying to Billy, "Fuck you." I don't know what was going through Reggie's mind when he did it. Maybe he saw it as a final test to see what Billy would do. And so Billy suspended him for five days, and during those five days we won all the games, and for the first time all year the clubhouse was peaceful. And the day Reggie came back, instead of going out and taking batting practice, he held a press conference in the clubhouse. And that's the thing that pissed Billy off the most. Billy felt that Reggie had been away for five days and was rusty, and he should have been out on the field before the game getting ready. All the players knew Reggie should have been out there, and perhaps somebody should have said something to him, but he was standing in the clubhouse in front of all those reporters, and something like that would have just made more headlines, so none of us did. I suppose it should have been Billy's job to tell him, but Billy has always been reluctant to confront people, so it didn't happen. It was after that game that Billy exploded, calling Reggie a born liar and George a convicted one.

The next morning I found out about the comment. We were in Kansas City, and as I was walking through the mall in the hotel, Billy called me aside. He said, "I'm calling a press conference at four o'clock this afternoon. I'm going to resign." I told him, "It's probably better for you that you do, the way things have been going." He told me he had had a test done and that he had a spot on his liver. I said, "It's probably better for you this way." I was almost relieved for Billy. He seemed close to having a nervous breakdown, and he had been acting a little strange — suspending Reggie and then calling Reggie and George liars. I could see he was acting a little irrational. It was best he get away from the game and view it from a different perspective.

A few hours later he called his press conference. That night Dick Howser managed the team, and the next night we got to the ballpark and Bob Lemon was in the manager's office. And right after that, we got over our injuries, and we had a set lineup for the next two months, and we marched through the East and beat everybody. It was much quieter with Lem there. If anyone said anything about Lem, he'd let it roll off his back.

And then a few days later, on Old-Timers' Day, it was

announced that Billy was coming back to manage in 1980. That's when I first came out with the line about how some kids dream of joining the circus and others dream of playing baseball, and that I was able to do both. George didn't like my referring to his team as a circus. Even though he was running it like a circus. I didn't think it was so bad, especially compared to the comment Billy had made a couple of days before. The circus draws a lot of people and is fun to watch.

When we came to Old-Timers' Day, we were told there was going to be a special announcement. Who knew what? It could have been anything. The last thing I was thinking about was that Billy was going to be rehired. Normally Joe DiMaggio is the last old-timer announced, because he had to be last or he wouldn't show up, but this time they must have told him what was going on, because after DiMaggio, the PA announcer said, "And the new manager for 1980," and we were all sitting in the players' lounge watching the introductions, and here came Billy out of the dugout, and he ran out onto the field, and the people were screaming and yelling, and I said to myself, "What in the hell is going on here?" We looked at one another and kind of laughed. Except for Reggie, of course. But despite how bizarre it was, I really wasn't shocked. Every week there was something unusual that outdid something from the week before. The strange had become common.

In 1982 we were supposed to be the Team that George Built. He bragged in the papers that all the trades during the off season had been engineered by him. His was going to be a new approach to Yankee baseball. Throughout our history we have been known as the Bronx Bombers, but for the first time, under the leadership of George Steinbrenner, the Yankees were going in for speed, as though we were playing on Astroturf. George had told everyone he couldn't afford to pay Reggie the million a year he wanted, and then he gave a million a year each to his so-called speed men, Ken Griffey and Dave Collins.

George smugly announced that we were going to win the

pennant by stealing bases. During spring training he made us wear sweatsuits and run around a lot, instead of playing baseball. I told one reporter, "You can now call us the South Bronx Striders." He didn't like that at all.

When we got to spring training, it was pretty clear we didn't have the kind of speed George was bragging about. Also, if you're going to run, you have to have an aggressive manager, and Bob Lemon is not that type, and neither is Gene Michael. When the season started, we hardly ever stole a base.

During spring training, he told the reporters, "This is the best team I ever put together." A week later he traded seven or eight players, shipped them out wholesale. None of the veterans could figure out why. He got rid of Bucky Dent, who was the heart of our infield, and he traded away Ron Davis, who was one of the best middle relief men we ever had. And who did he get for Davis? Roy Smalley, who's a better hitter than Bucky, but not half the fielder. Lou Piniella, Bobby Murcer, Goose Gossage, and I would sit around and try to figure it out.

To make morale even worse, he made us come to spring training two weeks early. He wrote each of us a letter that in essence said, "You're invited, but you better show up." I have a feeling that is one of the reasons he made me captain. He figured I wouldn't show, so he figured if he made me captain, I would have to come. Spring training is too long as it is. All the early practice did was enhance the opportunity for some-body to get hurt. And make all the players resentful. And tire them out at the end of the season.

Not much made sense in 1982. As I said, George paid Dave Collins about a million dollars a year to come here. Collins was a nice kid. His entire career he had been an outfielder, and when he came to New York, George made him a first baseman. Dave is five foot nine. Early in spring training, he said to me, "Don't you think I'm a little short to be playing first base?" I said, "Maybe we can put a couple of phone books under the bag and get you up to where we can see you."

George told everyone that our manager, Bob Lemon, would be there all year, promised Lem he would have the job all year, and two weeks into the season, he was fired. Gene Michael was made manager, and he lasted until August, and he was fired. Clyde King became manager. George never seemed satisfied with who we had. He never let anything stay the way it was. In the middle of the season he decided to dump his concept of the Yankees as a speed team, and he turned over the roster one more time. We must have gone through forty-five different players, and it is impossible to win that way. I once saw a statistic on the 1927 Yankees, the greatest team of them all. They had the same twenty-five guys all year. They went to spring training, management decided who they wanted to keep, and that was it. George is always preaching tradition. Hell, let's get back to tradition and keep the same players together.

George may pride himself on being a hotshot shipbuilder, but when the Yankee ship began going down, George just ran for the lifeboats. He couldn't accept that things had not worked out the way he wanted them to. He couldn't accept the notion that he wasn't the baseball genius he thought he was. His reaction was to blast all his players in the papers.

He ruined Davey Collins. Davey was unsure of himself to begin with, and then he was given a new position, and then he began reading the derogatory things George was saying about him, and by the end of the season he was walking around totally lost.

George was even on Dave Winfield's ass. Dave plays hard every day, and you have to admire him. Winfield, who has a ten-year contract, didn't even blink. When it was clear that the season was a disaster, George decided to pin the blame on Winfield. He took him on, questioned his integrity, questioned a lot of other things about him, but he didn't fold. He came back and had a good year, and he's doing it again this year. Billy ought to rest him every once in a while, because he plays the game so hard. He's out there every day, and he produces.

Last year the fans finally got wise to what George is all

about. The "bottom line" finally caught up with him. We were in New York, playing a game against the Angels. Reggie came to bat. Say what you want about Reggie, he is a very exciting ballplayer. Reggie had struck out the first couple times, and George was sitting in the stands behind the dugout gloating.

Then Reggie hit a long home run, reminding the fans what the Yankees were lacking — Reggie's power — reminding them that it was George's decision to let Reggie go. As Reggie was circling the bases, the fans turned on George. They started chanting, "Steinbrenner sucks. Steinbrenner sucks."

After the game he told reporters, "I couldn't believe the New York fans could use such language." It made me laugh. I thought to myself, "Where has he been for all these years? Doesn't he come to the park?" He must live in a dreamworld.

George, after all, was the one who had trained those fans. Over and over he told them, "The only thing that counts is the bottom line." The team was playing poorly, and the fans were picking up on the bottom line.

George had gotten rid of the powerful personalities on the team. But when he did that, he was taking a big chance. In the past he always allowed himself a buffer, someone to take the heat or the blame if things didn't work out. He had Al Rosen, and then Cedric Tallis. But then he let everyone know he was the one calling the shots, making the deals. He figured that when the Yankees won, he would get all the credit. Unfortunately, it didn't quite work out that way, and the fans knew where to point the finger of blame. The result was "Steinbrenner sucks." He underestimated them. He always does. He doesn't give them enough credit for being knowledgeable. They understood exactly where it was at.

Jim "Catfish" Hunter and Armen Keteyian

A Day to Remember

Catfish: My Life in Baseball

'Round about 11 A.M., a good hour before the parade was set
to start, it seemed like half of Hertford, North Carolina, had
showed up at the Harris Shopping Center parkin' lot. Over
where a sign said "Shop With the Friendly Folks," the
Perquiman High School Band, decked out in black and gold,
was filling the air with the sound of tubas and trumpets.
Antique cars were polished to a see-yourself shine; Little
Leaguers laughed and pawed at each other. Even some of the
boys from the Bear Swamp Hunting Club had showed up,
their hound dogs barkin' in the back of a pickup.

The Harris Center, in case you were wonderin', is on
Grubb Street, 'bout three blocks west of downtown Hertford,
right across from Keel's Shoe Repair & Trading Post, spittin'
distance from the Hertford Volunteer Fire Department, of
which I am an honorary member. At the moment, one of the
department's trucks sits idling in the lot. A cardboard sign
was taped to the driver's door. It said:

May 9, 1987
Jim "Catfish" Hunter Day

That's me. Both of me, actually. Jim and Catfish. Around
Hertford, a farming community of 2200 folks in the northeast-
ern corner of North Carolina, I'm Jim or Jimmy Hunter.
Uncomplicated, country born and raised, given to saying

"rivah" for river and "dat" for that, and droppin' the "g" from just about everthin' I say (as if you hadn't already noticed). Jimmy's one of those what-you-see-is-what-you-get kind of guys — a man who takes particular pride in being the best damn deer hunter, fisherman, farmer, dog breeder, and family man he can be. Simple as that.

Catfish, well, that's another story. Cat, if you don't mind me stayin' in the third person for a minute, doesn't hang around Hertford. Never has. Never will. He's a bit more slick than Jimmy, kinda country cool, I'd guess you'd say. Cat, you see, did his swimmin' in city waters. His claim to the Hall of Fame was pitchin', pure and simple. Throwin' strikes. Gettin' folks out. Winnin' ball games.

But for all his drive and desire, I believe you're goin' to discover that Cat was never what you'd call a real homebody. A TV-watcher. A letter-writer. A lobby-sitter. No, Cat was actually a pretty playful fella — had to be hanging around with the likes of Lew Krausse, Rene Lachemann, Dick Green, Sal Bando, Thurman Munson, and Sweet Lou Piniella. (I'd like to have been able to change the names to protect the innocent, but in that group, well . . . there was so little innocence.)

The nickname "Catfish" was born — and I bet you already knew this — in the fertile mind of one Charles O. Finley. "O as in Owner," said Mr. Finley. True, but the way that man operated, it could just as well have meant "Obstinate" or "Outspoken" or "Outrageous." Yes, sir, Mr. Finley was as unique an owner as you'll ever want to meet. Unless, of course, you hit baseball's version of the daily double and also had the pleasure of playing for one George M. Steinbrenner III. As baseball commissioner Peter Ueberroth said preceding my induction into the Hall of Fame last summer, just playing for those two men was enough to qualify anyone for a place in the Hall.

And, funny thing is, Charlie and George are still at it. Still playing king of the hill. Still tryin' to prove to each other that one's imprint on the game will be bigger than the other's.

I discovered that fact right after I'd been inducted into the Hall of Fame last July. The Cooperstown committee had cautioned all the inductees about walkin' down Main Street during the day — you'll get mobbed by the crowds, they said. So, naturally, right after the ceremony there's George on one side of the street, signing autographs, followed by a pack of parents and kids a block long. And who's on the other side but Charlie, scribbling away, playing the Pied Piper, just like George. Kim and Paul, my two youngest children, told me they'd finally wiggled their way up next to Mr. Finley. This is what he said to them:

"Is he still over there signing autographs?"

"Yes, sir," came the reply.

"Well," said Charles O. Finley, "I'm gonna sign 'em as long as he does."

Now at this point some of you folks might want to skip ahead a few paragraphs. Chances are you've heard this next story before. Lord knows I've only told it about seven million times in the last twenty-four years. I've told it fast. I've told it slow. I've told it funny. I've told it flat. But very few times have I told it like the first time, the way I explained it to the Associated Press writer who phoned me just after I had signed with the Kansas City A's on June 8, 1964, like how I'm gonna tell it this time.

It starts out with me signing a $75,000 "bonus baby" contract with the A's.

"Do you have a nickname?" asked Finley over the phone.

"No, sir," I said.

"Well, to play baseball you've got to have a nickname," he said. "What do you like to do?"

"Hunt and fish," I told him.

"Fine," said Finley. Barely pausing for breath, he continued, "When you were six years old you ran away from home and went fishing. Your mom and dad had been looking for you all day. When they finally found you, about, ah, four o'clock in the afternoon, you'd caught two big fish . . . ahh . . . catfish . . . and were reeling in the third. And that's how you got your nickname. Okay?"

"Yes, sir, Mr. Finley," I said.

"Good," came the reply. "Now repeat it back to me."

Reggie Jackson with Mike Lupica

I Was Just Leaving . . .

Reggie

I rode to Yankee Stadium the next day to clear out my locker.

For all intents and purposes, it was the last time I would go there as a Yankee, and I knew it. And despite the fact that I knew it was time to go, there was a nostalgia about the day, a sadness. We had had ourselves a time.

It was a gray October day as I made the ride up Madison Avenue, the same ride I had made so many times over the five years, in good times and bad, sometimes driving faster than I should have because I couldn't wait to get to the park and get a bat in my hands, sometimes crying as I had that terrible day in 1977. I remembered all the summer days when there'd be groups of black kids on the corners as I got farther and farther uptown, into Harlem; they'd recognize the Rolls, and yell out my name, coming over and slapping me five through the open window when I stopped at a light on my way to the Madison Avenue Bridge. I remembered driving the same route the night I hit the three dingers against the Dodgers, hearing on the radio that Steinbrenner had sweetened Billy's contract and given him a raise. Lots of rides. To the House That Ruth Built and that I'd helped keep filled.

I thought that day about having been a Yankee, and how even though we'd been the greatest show on earth, we'd made the image of the Yankees go wrong somehow. The Yankees are the most famous team in the world. Hell, the nickname for Americans is "Yankees." It's such a prestigious

name, such an important name in its way because of the
history attached to it. You can go anywhere in the world, and
"New York Yankees" means something. You can talk about
Red Auerbach and the Boston Celtics, and you can talk about
the Dallas Cowboys, but they're not the Yankees. The Yankees were Ruth, DiMaggio, Mantle, Gehrig, Berra, Howard,
Munson, Maris and Ford. I'm talking about *names*. You can
make up an arbitrary list of the most famous athletes in the
history of this country, and there'll be at least three Yankees
near the top — Ruth, DiMaggio, Mantle — and probably
four, because Gehrig belongs in there, too.

You can put my name on the list, but maybe with an
asterisk.

I was grateful to have been a Yankee, will always feel that
a part of me is a Yankee, but as I rode up Madison Avenue
that day, I wished we all could have done it better.

I was grateful for the money, grateful for the fame, which
then produced more money. I was black. I'd come from the
most humble background possible, been born poor. I had
climbed away from that and become wealthy beyond my
wildest imagination, and the Yankees had had a lot to do with
that. I will be making money from the Yankees for a long
time. In that sense, it's difficult for me to paint Steinbrenner
as a despicable person. The man hired me. The man paid me.
We had a wild ride together.

I just wish he didn't have to negate what good he did all the
time. He created money, he created jobs, he created interest, he brought the Yankees back from the grave. But he was
always turning right around and destroying what he'd created.
And it's a damn shame.

I don't think he's ever going to change, either. Too late for
that. I was the least surprised person in the United States of
America when he brought Billy back to manage for the 1983
season, and when he fired him after the 1983 season. The
merry-go-round just keeps whirling. George keeps knocking
people down as he grabs for the brass ring.

When I got to the clubhouse, I took my time packing.
There were writers there, and I talked to them for a while. I

shook hands with Pete Sheehy, the clubhouse man who was just a little bit younger than God. I chatted with some of the guys — Bucky, Cerone, Tommy John.

I told them I would see them down the road.

I walked out to the dugout and took one last look at the field. I knew I'd be back because I planned to stay in the American League, but I knew it wasn't going to be the same.

Dingers.

Dugout fights.

REG-gie.

Then I took the elevator upstairs to say goodbye to George M. Steinbrenner. It was business as usual in his office. He was flying off to somewhere or other. Bill Bergesch was there and Cedric Tallis, some of his p.r. people, secretaries. The frantic world of George. He asked me if I wanted to ride to the airport with him but I told him I was going to stay around New York for one more day.

One of the New York newspapers was on his desk. In it were stories about me *not* apologizing after George *had* apologized. George said. Reggie said. Et cetera. Et cetera.

George pointed to the paper.

Smiling.

"Same old stuff, right?" he said.

"Same old stuff," I said.

He asked me if I was all through downstairs. I said I sure was. He said, "Walk me down to my limo."

He said in the elevator that he'd be talking to me real soon about a new contract, that he'd be in touch with Gary Walker as soon as he got out from under all the end-of-season work he had. I just nodded. I knew he was bullshitting and so did he.

The limo was waiting near the big blue sign outside the Stadium that says, "Press." Long black stretch limo. First class for George always, from Reggie to cars.

We shook hands.

"I'll be in touch," he said, then he got into the car, and the car pulled away.

It's the last time I ever spoke to him.

Thomas Boswell

Shortstop: Don Mattingly

The Heart of the Order

It's tough to win a batting title your first full season, follow that with a Most Valuable Player Award and still remain somewhat unknown. To do so while playing for the New York Yankees ought to be impossible. But then, Don Mattingly's a tough guy. Tough to know, tough to predict, tough to evaluate. Toughest to get out.

Most twenty-four-year-olds would recall the winter night when they received the MVP plaque as one of glory. Mattingly says, "I don't remember much about it, except our son Taylor lost his pacifier and we were up all night with him. That'll bring you back to earth."

Just when you think you have the Don of the Bronx pegged as a phlegmatic stoic, he comes to a banquet after the Super Bowl wearing punk sunglasses and a headband with "Steinbrenner" on it. "Did it because Pete Rozelle was there," he says. That argument with George III over his new $1.37 million contract — close to a million-buck raise in a year — couldn't have anything to do with it?

If you guess along with Mattingly, you'll be the one who gets burned. That's the pitchers' book on the compact five-foot-eleven, 185-pound first baseman — little good it does them. Mattingly takes things as he finds them, then reacts. Except, occasionally, when he gets a step ahead of you, sets you up, and leaves you wondering, "Who's behind that mask anyway?"

Ask what pitcher and what pitch are hardest for him and he pulls a perfect Mattingly. "John Candelaria. Haven't got a clue to him yet. And high fastballs on the inner half. Write that down." True, Candy Man owns him. But the pitch Mattingly hits best is the fastball in his wheelhouse. If he tells this white lie often enough, some dumb pitcher somewhere is going to believe it.

Nobody has figured out Mattingly yet, that's true. Two years ago, he was just a prospect who'd hit .283 as a rookie but with no power (4 homers in 279 at bats). Then the Yankees hoped he might be a perennial .300 hitter. Now that estimate's radically revised.

"Who do you compare him to?" says former Yankees star Roy White. "Compare him to anybody you want. Stan Musial, Ted Williams, Joe DiMaggio."

For historical reference, the Musial analogy works. Left-handed hitter. Eccentric closed and coiled stance. Sprays the ball. Tons of doubles. Not too many walks. Hard to strike out.

"He doesn't look like Musial, but he hits like him," says Orioles manager Earl Weaver. "Musial was the best at adjusting once the ball left the pitcher's hand. He'd hit the pitcher's pitch. Williams was the best at making them throw his pitch. He didn't believe in adjusting. If it wasn't what he wanted, he knew enough to walk to first base. That's why he hit .406.

"Once every coupla games, a Musial or Mattingly is going to adjust and put that tough pitch in play instead of walking and you're going to get some extra outs. But he's also going to drive you crazy by popping a perfect fastball on the fists down the left-field line for a double."

The difference between Stan the Man and Mattingly is that, at similar ages, Mattingly is undeniably ahead. Sure, Musial averaged 209 hits, 79 extra-base hits and a .352 average in his first two big years. But Mattingly has been in that stratospheric range, too, for the last two years: 209 hits, 77 extra-base hits and a .333 average.

Plus.

Plus, Mattingly hit 23, then 35 homers and drove in 110, then 145 runs. When Musial was twenty-three, twenty-four years old, he was a comparative stripling, hitting about a dozen homers and driving in 80 or 90 runs.

"The power's been evolutionary. A surprise, I never expected to hit thirty-five," says Mattingly. "I learned the weight shift from Lou Piniella. He taught me to use my body more, look for pitches, set up pitchers and pull the ball."

The last Yankee to drive in more runs than Mattingly was DiMaggio in '48. Nobody in the American League has led the majors in doubles back to back since Tris Speaker. Special players do special things. Immediately.

Another Mattingly distinction is a Gold Glove. "Day game after a night game. Mattingly's still out there taking his hundred ground balls," says Coach Jeff Torborg. When Mattingly botched one last July, it ended a streak of 1,371 plays without error. Try that playing catch.

Sometimes he sneaks out to shortstop during the New York Yankees' batting practice to take grounders and fire clean, accurate, right-handed pegs to first base. Usually nobody notices him because he's built like a shortstop, moves nimbly like a shortstop and wears an inconspicuous infielder's number — 23.

Because Don Mattingly throws left-handed, very few people realize he is out at shortstop — learning, polishing, plotting, dreaming.

"He's always wanted to play shortstop right-handed. It's his fantasy," says Roy White. "It's amazing to watch him. You know, he looks like a pretty good shortstop."

Encircling Mattingly in comparisons only highlights his glow. He's Wade Boggs with power. Eddie Murray with hustle. George Brett but younger and in a home run park with Rickey Henderson on base and Dave Winfield on deck.

None of these parallels charm Mattingly much. "I appreciate it . . . but it doesn't help me on the field. So let it go. I'd compare myself more to Bill Buckner. He's consistent, hard-nosed, good in the clutch. I love the way he plays. If it's biting it takes, then it's biting; if it's scratch, then scratch . . . I'll take a ground ball off the chest, get my uniform dirty."

Why Buckner? When Mattingly was a teenager in Evansville, Indiana, Buckner was hitting .300 for the Cubs, the Midwest's darlings. Why the passion for consistency — the neither-rain-nor-sleet approach to performance? Well, (okay, laugh) his dad was a postman.

Mattingly's the easiest sort of player to praise — the quiet gamer with eye black like a punt returner and low, unstylish stirrups below his pants. "Half the time you forget he's even here," says White.

"What I do on the field, that's me," says Mattingly. "If I take care of my game, everything falls in place. The game is the thing you can control. Especially in New York, where so much stuff can clutter you up."

Like Ron Guidry, who clings to the bayou, Mattingly is defiantly anti-style. Just by existing, Mattingly is a standing critique of Henderson. A Yankees prankster has tacked a sign above Henderson's locker here: "O Lord, help my words to be gracious and tender today, for tomorrow I may have to eat them." No one ever snipes at Mattingly.

As they say, no brag, just fact. "I feel like I earned the MVP. I've worked hard," says Mattingly, "I kind of expected it. If I didn't win it last year, I didn't know when I ever would. I don't know if I'll ever do that again."

Don't bet against him. He adjusts. Mattingly abandoned a written "book" on pitchers. "Too monotonous . . . Actually, they're all tough, or none of them are. I get everybody or everybody gets me." What he really discovered was that a chronicle on catchers helped more. When lefties troubled him, he found a way to trouble them back: though he hits 60 points less against them, he slugs more homers in far fewer at bats.

If Mattingly has a flaw, it's probably ineradicable because it runs to the core. Will he, like Buckner, be too tough to stay in one piece? Last spring, arthroscopic knee surgery. This spring, a bone bruise to the thumb that has him benched. So far, not much. But will it add up?

Come back in 2001 for that. Then we'll really see how well he stacks up with Musial. For now, let Scott McGregor speak for a multitude of pained pitchers who have gotten to know Don Mattingly far too well, far too quickly. "How does he strike me?" says the Oriole. "All over the place. He just waxes you and goes home."

THE ATMOSPHERE WAS GRIM

In *Northward Toward Home,* Willie Morris recalls that the atmosphere was grim when friends and neighbors in his small southern town found out he'd been using a short-wave radio to predict the outcome of ballgames and preempt "the unmitigated eloquence" of the Old Scotchman, who'd held the allegiance of fans throughout the South with his technically delayed but rhetorically matchless broadcasts.

In the pieces that follow, by two of the most brilliant chroniclers of the modern baseball scene, Roger Angell and George F. Will, we become painfully aware that even the most powerful myths are fragile things, since so much of their durability is based on something as rare and intangible as simple human virtue.

Willie Morris

From *Northward Toward Home*

I can see the town now on some hot, still weekday afternoon in mid-summer: ten thousand souls and nothing doing. Even the red water truck was a diversion, coming slowly up Grand Avenue with its sprinklers on full force, the water making sizzling steam-clouds on the pavement while half-naked Negro children followed the truck up the street and played in the torrent until they got soaking wet. Over on Broadway, where the old men sat drowsily in straw chairs on the pavement near the Bon-Ton Café, whittling to make the time pass, you could laze around on the sidewalks — barefoot, if your feet were tough enough to stand the scalding concrete — watching the big cars with out-of-state plates whip by, the driver hardly knowing and certainly not caring what place this was. Way up that fantastic hill, Broadway seemed to end in a seething mist — little heat mirages that shimmered off the asphalt; on the main street itself there would be only a handful of cars parked here and there, and the merchants and the lawyers sat in the shade under their broad awnings, talking slowly, aimlessly, in the cryptic summer way. The one o'clock whistle at the sawmill would send out its loud bellow, reverberating up the streets to the bend in the Yazoo River, hardly making a ripple in the heavy somnolence.

But by two o'clock almost every radio in town was tuned in to the Old Scotchman. His rhetoric dominated the place. It hovered in the branches of the trees, bounced off the hills, and came out of the darkened stores; the merchants and the old men cocked their ears to him, and even from the big cars that sped by, their tires making lapping sounds in the softened highway, you could hear his voice, being carried past you out into the delta.

The Old Scotchman's real name was Gordon McLendon, and he described the big-league games for the Liberty Broadcasting System, which had outlets mainly in the South and the Southwest. He had a deep, rich voice, and I think he was the best rhetorician, outside of Bilbo and Nye Bevan, I have ever heard. Under his handling a baseball game took on a life of its own. As in the prose of the *Commercial Appeal*'s Walter Stewart, his games were rare and remarkable entities; casual pop flies had the flow of history behind them, double plays resembled the stark clashes of old armies, and home runs deserved acknowledgment on earthen urns. Later, when I came across Thomas Wolfe, I felt I had heard him before, from Shibe Park, Crosley Field, or the Yankee Stadium.

One afternoon I was sitting around my house listening to the Old Scotchman, admiring the vivacity of a man who said he was a contemporary of Connie Mack. (I learned later that he was twenty-nine.) That day he was doing the Dodgers and the Giants from the Polo Grounds. The game, as I recall, was in the fourth inning, and the Giants were ahead by about 4 to 1. It was a boring game, however, and I began experimenting with my father's short-wave radio, an impressive mechanism a couple of feet wide, which had an aerial that almost touched the ceiling and the name of every major city in the world on its dial. It was by far the best radio I had ever seen; there was not another one like it in town. I switched the dial to short-wave and began picking up African drum music, French jazz, Australian weather reports, and a lecture from the British Broadcasting Company on the people who wrote poems for Queen Elizabeth. Then a curious thing happened. I came across a baseball game — the Giants and the Dodgers, from the Polo Grounds. After a couple of minutes I discovered that the game was in the eighth inning. I turned back to the local station, but here the Giants and Dodgers were still in the fourth. I turned again to the short-wave broadcast and listened to the last inning, a humdrum affair that ended with Carl Furillo popping out to shortstop, Gil Hodges grounding out second to first, and Roy Campanella lining out to center. Then I went back to the Old Scotchman and listened to the rest of the game. In the top of the ninth, an hour or so later, a ghostly thing occurred; to my astonishment and titillation, the game ended with Furillo popping out to short, Hodges grounding out second to first, and Campanella lining out to center.

I kept this unusual discovery to myself, and the next day, an hour before the Old Scotchman began his play-by-play of the second game of the series, I dialed the short-wave frequency, and, sure enough, they were doing the Giants and the Dodgers again. I learned that I was listening to the Armed Forces Radio Service, which broadcast games played in New York. As the game progressed I began jotting down notes on the action. When the first four innings were over I turned to the local station just in time to get the Old Scotchman for the first batter. The Old Scotchman's account of the game matched the short-wave's almost perfectly. The Scotchman's, in fact, struck me as being considerably more poetic than the one I had heard first. But I did not doubt him, since I could hear the roar of the crowd, the crack of the bat, and the Scotchman's precise description of foul balls that fell into the crowd, the gestures of the base coaches, and the expression on the face of a small boy who was eating a lemon popsicle in a box seat behind first base. I decided that the broadcast was being delayed somewhere along the line, maybe because we were so far from New York.

That was my first thought, but after a close comparison of the two broadcasts for the rest of the game, I sensed that something more sinister was taking place. For one thing, the Old Scotchman's description of the count on a batter, though it jibed 90 percent of the time, did not always match. For another, the Scotchman's crowd, compared with the other, kept up an ungodly noise. When Robinson stole second on short-wave he did it without drawing a throw and without sliding, while for Mississippians the feat was performed in a cloud of angry, petulant dust. A foul ball that went over the grandstand and out of the park for short-wave listeners in Alaska, France, and the Argentine produced for the firemen, bootleggers, farmers, and myself a primitive scramble that ended with a feeble old lady catching the ball on the first bounce to the roar of an assembly that would have outnumbered Grant's at Old Cold Harbor. But the most revealing development came after the Scotchman's game was over. After the usual summaries, he mentioned that the game had been "recreated." I had never taken notice of that particular word before, because I lost interest once a game was over. I went to the dictionary, and under "recreate" I found, "To invest with fresh vigor and strength; to refresh, invigorate (nature, strength, a person or thing)." The Old Scotchman most assuredly invested a game with fresh vigor and strength, but this told me nothing. My deepest suspicions were confirmed, however, when I found the second definition of the word — "To create anew."

So there it was. I was happy to have fathomed the mystery, as perhaps no one else in the whole town had done. The Old Scotchman, for all his wondrous expressions, was not only several innings behind every game he described but was no doubt sitting in some air-conditioned studio in the hinterland, where he got the happenings of the game by news ticker; sound effects accounted for the crack of the bat and the crowd noises. Instead of being disappointed in the Scotchman, I was all the more pleased by his genius, for he made pristine facts more actual than actuality, a valuable lesson when the day finally came that I started reading literature. I must add, however, that this appreciation did not obscure the realization that I had at my disposal a weapon of unimaginable dimensions.

Next day I was at the short-wave again, but I learned with

much disappointment that the game being broadcast on short-wave was not the one the Scotchman had chosen to describe. I tried every afternoon after that and discovered that I would have to wait until the Old Scotchman decided to do a game out of New York before I could match his game with the one described live on short-wave. Sometimes, I learned later, these coincidences did not occur for days; during an important Dodger or Yankee series, however, his game and that of the Armed Forces Radio Service often coincided for two or three days running. I was happy, therefore, to find, on an afternoon a few days later, that both the short-wave and the Scotchman were carrying the Yankees and the Indians.

I settled myself at the short-wave with notebook and pencil and took down every pitch. This I did for four full innings, and then I turned back to the town station, where the Old Scotchman was just beginning the first inning. I checked the first batter to make sure the accounts jibed. Then, armed with my notebook, I ran down the street to the corner grocery, a minor outpost of baseball intellection, presided over by my young Negro friend Bozo, a knowledgeable student of the game, the same one who kept my dog in bologna. I found Bozo behind the meat counter, with the Scotchman's account going full blast. I arrived at the interim between the top and bottom of the first inning.

"Who's pitchin' for the Yankees, Bozo?" I asked.

"They're pitchin' Allie Reynolds," Bozo said. "Old Scotchman says Reynolds really got the stuff today. He just set 'em down one, two, three."

The Scotchman, meanwhile, was describing the way the pennants were flapping in the breeze. Phil Rizzuto, he reported, was stepping to the plate.

"Bo," I said, trying to sound cut and dried, "you know what I think? I think Rizzuto's gonna take a couple of fast called strikes, then foul one down the left-field line, and then line out straight to Boudreau at short."

"Yeah?" Bozo said. He scratched his head and leaned lazily across the counter.

I went up front to buy something and then came back. The

count worked to nothing and two on Rizzuto — a couple of fast called strikes and a foul down the left side. "This one," I said to Bozo, "he lines straight to Boudreau at short."

The Old Scotchman, pausing dramatically between words as was his custom, said, "Here's the pitch on its way — There's a hard line drive! But Lou Boudreau's there at shortstop and he's got it. Phil hit that one on the nose, but Boudreau was right there."

Bozo looked over at me, his eyes bigger than they were. "How'd you know that?" he asked.

Ignoring his query, I made my second prediction. "Bozo," I said, "Tommy Henrich's gonna hit the first pitch up against the right-field wall and slide in with a double."

"How come you think so?"

"Because I can predict anything that's gonna happen in baseball in the next ten years," I said. "I can tell you anything."

The Old Scotchman was describing Henrich at the plate. "Here comes the first pitch. Henrich swings, there's a hard smash into right field! . . . This one may be out of here! It's going, going — *No!* It's off the wall in right center. Henrich's rounding first, on his way to second. Here's the relay from Doby . . . Henrich slides in safely with a double!" The Yankee crowd sent up an awesome roar in the background.

"Say, how'd you know that?" Bozo asked. "How'd you know he was gonna wind up at second?"

"I just can tell. I got extra-vision," I said. On the radio, far in the background, the public-address system announced Yogi Berra. "Like Berra right now. You know what? He's gonna hit a one–one pitch down the right-field line — "

"How come you know?" Bozo said. He was getting mad.

"Just a second," I said. "I'm gettin' static." I stood dead still, put my hands up against my temples and opened my eyes wide. "Now it's comin' through clear. Yeah, Yogi's gonna hit a one–one pitch down the right-field line, and it's gonna be fair by about three or four feet — I can't say exactly — and Henrich's gonna score from second, but the throw is gonna get Yogi at second by a mile."

This time Bozo was silent, listening to the Scotchman, who described the ball and the strike, then said: "Henrich takes the lead off second. Benton looks over, stretches, delivers. Yogi swings." (There was the bat crack.) "There's a line drive down the right side! It's barely inside the foul line. It may go for extra bases! Henrich's rounding third and coming in with a run. Berra's moving toward second. Here comes the throw! . . . And they *get* him! They get Yogi easily on the slide at second!"

Before Bozo could say anything else, I reached in my pocket for my notes. "I've just written down here what I think's gonna happen in the first four innings," I said. "Like DiMag. See, he's gonna pop up to Mickey Vernon at first on a one–nothing pitch in just a minute. But don't you worry. He's gonna hit a 380-foot homer in the fourth with nobody on base on a full count. You just follow these notes and you'll see I can predict anything that's gonna happen in the next ten years." I handed him the paper, turned around, and left the store just as DiMaggio, on a one–nothing pitch, popped up to Vernon at first.

Then I went back home and took more notes from the short-wave. The Yanks clobbered the Indians in the late innings and won easily. On the local station, however, the Old Scotchman was in the top of the fifth inning. At this juncture I went to the telephone and called Firehouse No. 1.

"Hello," a voice answered. It was the fire chief.

"Hello, Chief, can you tell me the score?" I said. Calling the firehouse for baseball information was a common practice.

"The Yanks are ahead, 5–2."

"This is the Phantom you're talkin' with," I said.

"Who?"

"The Phantom. Listen carefully, Chief. Reynolds is gonna open this next inning with a popup to Doby. Then Rizzuto will single to left on a one–one count. Henrich's gonna force him at second on a two-and-one pitch but make it to first. Berra's gonna double to right on a nothing-and-one pitch, and Henrich's goin' to third. DiMaggio's gonna foul a couple off and then double down the left-field line, and both Henrich and

Yogi are gonna score. Brown's gonna pop out to third to end the inning."

"Aw, go to hell," the chief said, and hung up.

This was precisely what happened, of course. I phoned No. 1 again after the inning.

"Hello."

"Hi. This is the Phantom again."

"Say, how'd you know that?"

"Stick with me," I said ominously, "and I'll feed you predictions. I can predict anything that's gonna happen anywhere in the next ten years." After a pause I added, "Beware of fire real soon," for good measure, and hung up.

I left my house and hurried back to the corner grocery. When I got there, the entire meat counter was surrounded by friends of Bozo's, about a dozen of them. They were gathered around my notes, talking passionately and shouting. Bozo saw me standing by the bread counter. "There he is! That's the one!" he declared. His colleagues turned and stared at me in undisguised awe. They parted respectfully as I strolled over to the meat counter and ordered a dime's worth of bologna for my dog.

A couple of questions were directed at me from the group, but I replied, "I'm sorry for what happened in the fourth. I predicted DiMag was gonna hit a full-count pitch for that homer. It came out he hit it on two-and-two. There was too much static in the air between here and New York."

"Too much *static?*" one of them asked.

"Yeah. Sometimes the static confuses my extra-vision. But I'll be back tomorrow if everything's okay, and I'll try not to make any more big mistakes."

"Big mistakes!" one of them shouted, and the crowd laughed admiringly, parting once more as I turned and left the store. I wouldn't have been surprised if they had tried to touch the hem of my shirt.

That day was only the beginning of my brief season of triumph. A schoolmate of mine offered me five dollars, for instance, to tell him how I had known that Johnny Mize was going to hit a two-run homer to break up one particularly close game for the Giants. One afternoon, on the basis of a lopsided first four innings, I had an older friend sneak into The Store and place a bet, which netted me $14.50. I felt so bad about it I tithed $1.45 in church the following Sunday. At Bozo's grocery store I was a full-scale oracle. To the firemen I remained the Phantom, and firefighting reached a peak of efficiency that month, simply because the firemen knew what was going to happen in the late innings and did not need to tarry when an alarm came.

One afternoon my father was at home listening to the Old Scotchman with a couple of out-of-town salesmen from Greenwood. They were sitting in the front room, and I had already managed to get the first three or four innings of the Cardinals and the Giants on paper before they arrived. The Old Scotchman was in the top of the first when I walked in and said hello. The men were talking business and listening to the game at the same time.

"I'm gonna make a prediction," I said. They stopped talking and looked at me. "I predict Musial's gonna take a ball and a strike and then hit a double to right field, scoring Schoendienst from second, but Marty Marion's gonna get tagged out at the plate."

"You're mighty smart," one of the men said. He suddenly sat up straight when the Old Scotchman reported, "Here's the windup and the pitch coming in . . . Musial *swings!*" (Bat crack, crowd roar.) "He drives one in to right field! This one's going up against the boards! . . . Schoendienst rounds third. He's coming on in to score! Marion dashes around third, legs churning. His cap falls off, but here he *comes!* Here's the toss to the plate. He's nabbed at home. He is *out* at the plate! Musial holds at second with a run-producing double."

Before I could parry the inevitable questions, my father caught me by the elbow and hustled me into a back room. "How'd you know that?" he asked.

"I was just guessin'," I said. "It was nothin' but luck."

He stopped for a moment, and then a new expression showed on his face. "Have *you* been callin' the firehouse?" he asked.

"Yeah, I guess a few times."

"Now, you tell me how you found out about all that. I mean it."

When I told him about the short-wave, I was afraid he might be mad, but on the contrary he laughed uproariously. "Do you remember these next few innings?" he asked.

"I got it all written down," I said, and reached in my pocket for the notes. He took the notes and told me to go away. From the yard, a few minutes later, I heard him predicting the next inning to the salesmen.

A couple of days later, I phoned No. 1 again. "This is the Phantom," I said, "With two out, Branca's gonna hit Stinky Stanky with a fast ball, and then Alvin Dark's gonna send him home with a triple."

"Yeah, we know it," the fireman said in a bored voice. "We're listenin' to a short-wave too. You think you're somethin', don't you? You're Ray Morris' boy."

I knew everything was up. The next day, as a sort of final gesture, I took some more notes to the corner grocery in the third or fourth inning. Some of the old crowd was there, but the atmosphere was grim. They looked at me coldly. "Oh, man," Bozo said, "*we* know the Old Scotchman ain't at that game. He's four or five innings behind. He's makin' all that stuff up." The others grumbled and turned away. I slipped quietly out the door.

My period as a seer was over, but I went on listening to the short-wave broadcasts out of New York a few days more. Then, a little to my surprise, I went back to the Old Scotchman, and in time I found that the firemen, the bootleggers, and the few dirt farmers who had short-wave sets all did the same. From then on, accurate, up-to-the-minute baseball news was in disrepute there. I believe we all went back to the Scotchman not merely out of loyalty but because, in our great isolation, he touched our need for a great and unmitigated eloquence.

Roger Angell

Excerpt from Asterisks

The New Yorker, November 30, 1981

No other sport can match baseball's flair for the appropriate. The last news of the 1981 season, by all odds the worst in the history of the pastime, was made away from the field by a nonparticipant in the games, and it simultaneously demeaned the players and insulted the fans. Perfect. The coda was sounded a few minutes after the Los Angeles Dodgers had captured the World Series at Yankee Stadium by winning the sixth game, 9–2, thus completing their well-deserved turn-around victory against the famous and lordly American League champions. The Series was not very well played, to be sure — there were thirteen official errors, and a great many more malfeasances on the base paths and at the plate, where the Yankees established an all-time record for autumn unopportunism by stranding fifty-five base runners — but the spirited Dodgers did come from behind in each of the four games they won, as well as in the Series itself, and also in two previous rounds of league championship eliminations. Their World Championship was a sweet one for the Dodger supporters, since it offered some redress for the team's thrashings by these same Yankees in 1977 and 1978, and also brought the sport's ultimate reward to the infield of Garvey, Lopes, Russell, and Cey, who have played together as regulars, almost unimaginably, for very close to a full decade. Enough there, one might conclude, to satisfy the sense of balance and sporting justice — a feeling of a certain fitness of things — that most followers of the game are able to find at the close of each summer's long proceedings, no matter who has won or lost. But George Steinbrenner, the owner of the Yankees, is not a man in search of such rewards. A few minutes after the players had quit the littered, chilly field at the Stadium and the let-down but unenraged local fans had begun to find their way home to winter and its discontents (a good many of them, in fact, had sensibly walked out on the game in the seventh and eighth innings), he issued this statement to the press: "I want to sincerely apologize to the people of New York and to fans of the New York Yankees everywhere for the performance of the Yankee team in the World Series. I also want to assure you that we will be at work immediately to prepare for 1982." The release went on to praise the Dodgers and the Dodger organization for their season and their victory, but this, of course, did not allay what had come before: an implication that this Series had been not won but lost; an insinuation that the Yankee players had somehow disgraced themselves, and that punishment would now be meted out to them by their employer; a supposition that Yankee fans, and perhaps most fans, had no interest in baseball beyond seeing the Yankees win again; and the continuing evidence (with its familiar accompanying sinking sensation in this recipient) that the *real* Yankee news would continue to be made not by the team's batters and fielders and pitchers but by the man on top, George M. Steinbrenner.

True fans are eager to draw moral conclusions from every possible baseball event, right down to an intentional base on balls, and this shabby little postlude must have struck many of them as a deserved termination of the season just past, which saw the game closed down altogether for fifty-nine days in midsummer by a bitter and entirely avoidable players' strike, and then resumed under a patchwork plan that not only crammed an extra round of post-season elimination playoffs into the already overextended league schedules but also managed to disqualify the teams with the best and third-best records of the year (the Reds and the Cardinals) from further competition while admitting the seventeenth-best team (the Kansas City Royals) to those same playoffs. (This set of rules, however, was better than the one first put into effect by the men of baseball; that plan would have made it possible, under certain conditions, for a team to qualify for the playoffs by intentionally losing games to a carefully chosen opponent. This little blemish was first noticed by White Sox manager Tony LaRussa, who is a practicing attorney, and he and several other pilots said they would not hesitate to win by such means if the chance should come their way. As LaRussa had predicted, this admission won them a tongue-lashing by various front-office moralists, but the pragmatic logic was inescapable, and the league officials glumly regathered and in time hatched a lesser hippogriff.) Writing this, I have noticed that several parts of my preliminary rundown of the 1981 season already require further explanation at some point if they are to be understood by anyone except the most dogged recent students of the game, but that, too, is in the nature of baseball just now. This was the season of the parenthesis and the asterisk, to explain the meagre statistics that will now go up next to every player's 1981 record — a time when the center of the game shifted away from the old patterns and easy clarities of the field and over to boardrooms and to press conferences and to the blazered, three-button clarifying statement — and there is absolutely no telling how many life-long fans lost interest along the way and wandered off in search of better amusement.

The Yankee clubhouse after that last Series game offered customary scenes of murmurous disappointment, with some half-undressed players staring at the carpeted floor in front of their cubicles and now and then tipping back their cans of beer, the flatter beverage for this part of October. A crowd of writers surrounded Reggie Jackson, of course. He sat at ease at a table in the middle of the room, in his long-sleeved undershirt and (perhaps for the last time) his pin-striped Yankee uniform pants, and, with his hands behind his head, talked about the events just past — his fifth World Series, his twenty-seventh Series game, his sixty-seventh post-season contest. He had missed the first three games of this particular Series with an injury but had come back to knock a home run in Dodger Stadium, and also to commit a horrendous (or delightful, if you were a Dodger fan) error when he lost a fly ball in the sun; he batted .333 for the Series but had gone hitless in his last eight at-bats, when the Yankees were dying for runs. Jackson holds a hatful of all-time individual World Series records, including his slugging average of .755, but this was the first losing Series he had ever played in.

"I have nothing to apologize for," he said calmly. "I tried my best. It's too bad to lose, but we didn't lose it — we got beat. When you go hard on every pitch and every game and you get beat, you just feel the hell with it, it's over."

Reporters broke in to ask about plays and pitches that might have turned things around if they had gone the other way, about the lack of the designated hitter in this World Series, and so forth.

"No, you don't understand," Reggie said. "The d.h. didn't make any difference. Don't you see? *They beat us.*"

Jackson would become a free agent — for the second time — in a few weeks, and there was already a strong clubhouse and press-box feeling that his disappointing .237 season and his age (he is thirty-five) and his salary demands meant that he had played his last game for the Yankees. But this, too, did not seem to concern him. "I'm going to play a few more years," he said. "I'll be back in the World Series, hitting them over the fence. Where? I have no idea."

Another crowd of reporters in the Yankee clubhouse — it was just as large as Reggie's audience, perhaps larger — now began to follow George Steinbrenner as he walked about the long room with his purposeful stride and his thrusting, preoccupied stare. There were a couple of security cops with him, clearing the way, and two or three younger Yankee businessmen behind him, and although he was there only to murmur a few words of reassurance to some of his players, the reporters and photographers and local TV crews scrambled after him, pushing each other and sometimes tripping over the cables on the floor in their eagerness for another far-out quote or another scandalous story. Already in this Series he had publicly second-guessed his manager, Bob Lemon, after the Yankees began to lose, and had let the press know that several Yankees might not be back next year if the team didn't recover. He had also broken his hand in a fistfight with some drunken Dodger fans in a Los Angeles hotel elevator (he said; there were no witnesses to the incident) when they cursed his team and vilified New York City. Two weeks before, during the American League subdivisional playoffs, he had violently upbraided his troops for their baserunning mistakes and poor play against the Milwaukee Brewers. His first baseman, Bob Watson, a twelve-year veteran, had committed an error on a throw in that series, and Steinbrenner had ordered him to take a hundred ground balls in practice the next day. Back in September, he had fired his previous manager, Gene Michael, who had told reporters that he could hardly function because of Steinbrenner's constant threats of dismissal if the team didn't do better, and who refused to abase himself by apologizing to his boss for saying such a thing. Late last year, Mr. Steinbrenner dropped another manager, Dick Howser, whose club had won a hundred and three games and a divisional title but had then lost to the Royals in their league playoff. Bob Lemon, in fact, was the eighth manager to be hired or rehired (it was his second go-round) in the nine years since Mr. Steinbrenner acquired control of the club.

As I thought about this notorious and depressing state of affairs, it suddenly came to me, there in the Yankee clubhouse, that the real difference between Reggie Jackson and George Steinbrenner was not that one signed the paychecks and the other collected them, or that one played ball while the other could only watch it. It was, rather, the fact that Reggie Jackson, like every other major leaguer, understands defeat.

Sooner or later, and repeatedly over a career of any long
duration, every ballplayer makes a frightful, inexcusable error
out there in the open, or pops up with the bases loaded. Even
the best hitters go unrewarded two out of three times when
they step up to the plate; half the players on the field at the
beginning of each game will be disappointed when it is over;
and twenty-five of the twenty-six major-league clubs finish
their seasons as losers. Baseball is hard. The television
networks suggest to us that "the thrill of victory and the
agony of defeat" are almost a tossup proposition, but only
children fail to perceive the true odds. It is the enormous
probability of failure that gives all difficult sports their serious-
ness and their rare and thus splendid moments of triumph.
The reporters were right to follow Mr. Steinbrenner closely,
I decided, for he is a sportsman unsolaced by sport, or
perhaps by anything short of another victory or another
apology, which makes him dangerous company indeed — and
news.

The Dodger locker room was the quietest winning clubhouse I have visited in twenty-odd Octobers. The presenta-
tions and the network interviews were over by the time I
arrived, but Dodger players were still encountering each
other here and there in the heat and crush of the low-ceilinged
room, amid almost immovable throngs of writers and func-
tionaries and relatives and those mysterious front-running
strangers who always turn up at such occasions; two sweaty,
half-undressed young men would throw their arms around
each other and yell and laugh and perhaps exchange a swallow
of champagne from the bottles they were toting. Each of the
Dodger starters and heroes — Steve Garvey and Burt Hooton and Steve Yeager and Ron Cey (who had played in this
last game and singled twice, in spite of his terrible beaning by
a Goose Gossage fastball three days earlier) and the others —
had his own eight-deep circle of reporters and cameramen
around him, but they all looked more exhausted than triumphant. I started to leave, but then I spotted Steinbrenner's
opposite number — the Dodger owner, Peter O'Malley —
standing alone for the moment on an empty TV-interview

platform. He is a round-faced, extremely polite man, with round eyeglasses, a boyish smile, and a strong, Irish-jawed resemblance to his father, the late Walter O'Malley, whom he succeeded in office more than a decade ago. I congratulated him, and he thanked me and said, "Yes, isn't it wonderful? You wait and wait and then it comes. Do you know that this is the very same room that the 1955 Dodgers came back to after they'd beaten the Yankees for the very first time? It was the same for them — they won the Series away from home, like this, here in the Stadium. Roy Campanella and Gil Hodges and Pee Wee and Johnny Podres and all the rest of them. I was just a little boy then, so I wasn't here, but I've heard about it all my life, of course. I've been thinking about that team all day today." . . .

The strike began on June 12th and continued for seven weeks and a day, wiping out seven hundred and thirteen games — a third of the 1981 schedule. The financial losses, it has been estimated, exceeded seventy million dollars in ticket, concession, and broadcast revenues and twenty-eight million in players' salaries. The damage inflicted upon the status of baseball in the affections and attention and loyalty of its fans can never be measured — a circumstance that may permit the owners to skip this page in the ledger once again. If the strike proved anything, it was that the owners do not hold themselves accountable in any way to their customers. The crisis left a very sour feeling not just because of the loss of the dailiness and flow of summer baseball, or because of the bitterness and hostility of the negotiations, but because no one on the owners' side could ever put forward a brief, reasonable explanation of the deadlock or prevent its prolongation until the last moment at which some vestige of the season could be retrieved. From first to last, the crisis was an invention of the owners — the inevitable result of their determination to radically alter or put an end to the basic structure of player free-agency, and thus to win back by force what they had lost in bargaining and in the courts and through mediation. . . .

Miserable over the loss of their sport and angered by the

very high financial stakes involved in this family dispute over the division of baseball's revenues, the fans were never able to understand how these matters had been pushed to such an impasse — why some reasonable accommodation could not have been offered and accepted, in a time when the game's popularity and income and attendance were at close to an all-time high. That is, in truth, the hardest question of all. Its answer, for me, lies in the remarkable degree of wishful thinking and self-deception that permeated the front offices of baseball on the eve of the strike, and, even more, in the owners' extraordinary way of conducting their side of this labor dispute. A strike over the player-compensation issue almost took place last year, it will be recalled, and was averted only an hour or two before the strike deadline announced by the Players Association, when the news came that two or three teams had refused to board the planes that would take them on to the cities where they were scheduled to play the next day. The issue was then hastily put over for another year, by mutual consent. Last year, most of the owners and front-office people I talked to in spring training and early in the season had assured me that the stars of the game were far too well paid ever to go out on strike over such a trifling matter; they said this with immense self-assurance and usually with an accompanying half smile, as if they and I understood reality in such grownup matters. The near-miss apparently did not convince them of the serious-ness of the Players Association, for the little smiles were back again, I noticed, in early June this year. "They won't strike," one lifelong baseball executive told me just before the last game that was to be played in his team's ballpark until August 14th. "I know the players." But he didn't. He was telling me a wish. . . .

What is going on here, I believe, is the same old psycho-drama about American fathers and sons, work and play, money and sex and sports which is always being enacted deep within our national unconscious. The parable is constantly replayed — in 1977 by the then Mets board chairman

M. Donald Grant and Tom Seaver, the best pitcher in baseball, whom Grant preferred to trade away (even at the cost of destroying the team's future as a contending club) rather than pay him his worth in a rising market, or even talk business with him in any reasonably equal fashion; in 1981 by George M. Steinbrenner and the various Yankee managers and players, whom he must browbeat and humiliate in the pursuit of success or dismiss if they do not apologize for their expressions of resentment at such patronizing and patriarchal gestures. "I feel like a father scorned," Steinbrenner declared when he fired his unhappy but unrepentant manager, Gene Michael, in September — and he spoke, I think, for a great many other owners and front-office executives (and not a few senior baseball writers), who control every part of this game except the one that most matters: the moment when it must be handed over to the lucky, well-paid, and unforgivably young men who can actually play it. . . .

There were thirty-two post-season games in October — a total beyond sensible summary or clear recollection. Thinking back on them — even on the dozen-odd games I managed to catch in person — is a little like trying to bring back two or three days of non-stop television watching, I imagine: a kinetic blur, an assault of sound and light. I will touch down upon a few games and moments that are still imprinted on my bruised baseball cortex, and I apologize in advance to the actors and producers of the soaps and sit-coms that have slipped away, or that I couldn't tune in on because I was over on another channel, so to speak. The lack of clarity I sense when I think back on this October must be shared by millions of other fans, and if that is so it is a terrible loss. The special attraction of baseball for its true adherents depends most of all upon precision of detail and firmness of memory — who did what with two on in the top of the fifth; who was pitching; what the count was; where the single went; and exactly from where in the park Yaz threw to wipe out the desperately sliding Bob Allison — yow! — to end the inning. Television can bring all this — or most of it — to us in our living rooms, which is still almost a miracle to me, but television, of course, is the least *memorable* of all means of communication, mostly because it never stops. The baseball owners and decision-makers now seem determined to help feed the tube at all costs — to give it more and still more games and trumped-up sub-championships — but for every increase they can achieve in the number of sets turned on to the game, they must register an accompanying loss, I believe, in the number of minds tuned in to it: fewer games isolated in memory, baseball no longer known by heart. The new statistics are that we have from twenty-two to thirty-seven games in October now, where once we had no more than seven. Read 'em and weep. . . .

The strategies that had brought the Yankees and the Brewers through the pennant race and up to their meeting in the American League East playoff were exactly the same: get ahead and phone for help. The startling performance of both bullpens — Rollie Fingers for Milwaukee, that is, and Ron Davis and then Goose Gossage for the Yanks — put them almost beyond comparison, even with each other. The Yankees were 51–3 for the year in games in which they had led when they entered the eighth inning, while the Brewers stood at 51–1 by the same measurement. Fingers, in fact, had surrendered only one earned run at home this year. The Yankees took both games of the opening pair at County Stadium by racking up modest leads for their starters, Ron Guidry and Dave Righetti, and then turning things over to the Messrs. D. & G., who muffled the Milwaukees utterly. Twenty-six Brewers fanned. Rollie F., for his part, got no useful work until Game Three, back in the Bronx, which he won, if a bit shakily, with a three-inning, two-run stint. That game was stuffed with ructions and distractions — two fine running catches by Reggie Jackson, of all people, in right field; a sudden mid-game tackle of third-base ump Mike Reilly by a drunken fan (Graig Nettles instantly leaped in to assist the startled arbiter, and since my first glimpse of the action showed only Nettles and Reilly rolling in the dirt, I briefly held the mistaken but nonetheless interesting notion that Graig had simply gone bonkers out there); and late homers by Ted Simmons and Paul Molitor. I was pulling for the Brewers by now, I found, in part because their third baseman in these games was Sal Bando, a hero of mine ever since his glory days as the captain of the hairy and theatrical World Champion Oakland A's, almost a decade ago. He had already announced his retirement as a player at the conclusion of this season, no matter how the Brewers fared. "All through the game, I kept walking up and down in our dugout saying, 'Give me one more at bat, you guys! Give me one more game!'" he said cheerfully in the clubhouse.

Bando won yet another stay the next afternoon, when Pete Vuckovich and several other Brewer mound stalwarts, concluding with Fingers, held on grimly for a 2–1 decision, to even up the series. This was the game in which some heads-down baserunning took the Yankees out of two promising situations (one ending in a 7-5-3-4-6 play that erased Larry Milbourne just south of third base), and after which George Steinbrenner blew his cork at a postgame clubhouse meeting. Later on, when I told Bando about Steinbrenner's tirade, he said, "I played nine years for a man like that" — he meant Charlie Finley — "and it didn't help at all." Mr. Steinbrenner would argue the point, I suppose, because the Yankees captured the playoff the next night (so long, Sal!), with a 7–3 victory that featured wildly greeted home runs by Jackson, Oscar Gamble, and Rick Cerone. Reggie's was a missile to the third row of the right-field top deck, and he celebrated it in characteristic fashion: the curatorial pause by the plate for wonder and interior cataloguing, and then that little lick of the three middle fingers of the right hand as he trots past first base. I smiled as I watched, won back. Reggie is an old Oakland boy, too.

So many names and games had begun to wear me down, and I was not much bothered when the long-awaited league-championship series between the A's (the new Billy Martin A's, that is) and the Yankees turned out to be such a bomb. Playing in the Bronx temple, the first two young Oakland starters, Mike Norris and then Steve McCatty, pitched in gingerly, self-conscious fashion as their team dropped the opener by 3–1 to Tommy John, and then was blown away, 13–3, in a frightful laugher the next day. The only people on the premises who didn't seem to notice that the famous Billy Martin–George Steinbrenner "confrontation" had come to nothing — had no trace of meaning, in fact — were the NBC television directors and producers on the scene, who, according to friends of mine watching the games at home, kept interrupting their game coverage to present alternating close-up shots of Billy patrolling his dugout and George (seen with pseudo-menacing dimness at the back of his balcony box) biting his nails. Bush stuff. The clubs repaired to Oakland and to a long, close, slow, but not very good game (I saw it by television) that was settled at last when a reserve A's outfielder turned the wrong way on a deep fly ball, which fell in for three runs and the game and, at last, the pennant. The feature of the day out there had been the real feature of the Oakland season, come to think of it — the roaring-in-unison, roaring-by-sections, roaring-in-good-times-and-bad Oakland crowds, who seemed happy just to be given another A's ballgame, another picnic at the park, so late in the year. Their innermost convictions had been summed up, I think, in something the young Oakland catcher, Mike Heath, had said to me earlier in New York: "I won't feel terrible if we lose this thing, because we already did so great this year. Our real future is four or five years down the road. The best is still ahead." . . .

I live in New York, and it may be that the disappointment in the World Series that I feel and still hear about from so many friends is a regional failing. I doubt it, though. Good defense is the hallmark of good baseball, and in this set of games there were more muffed grounders and bounced pegs to first (or past it) than I can recall at any other grownups' tourney.

There were also a great many baserunning foul-ups, some flabby pitching by starters and relievers alike, two or three abysmally sustained individual inefficiencies at the plate or in the field, and a wholly unexpected air of deepening ineptitude by the Yankee team at the end, which almost tainted the taste of victory for the Dodgers and their supporters. But all this was the lesser part of what was wrong with these last and supposedly best games of the year. The 1981 Series may have looked bad at times, but it *felt* bad — trivial and almost drained of meaning — all the time, because it came after so much miserable baseball news this year. The owners and the players and the fans all wanted this Series to make up for everything, I believe, and, of course, it never had a chance.

It would be a shame, though, if this hovering aura were to diminish our admiration for the Dodgers. I was sharply critical of the Dodgers in 1977, and especially in 1978, when they lost successive World Series to the Yankees, and failed, one sensed, because they seemed immature and self-pitying and caught up in a delusive vision of themselves: the beach boys in the big city. Most of these 1981 Dodgers were the same regulars we had seen so often down the years, but in fact this team was quite different in its abilities — diminished hitting, less power, much better pitching — and in its motivation. The golden Californians had aged at last. Garvey, Cey, Russell, Lopes, Yeager, and Monday are all well into their thirties, and some of their skills appear to be in decline. Bill Russell batted .233 this summer; Lopes was at .206; and Yeager, no longer a regular, hit .209. "We had a silent feeling that this might be our last chance," Russell said when the Series was over. "We didn't mention it, but it was there." Even after the Dodgers had lost the first two games of the Series at the Stadium, there was no sign of foreboding or anxiety among them. Reggie Jackson noticed this, and observed that the earlier Dodgers had always seemed content simply to be in the Series at all but these Dodgers looked as if they wanted something more. "I'm concerned," he said, and he was right, as usual.

The games also altered my opinion of Tom Lasorda, whom

I had previously viewed as a strategist of indifferent powers, with a genius only for homily and public relations. In this Series, he managed his pitchers with insight and restraint — most notably in his patience with Valenzuela in the third game, when Fernando was very far from being at his best — and also worked his rotation so that he had Valenzuela, his ace, rested and ready for a seventh game, had the Series gone one more day. He got an exceptional performance from Yeager, who had been a starting catcher in only twenty-three games during the season, and he shuffled his batting order so that Dusty Baker, his slumping No. 3 hitter, was allowed to move down a bit and play under less pressure. There was no designated hitter this year (the artifice is mercifully benched in the Series in alternate years), and Lasorda gave us a sustained Chautauqua in the National League style of play — how to use the intentional base on balls, when to bat for your pitcher and (much harder) when not to, when to wheel in your pinch-hitters, when to wait, when to be swift. The Yankee brain trust — Bob Lemon and (one must assume) George Steinbrenner — looked more and more flustered and uncertain in its exercise of these ancient options, and it was the difference between the two clubs in this always uncertain terrain, it seems to me, that both won and lost the Series.

The opening pair of games, in New York, suggested only that the Yankees' autumn hegemony was unshakable. The Yankees, winning by 5–3 and 3–0, were given near-impeccable pitching by their two lefty starters, Guidry and John, and Goose Gossage fanned five Dodgers in his two-day, four-inning stint, for two saves. Graig Nettles and Willie Randolph came up with almost a half-dozen fielding gems in the opener, thus permitting the press-box Homers to trot out their hoary autumn maxim: it is the Yankees' *defense* that sets them apart from all other clubs. The Dodgers, to be sure, did rip the ball pretty hard, even while losing, but the big Yankee play was always there when needed; viz., Nettles' first-game, eighth-inning full-length airborne dive behind the bag at third to snare Garvey's line drive in the outermost inches of his glove and shut off the visitors in mid-rally. Nothing to it, folks.

Out at Chavez Ravine, the Dodgers won a wearing, three-hour, endlessly discussable 5–4 contest that began with an unmerciful pummelling of the celebrated rookie starters, Valenzuela and Righetti, who were whacked for seven runs (including homers by Cey, Watson, and Cerone) in the first three innings, but was actually settled by the Dodgers' superior stratagems and bat control and luck in the closer environs of the diamond. In the fifth, with Dodger base runners on first and second, and nobody out, Lasorda ordered Pedro Guerrero to swing away, of all things, and Guerrero hit a chopper that ricocheted off the pavementlike infield and sailed untouched over Aurelio Rodriguez's head, at third, for a double that brought in both runs and put the Dodgers in front for keeps. (Nettles, who was nursing a mashed thumb, was sitting out the game, but I don't think he could have made the play, either.) Luck of a sort, one might conclude, but the purer variety appeared, in disguise, an instant or two later, when a Dodger hitter rapped into a double play, thus permitting Lasorda to let Valenzuela bat for himself and remain in the game. The stolid, courageous youngster was not at all himself on this outing, but he hung on now, allowing no Yankee base runners past second base after the fifth inning, and he won on a bad day, which is the best sign of pitching class. The Yankees, for their part, simply looked bad on a bad day, stranding nine base runners and somehow contriving to send up the power-hitting Bobby Murcer to pinch-hit in a bunt situation. He bunted into a double play.

Everyone *except* the batters looked terrible the next day, when the Dodgers evened the Series by winning (8–7) a vast, untidy *smörgåsbord* of baseball — baseball of a hundred flavors — in which thirteen batters were stranded in the first four innings, and ten pitchers surrendered twenty-seven hits in all. Reggie Jackson, who had sat out the first three Series games with a strained muscle, had an adventurous afternoon, rapping out three hits, one of them a homer, but misplaying a high, short fly ball by Davey Lopes in the sixth which he lost

track of in the glazy late-season high sky of Chavez; the ball
struck him on the shoulder and bounded away, and Lopes, a
bit later, came home with the run that brought the Dodgers
even in the game for the first time. There were other
mistakes by the Yankees, in fielding and baserunning and
strategy (Jerry Mumphrey, the regular center fielder, somehow never got into the game at all, and neither did Gossage),
but their only unforgivable error was in not winning this
slummocky, bushfighting kind of ballgame, which was available, right up to the end, to the team that wanted it most.
The game was a thriller, I should add, and when it was over I
thought about the many thousands of Dodger-mad families,
homeward bound over the freeways, all exclaiming and
chattering and laughing as they replayed the long afternoon in
excited memory: Bill Russell's miserable throwing error, and
Jay Johnstone's glorious pinch-hit two-run homer, and Jay
coming out of the dugout and waving his hat to the folks
afterward, naturally ("*Did* he? I didn't even see that!"), and
Rick Monday's liner to center that was gloved but then
dropped by somebody out there (it was Bobby Brown), and
the horrible little flip past first base by Steve Howe ("He's so
cute!") at the end there, and, of course, Reggie Jackson
staggering and reeling and flinching under the glare of the sun
("I knew he'd drop it! I *knew* it, I tell you!"), and that great
yell when the ball did drop free, and then the glorious,
grateful, unfair, full-house chant at their old oppressor: "Reggie! Reg-gie! Reg-gie!" And Reuss would go tomorrow!

And go he did, in the best and swiftest contest of the
Series — a terse, almost austere pitchers' game, which
cleared away the detritus of so much rackety, too entertaining
baseball over the previous days. The Dodgers won it, 2–1,
on two sudden home runs — as close together as handclaps,
it seemed — hit in succession in the seventh against Ron
Guidry by Pedro Guerrero and Steve Yeager. There was no
preparation for such a thing — no premonitory high counts
on the mound or wavers in the field, which often suggest
where the break in this kind of game will come. Guidry, in

fact, had looked very nearly untouchable up to that instant, having zipped off his seventh swinging strikeout just prior to the crash. Then he was done — and so were the Yankees, one suddenly felt; as quickly as that, the outcome of the Series and the end of this year seemed settled. Reuss, who had survived three errors by his second baseman, Lopes, in the early going, pitched from his strength — a punishing low-level fastball that sails or dives cruelly just as it penetrates the strike zone — and from his gruff conviction that no mere mistakes, no distractions or accidents or bad luck, were going to alter the outcome for him that day. "That mound is my valley," he said afterward, "and nothing goes on in my valley unless I say so." Then he took the game-ball and put an identifying blue dot on it with a felt pen and tucked it away in his locker. "I'll write in the details this winter, back home," he explained. "After we've won."

This kind of reward — the clarity of a fine performance and a close game well won — did not come to us fans at the very end this year. The weary Dodgers, as I have written, were appropriately happy, if not ecstatic, with their championship when it arrived at last, and I don't think they much cared that the Yankees played so poorly in the final game, back at the Stadium, which went to the Dodgers by 9–2. But even Dodger fans might have preferred a classier termination. Burt Hooton pitched strongly enough and won, and Guerrero hit a single and a triple and a homer, and the Dodgers broke it open with three runs in the fifth and four more in the sixth, against the Yankees' suddenly paperlike middle relievers, including Ron Davis. The Yankees did almost nothing well there at the end, which leaves us with a most unsatisfactory residue of questions. Why did Bob Lemon throw away his most experienced, most resolute starting pitcher, Tommy John, for a pinch-hitter (and to no end) in the fourth inning, when the game was still tied, 1–1, and when it had already been made plain that his bullpen was not to be relied upon? Why did Lemon persist in marooning Dave Winfield in the No. 3 slot of the batting order throughout the Series when Dave, who had fielded and run and hit so well all summer, was clearly no longer himself and could only flail helplessly at the ball (he went one for twenty-two in the Series) from the depths of his late-season slump? Why was Jackson, by then almost entirely recovered from his injury, not in the lineup in the third game, when his left-side power might have made the difference against Valenzuela's screwball? And so on. Who was really running the Yankees this fall, and why did this Yankee team never remind us of its famous predecessors whose skills and money and reputation were always less, one understood in the end, than their fearsome manly pride? I think I know the answer to that question, but this is not the sort of baseball speculation I enjoy. It will bring very little comfort in the months just ahead, while we must wait and wonder what new hopes and pleasures we may rediscover in the game in its coming, badly needed springtime.

George F. Will

A One-Man Error Machine

Newsweek, August 6, 1990

This summer a suburban Washington dinner theater is putting on the 1955 musical *Damn Yankees*. At first I thought, what fun, I'll take the children. Then, pulling myself up from the time warp, I had second thoughts. The children would not get it — would not understand the role played by the Yankees. The evening would just confirm them further in their view that their father is a fossil.

You may dimly remember the *Damn Yankees* story. It is Faust for the modern age. The protagonist is a middle-aged, unathletic but ardent fan of the Washington Senators. (Remember your ancient history, from back when the saying was, "Washington — first in war, first in peace and last in the American League.") The fan sells his soul to the Devil for one sensational season as a major league player — a perfectly reasonable transaction, I think. In that season he (I am leaving out a lot) leads the Senators to victory. Over whom? Who else? That irresistible force, that Leviathan of the diamond, that Cadillac (another anachronism; today we would say Mercedes) of major league franchises. The Senators beat the perennially mighty and therefore universally detested Yankees.

That was then, this is now. Then Whitey Ford was pitching and Yogi Berra was catching and Mickey Mantle was belting the ball out of Yankee Stadium's ZIP code (oops! that was

pre-ZIP codes) and the memory of man ranneth not to when
the Yankees were other than awesome. Now the Yankees are
the worst team in baseball. Look to your non-laurels, Atlanta
Braves. The Bronx Bumblers have captured baseball's booby
prize. And the Yankees' owner, George Steinbrenner, is the
worst problem on the plate of the Commissioner of Baseball,
Fay Vincent, who must think the Devil is plaguing him.

An earthquake messed with Vincent's first World Series, a
lockout delayed his first Opening Day, it rained on his first
All-Star game, and this summer he has the migraine-inducing
duty to sift through Steinbrenner's wonderfully imaginative and glaringly incompatible and completely unconvincing
stories about why he gave $40,000 to an unsavory character
who gambles. Steinbrenner is almost certainly innocent of
gambling. And that about exhausts his innocence.

Steinbrenner is, shall we say, an acquired taste. He can be
charming when his interests are not engaged and he is dealing
with people not in his employ. The rest of the time, which
means most of the time, he is hard to take in even small
doses. Vincent, having engaged Steinbrenner in long discussions about rules and laws and ethics, must wince when he
reads the title of the book his predecessor, Bart Giamatti,
wrote about Americans and their games: *Take Time for
Paradise*. If this is paradise, Adam and Eve were smart to
leave.

Steinbrenner is a boor and a buccaneer, overflowing with
the animal spirits that fuel capitalism in its rawer forms. Such
spirits sometimes seek additional outlets in the ownership of
sports franchises. Vincent is a gentleman and a scholar.

He is a graduate of Yale Law School. (Pete Rose on Giamatti: "He's an intellectual from Yale, but he's very intelligent.") It is said that the study of law sharpens the mind by
narrowing it. However, Vincent is a voracious reader. Trying to find a biography he has not read is like naming, say,
the St. Louis Cardinals catcher in 1912: it is possible, but requires research. (By the way, the Cardinals catcher was Ivey
Wingo.) Vincent carefully measures the words he selects to

explain his measured responses to problems. In his delicacy and disdain for flamboyance baseball's eighth commissioner is utterly unlike the first.

The Commissioner's office is one of those institutions that is (in Emerson's words) the lengthening shadow of man. The man was Kenesaw Mountain Landis, a Chicagoan with a shock of white hair over craggy features and a mail-slot mouth. His was the visage of an Old Testament prophet who has looked around and is not amused by what he has seen. Landis was a judge, and looked like one. (Big deal. Has anyone ever looked more like a President than Warren Harding did?) Landis was a grandstanding judge — in baseball lingo, a hot dog. The Supreme Court overturned his $29 million fine of Standard Oil (in those days that was serious money). He tried to extradite the Kaiser because a Chicagoan died when a German submarine sank the *Lusitania*. Landis enjoyed stiff drinks of whisky but handed out stiff sentences to people who violated Prohibition. But he was just what baseball needed in its hour of maximum need — the aftermath of the Black Sox scandal, the fixed World Series of 1919.

Landis delivered rough justice, perhaps more rough than just. Eight players, some more dumb than dishonest, were banned from baseball for life; nothing happened to the gamblers. Then baseball picked itself up, dusted itself off, built Yankee Stadium, put Babe Ruth on center stage, and rollicked through the 1920s. That decade was the dawn of broadcasting and hence of hoopla. It was the Golden Age of American sport — Ruth, Jack Dempsey, Gene Tunney, Red Grange, Knute Rockne, Bobby Jones, Bill Tilden, Man o' War.

A Right

Landis became (with assists from Ruth and the lively ball) baseball's savior 70 years ago. From the owners he extracted an extraordinary empowerment for his office. A Commissioner may (note well: may, not must; it is a right, not a duty) take remedial measures against any "act, transaction or practice" that is "not in the best interests" of baseball. That clause is a huge grant of discretion. Like any such grant, it is a mixed blessing for the recipient.

The Commissioner's power is unconstrained, other than by the Commissioner's prudence. And it is unappealable, unless the Commissioner acts more capriciously than any Commissioner ever has. The sweep of the "best interests" clause generates pressure to use the power. The pressure often comes from people impatient to use fiats to cut through complex problems, sweeping like a scythe through procedural niceties. Nothing matches the impatience of a baseball fan fed up with his team's owner. No one is as fed up as Yankee fans.

The remedies available to the Commissioner acting in baseball's best interests run all the way up the escalation ladder to the expulsion of an owner from the ranks of ownership. But this power is like a nuclear weapon. Its only satisfactory role is as a deterrent. Using it today probably would involve unacceptable collateral damage.

Consider another analogy, from Constitutional law. The "best interests" clause of baseball's constitution resembles the "equal protection" and "due process" clauses of the Constitution. A willful judge can do almost anything he wants with such language — if he is indifferent to the damage done to the texture of the law and the stature of his office. But a judicious judge will exercise self-restraint. He will be a strict constructionist because judicial power is best preserved by being used reluctantly and economically.

The "best interests" clause has been invoked some 70 times in 70 years. It has been used to suspend a manager (the Dodgers' Leo Durocher in 1947, for consorting with gamblers). It has been used to bar two retired stars, Mickey Mantle and Willie Mays, from any contact with baseball as long as they were employed at an Atlantic City casino. It was used in 1976 to stop an owner, Charles Finley of the Athletics, from conducting a fire sale of players, a sale that would have instantly degraded the franchise. (Finley was furious about the coming of free agency. Blocking the sale did not prevent Finley from wrecking his team. The law has limits. The Athletics have risen from the ruins, several times. Nothing is forever, not even ruination.)

Now, would it be in baseball's best interests were Steinbrenner to sell the Yankees? Hey, ask me a hard one. Baseball is a game of inches but this is not a close call. Of course Steinbrenner is bad for baseball's grandest franchise, and hence for the game. But that fact does not entail the conclusion that Vincent should hurl Steinbrenner into outer darkness forever. A mere monetary fine would be derisory; permanent expulsion would be disproportionate; a substantial suspension — say, through 1991 — would be about right.

Steinbrenner's sins are manifold and manifest. There is the scarlet sin of his transaction with the gambler. And there are the scores of mundane sins of stupidity which have reduced the Yankees to rubble. No one of these sins seems to warrant the nuclear weapon of forcing him to sell, however much that might make Vincent the toast of the Bronx (and, truth be told, of Steinbrenner's fellow owners). But there are precedents that should make Steinbrenner nervous, and it is in baseball's best interest that he should be nervous.

In 1943 and again in 1953, owners of the Phillies and Cardinals, respectively, were forced to sell their teams, the former because he bet on games, the latter because he was convicted of tax evasion. But back then a franchise was an economic entity akin to a corner candy store. Today it is more like Neiman-Marcus. A difference in degree becomes a difference in kind. To force one of today's owners to sell, even at a fair market price (the Yankees would bring at least $200 million), might trigger judicial sympathy for any Steinbrenner claim that he was being deprived of property without due process. Courts traditionally have been wary about intervening in the internal governance of private associations. But in the current climate of judicial hubris, a judge can almost always be found who will try to fine-tune any controversy.

(Here is a pretty judicial pickle. Imagine trying to assemble an impartial jury of New Yorkers to hear Steinbrenner's case.

"Tell the court, Mr. Prospective Juror, do you have any strong opinions about the owner who masterminded the trade of Fred McGriff from the Yankees to the Blue Jays in exchange for a couple of no-names? Stop snarling, Prospective Juror.")

It is baseball's double misfortune that Steinbrenner is not just an owner, but the owner of the Yankees. Damn them to your heart's content, they have been important to the game's health.

From 1926 through 1964 they had 39 consecutive winning seasons. (The longest current streak is the Blue Jays' seven.) In those 39 years the Yankees finished first 26 times. From 1949 through 1958 they won nine pennants. They finished second in 1954, when the Cleveland Indians (yep; you can look it up) set a League record with 111 wins in a 154 game schedule. If the Yankees' 103 wins had been, as such a total usually is, enough to win in a walk, the Yankees would have been in 10 consecutive World Series.

Competitive balance has been excellent in the last dozen seasons. Balance is better for baseball than the sort of dominance the Yankees enjoyed. But baseball benefits from occasional mini-dynasties. The Athletics and Reds were such in the 1970s; the Athletics are today. The Cinderella story of the 1990 White Sox is especially fun because they are challenging Oakland's gang of forearms: Ozzie Guillen against José Canseco — Peter Pan meets Godzilla.

It was good for baseball when the most glamorous team, the Yankees, had glamour. To be blunt, Steinbrenner's mismanagement of the Yankees matters much more than the mismanagement of the Braves. The Yankees, the source of so much of baseball's most stirring history — Ruth, Gehrig, DiMaggio, Mantle — are simply irreplaceable as carriers of a tradition that lends derivative glory to teams that compete against them.

Of course nothing lasts. The ravages of time are lethal, especially when assisted by the ravages of a Steinbrenner. The Yankees were once, it seemed, one of those rare institutions that could not be ruined. Wrong. Such institutions are not rare; they are, because there are Steinbrenners, non-existent. The Yankees had a huge market, a vibrant farm system, a fat treasury, an inspiriting tradition. And yet they were brought low by the 10-thumbed touch of their owner.

Madcap Misadventures

Some serious folks from the Harvard Business School have studied the Oakland Athletics' current management. They say it is a model of sound practices. Steinbrenner could serve as the reverse, as baseball's dumb-o-meter: study his decisions, do the opposite, and you will do well. There is no need to rehash here all the talent-squandering trades, the morale-shattering tirades and other madcap misadventures that have made Steinbrenner's regime resemble Mussolini's Italy — despotism tempered by anarchy. Suffice it to say you can cover your Yankee scorecard with a slew of "E-O" notations — error by the owner.

Baseball is so hard to play, it is extremely difficult to judge baseball talent. Even professionals make misjudgments. (Three of today's players who probably are headed for the Hall of Fame, Roger Clemens and José Canseco and Ryne Sandberg, were not picked in baseball drafts until the 12th, 15th and 20th rounds, respectively.) Amateurs like Steinbrenner should butt out. Steinbrenner should have been a football owner. The NFL's farm system is run by big universities. And how hard is it, anyway, to judge the beeftrusts who become linemen? Weigh them, time them, sign them.

But Steinbrenner is not just error-prone, he is an error machine. He is because he lacks an attribute essential for baseball (and, not coincidentally, for democracy): patience. Baseball is an appropriate national pastime for this democratic nation precisely because it both requires and teaches what Americans often lack: patience. (The American prayer: "Lord give me patience — and I want it *right now!*") Democracy rests on persuasion, which takes time. Democracy involves constant compromising, which means partial failure to get one's way. Democracy is the politics of the half-loaf. And baseball? The best team is going to get beaten about 60 times this year, and is going to be hammered many of those times. Steinbrenner has a football temperament. In the NFL, your team only plays 16 games, so if it loses three games in the early going, it is rational — well, by football standards — to slit your wrists.

The late Edward Bennett Williams, the Washington attorney who bought the Baltimore Orioles in 1979, had been president of the Washington Redskins. He had a football frame of mind. But after he spent lavishly and futilely on free agents for the Orioles he learned a lesson. "There are," he said, "three things money can't buy — love, happiness and an American League pennant." One cause of Steinbrenner's downfall is that at first he seemed able to buy success. His swashbuckling impatience seemed validated by spending (for Reggie Jackson and Catfish Hunter, especially) that helped produce the 1977 and 1978 winners. But baseball is a great leveler, punishing the impatient who throw money rather than intelligence at problems.

(And yet . . . Perhaps Steinbrenner should keep control of the Yankees. The Yankees get about $55 million a year in local broadcast revenues. Some other teams get only $5 million or less. Perhaps Steinbrenner's incompetent squandering of his money prevents the Yankees from disrupting the League's balance.)

Steinbrenner will be punished by Vincent for his association with a gambler. And the shipwreck of the Yankees is condign punishment for Steinbrenner's utter lack of baseball sense. Alas, Yankee fans, too, are being punished. But life is unfair and the Commissioner can do nothing about that defect in the universe. And he can not make baseball blunders punishable offenses.

Today baseball is better than ever, on the field and in the front offices. You might not think so, reading the sports pages. Recently they have read like refugees from *The Wall Street Journal* — money, contracts, labor strife — and police blotters — gambling, drugs. But there have always been dumb and coarse owners (and congressmen and senators and journalists and . . .). They have to be lived with, and survived. Steinbrenner will be.

It is said democracy is a splendid thing that the people who run it do their level best to ruin. Baseball is like that. But listen to the levelheadedness of George Anderson, the philosopher of the Detroits. (That is how some old-time baseball people talk — never about the Tigers and Red Sox, only about the Detroits and Bostons.) Anderson, known as Sparky in his capacity as manager of the Detroits, says: "We try every way we can do to kill the game, but for some reason, nothing nobody does never hurts it." Still true, so far, but stay tuned.

Epilogue: The Luckiest Man on the Face of the Earth

We end with some of the most familar words ever spoken by an American athlete. In the era of Pete "Don't Say It Ain't So" Rose and Neon Deion, it might be helpful for us to reflect on a few words that didn't come from an ad shop, a PR department, a ghostwriter, or a Hollywood script — although these particular words have been immortalized in a movie aptly titled *The Pride of the Yankees.*

These are words from the heart — which must, in the end, be where we finally find that mythical place called America.

"For weeks I have been reading in the newspapers that I am a fellow who got a tough break. I don't believe it. I have been a lucky guy. For 16 years into every ballpark in which I have ever walked, I received nothing but kindness and encouragement. Mine has been a full life. . . . I have a wonderful wife, I have a wonderful mother and father, and wonderful friends and teammates. I have been privileged to play many years with the famous Yankees, the greatest team of all times. . . . I may have been given a bad break, but I have an awful lot to live for. All in all, I can say on this day that I consider myself the luckiest man on the face of the earth."

Here at last! An all-new anthology celebrating the most successful team in the history of baseball — the New York Yankees. The Yankees have appeared in the World Series an astounding 33 times and have won in 22 of them. Their unparalleled accomplishments have inspired a nationwide legion of fans and some of the best writing the sport has ever seen.

Contributors include:

Roger Angell	Reggie Jackson
Yogi Berra	Armen Keteyian
Thomas Boswell	Tony Kubek
Jim Bouton	Frederick G. Lieb
Brendan C. Boyd	Mike Lupica
James P. Dawson	Sparky Lyle
Dock Ellis	Willie Morris
Peter Golenbock	John Mosedale
David Halberstam	Graig Nettles
Donald Hall	Terry Pluto
Fred C. Harris	Shirley Povich
Lesley Hazleton	Grantland Rice
Ernest Hemingway	Red Smith
Tom Horton	Casey Stengel
Richard Hugo	George Vecsey
Jim "Catfish" Hunter	George F. Will

This all-star collection includes the finest pieces on the park (beloved Yankee Stadium, both old and new) and the plays, the great games and the great names — Ruth, DiMaggio, Gehrig, Berra, Mantle, and many more.

COVER DESIGN: KANDY LITTRELL

COVER PHOTOGRAPH: COURTESY OF THE NATIONAL BASEBALL LIBRARY, COOPERSTOWN, N.Y.

ISBN 0-395-58777-8

0491
6-94548

9 780395 587775